Cameroon Grassfields Civilization

Jean-Pierre Warnier

Langaa Research & Publishing CIG
Mankon, Bamenda

Publisher:
Langaa RPCIG
Langaa Research & Publishing Common Initiative Group
P.O. Box 902 Mankon
Bamenda
North West Region
Cameroon
Langaagrp@gmail.com
www.langaa-rpcig.net

Distributed in and outside N. America by African Books Collective
orders@africanbookscollective.com
www.africanbookcollective.com

ISBN: 9956-727-90-3

DISCLAIMER
All views expressed in this publication are those of the author and do not necessarily reflect the views of Langaa RPCIG.

Preface

Grassfields Research Encounters: One Person's Anthropologist is Only in the Womb
Francis B. Nyamnjoh

This book is a timely gesture of restitution by one of the foremost ethnographic historians of the Cameroon Grassfields. It is the crowning moment of a journey rich in encounters and mutual shaping, between a scholar and the people and places he came to know and cherish for forty years. The book is distilled from intellectual curiosities and conversions kindled and fuelled by relationships forged and entertained across different countries (France, USA, UK, Nigeria and Cameroon) and within different regions in Cameroon. It is a book I am pleased to be associated with.

Jean-Pierre Warnier's ethnological encounter with Mankon as field location was not initially planned, negotiated or made by personal choice. Nor were his subsequent returns to continue his research, expanded to include the political, material and economic history, linguistics and archaeology of the entire Grassfields region. Circumstances and a series of chance encounters brought him to the region, and have stimulated his intellectual and social engagements with Mankon, the Grassfields and Cameroon for 40 years. In his introduction to this impressive seminal collection of essays produced and perfected in the course of these encounters, Warnier provides a snippet view of the forces and individuals that influenced the turn taken by his research curiosities and interests, and that tells us why he has come to cherish anthropological research not as analyses of a given people, but rather, as analyses of an anthropologist's interactions with given subjects and groups.

Indeed, circumstances beyond his control brought Jean-Pierre Warnier and Mankon together. First, his scanty finances as a doctoral student at the University of Pennsylvania excluded his contemplation of field sites in Oceania and Asia, and with the Americas the preserve of North American anthropologists, he was left with Africa as the option. Even then, his choice of Ivory Coast was turned down by his assigned supervisor – Professor Igor Kopytoff –, who, writes Warnier, "…directed me to Cameroon where Ngwa'fo, king of Mankon, had informed Elizabeth Chilver, a historian from Oxford, of his wish to have an anthropologist conduct some research in his kingdom." So Jean-Pierre Warnier found himself in Mankon in May 1971, at the beginning of a series of encounters and mutually beneficial interactions between him, individuals and groups in the kingdom of Mankon. The power of circumstances shaped his view of research from the outset, as a process that consists in putting an individual in a given situation and then looking at what happens. In his perspective, "encounters with other subjects provide the impetus and the orientation of the research," and the richer these encounters, the greater the impetus and orientation to one's research.

In December 2009 Fo Angwafo III celebrated his 50 years as king, exactly 38 years after Jean-Pierre Warnier was made to answer his request to Sally Chilver for an anthropologist to document the ways of his kingdom. This was an occasion the planning of which Warnier had followed up closely, and which he attended, along with two filmmakers from the University of Vienna, working for Austrian television, as he sought to document the event as the crowning event of his 38 years of ethnological encounters with Mankon. In his autobiography published to coincide with the jubilee, Fo Angwafo III acknowledged Jean-Pierre Warnier, and the role he had played as the king's courtyard in placing the things and achievements of the palace on the radar of scholarly attention and recognition:

I am grateful for this collaboration on the cultural heritage of Mankon, just as I am grateful to all those anthropologists, historians and others who have never relented in their documentation of ways and encounters with others. Amongst these, I am particularly thankful to Jean-Pierre Warnier, a French anthropologist and historian who has written extensively on various aspects of Mankon since the 1970s, and who has always sent copies of his writings to the palace, where he is known as *Sangto'* – the Palace Courtyard – a title I gave in 1974 in recognition of his achievements for Mankon. My acknowledgement also goes to *Mafo Sangto'* Jacqueline Leroy, his wife at the time, for her two detailed books and a number of articles on the Mankon language. It is pleasing to know that they have remained committed and active in their study of and interaction with Mankon, inspiring our own scholars to rise to the challenge of recording the happenings and realities of our society. (Fo Angwafo III 2009:69).

Mankon and the Grassfields, Jean-Pierre Warnier was to find out, were far from being bounded communities that thrived on exclusionary articulations of belonging. He writes, "Mankon, like most, if not all, surrounding kingdoms, was a composite one. 30% of the women married in Mankon around the turn of the 20th century came from another local community, and quite a few descent groups came from various neighbouring regions." This was a similar finding to Igor Kopytoff's whose study of the Aghem of the same region provided the basis for his classic on "African Frontier" societies (Kopytoff 1987). The composite nature of Grassfields kingdoms is hardly surprising, given this widely shared saying in the region: A child is one person's only in the womb (Nyamnjoh 2002). Indeed, if my own experience and identity are anything to go by, these observations by Kopytoff and Warnier were most pertinent.

My own encounter with Mankon and Fo Angwafo III almost coincided with Warnier's. We are both familiar with and indeed recognised to belong in Mankon, even if, conventionally, we are likely to be thought of and referred to as non-Mankon. We came to Mankon via different routes, around the same time; Jean-Pierre Warnier in May 1971, I in August 1973. Fo Angwafo III opened up to accommodate him and his wife as Sangto' and Mafo Sangto', and me as a son, giving me a mother in the palace. We were not simply accommodated as strangers or ankyeni "good enough to be absorbed and eaten". The fact that both our sons were named Anye by Fo Angwafo III, his name before he assumed the throne in 1959 – meant that the Fon, as "Pot-King", had shared with us his "vital piggy-bank". He had allowed us to draw on him as a "container" for our own sustenance. What the Fon gives out is always more important than what he takes in (Warnier 2007).

As the following excerpt from a paper I published in 2002 demonstrates, not only are Grassfields kingdoms composite, Grassfields identities are multiple and flexible, suggesting a readiness to accommodate that speaks more of conviviality than conflict, and an idea of origin and belonging that builds on encounters and relationships than simply on essences:

Such adaptability or dynamism is displayed both towards macro level changes and towards developments within the family among children. Continuity and change are alike determined by mutuality in concessions. Turning to social structure and agency at the level of the family, I now want to consider how conviviality is negotiated over time; thus providing for both meanings of a child is one person's only in the womb. Limiting oneself to one of these meanings denies either the impact of history as a process or the resilience of tradition ('the womb') in the regeneration of social structures or the life of the individual.

At the level of the family, I illustrate with examples of marriages in Mankon that show how people negotiate tradition with modernity through conviviality, and how competing understandings of agency or subjectivity are compromised. To understand my Mankon example better, here is a brief biographical account of my association with fon Angwafo III; a further illustration of how ideas of cultures and identities as homogenous wholes often hide more than they reveal.

I was born in December 1961 in Bum, where I spent the first ten years of my life. My biological father was Ndong, a rich cattle owner of Bafmen origin whom I was to meet for the first time in my third year in college. My mother got married to Nyamnjoh when I was three years old, her father having turned down Ndong's offers to marry her because Ndong was not of Bum. My mother's elder sister was married to fon Yai of Bum, and together with his 20 other wives they lived in his LakaBum palace, some 30 kilometres away from Fonfuka where I attended primary school. Without children of her own to send to school, my aunt had persuaded her husband to sponsor me instead. He had accepted but had also insisted that I spend my holidays in LakaBum, and work for him like all the other young men and women he sponsored, including his own biological children. Although not of royal blood as such, I was to spend my childhood and adolescence with two fons in two different fondoms, fon John Yai and fon Solomon Angwafo III, of Bum and Mankon respectively. Both fons have fathered me socially, and both fondoms claim me and my achievements (or the lack thereof) equally. Through me, they have prided themselves at having a son in the corridors of modern opportunities on the national and international levels. And so too I have had to identify with them, for one personal reason or another, in the course of my life.

In both Bum and Mankon, I am a prince in every sense but blood, since neither fon is my biological father. When I discovered the latter in my third year in college, he showed more interest in trying to claim me by undoing the impact of all the others on my life and upbringing, than in seeking to catch up with them. But when I refused to change my name from Nyamnjoh to Ndong and to become reinvented by him, he lost interest and I kept some distance. My reaction to similar pressure by the fon of Bum to adopt his name, was however not the same. Instead of giving up the name Nyamnjoh as he repeatedly instructed, claiming it was the name of a commoner, I at one point added Yai to my list of names, and some of my school certificates did actually bear 'Francis Beng Yai Nyamnjoh'. I also remember at one point adopting the nickname 'Frank Human' in exasperation, and asking my classmates and friends to call me that instead of all these names that different claimants were seeking to impose on me for their own strategic reasons. Later on however, I decided to shade Yai from my list of names, and to stick to the rest. (It was normal for a child to have three names where I grew up – the name at birth, the family name and the Christian name upon baptism.) I was conscious I was different from other children whenever people asked me questions to which they were used to receiving simple, straightforward, cliché answers: 'Where do you come from?', 'Who is your father?', 'What is your name?' I found myself having to explain all the time, to prove that I was not lying by claiming this parentage or that identity, when my name or other indicators pointed elsewhere.

If there is any such thing as an identity crisis, mine was not felt from within, but was rather imposed by others. I feel an insider to both communities, and according to many cultural indicators, I may even be more of an insider than most people exclusively assumed to be of either cultures, given my connections with the palaces and their institutions as embodiments of culture. But if one were to stick to traditional ideas of belonging as some have, I would definitely not be classified as Mankon or Bum, but as Bafmen, the home village of Ndong, my biological father. According to the same logic, neither my aunt in the Bum palace nor my social mother in the Mankon palace, would qualify to claim me as a son (which they do), their love and commitment notwithstanding. Frozen ideas of identity and culture are like labelling in order to include or to exclude; it is like seeking to confine the child in the womb.

My completion of primary school coincided with the marriage of a princess of Bum to fon Angwafo III of Mankon, a childhood friend and school mate of fon John Yai of Bum. So I was sent to stay with fon Angwafo III who became my guardian during my first two years at Sacred Heart College, Mankon. Fon John Yai soon became irregular with payment of fees for my college education, and I was threatened with dismissal. Fon Angwafo III, who cherished education particularly, given his own brilliant achievements in this regard, could not understand why his friend was irregular with the fees. One day I was actually sent away from college, and went to see him in tears. He sat me down and listened. It was only then that he learnt for the first time that I was not a prince of Bum by blood. Faced with the prospect of having me dismissed from school for nonpayment of fees, he decided to sponsor me thenceforth. And did so right into my MA degree at the University of Yaounde, where I subsequently won a government scholarship for PhD at Leicester University in the UK. Not once did he suggest that I change my name to bear Angwafo, nor did he encourage me when I hinted I was willing to consider doing so. With Ndong at the margins, I was left with three active fathers, two royal and one commoner, and in my own little way have sought to satisfy their competing demands for attention ever since. They have each allocated me a piece of land in their villages on which to build my house, as is traditional in the Grassfields. When I married in December 1990, they all were part of the process and all attended the ceremony and each participated in his capacity as a father. Two of my mothers were present as well; only the biological one was absent, having died in 1989. (Nyamnjoh 2002:126-129).

If Jean-Pierre Warnier participated in the 50th jubilee as an anthropologist, filmmaker and Sangto', I was present and active as a son, and also as one who had collaborated with Fo Angwafo III in writing his biography. In working with the Fon on his biography, I drew extensively on anthropological and historical sources, including the works of Jean-Pierre Warnier, as well as the works of Mankon historians such as Nicodemus Awasom and Thaddeus Achu Anye, who had drawn significant inspiration from Warnier's work.

Warnier writes, "Teaching is one of the best ways of learning." He is a great teacher, and an even greater learner. The tribute he pays his former doctorate students – Dieudonné Miaffo and Séverin Cecil Abega – is evidence of a teacher who understood the added "considerable surplus value" to teaching that came with learning from the "first-hand knowledge" his students commanded of their own societies. It is also a statement on the modesty of such a highly learned scholar. I am grateful that Jean-Pierre Warnier initiated me into anthropology at the University of Yaounde where he supervised my Maîtrise dissertation in 1985 on Change in the Concept of Power Among the Bum, the same year he left to take up a position as Professor of Ethnology at the Université René-Descartes (Paris V) in France. It was as his student in Yaounde that Michael Rowlands graced my modest student accommodation with his presence, directed by Warnier to meet me for an interview. That was shortly before I left for England to do my PhD, in the course of which Michael Rowlands remained a steady friend and support. Les amis de mes amis sont mes amis (the friends of my friends are my friends), the saying goes, and how apt! Put anthropologically, the contacts of my contacts are my contacts or, the networks of my friends are my networks – a logic Facebook has mastered superbly.

Just like the rich, flexible encounters and relationships of our lives individually, Warnier's encounters and relationships with me and others in the Grassfields, the rest of the country and beyond have been unending chains of personal and collective networks of sociality, academic and otherwise. The full weight of this statement comes with the "What if..." questions: What if Jean-Pierre Warnier had been rich enough as a student to contemplate fieldwork in Oceana and Asia? What if Sally Chilver had not met Igor Kopytoff or Fo Angwafo III? What if the French bureaucracy had welcomed Jean-Pierre Warnier back with open arms upon the completion of his PhD? What if Martin Njeuma, Dean of the Faculty of Letters and Human Sciences at the University of Yaounde, had not invited Jean-Pierre Warnier to teach in 1979? We can go on and on, only to end up with the conclusion that Warnier stresses in this volume: Circumstances shape encounters and encounters give impetus and orientation to research and scholars on the move.

It is through Warnier that I met Séverin Cecil Abega, with whom I was to have exciting intellectual conversations of a comparative nature. He sought to understand the Grassfields, just as I invested in understanding the forest zones of southern and eastern Cameroon from where he hailed and where his fieldwork was based. He fed me expressions in local Beti languages when I was writing Souls Forgotten (Nyamnjoh 2008), an ethnographic novel set between Yaounde and the Grassfields. When I completed my PhD and paid Warnier a visit in France (during which we went hunting and fishing together with his son Louis (Anye or the extension of Fo Angwafo III and the kingdom of Mankon in France) at his home villages of Besse and Anger before my return to Cameroon, he introduced me to Chandon-Moët (a Jesuit priest from his region of France), Dean of Social Sciences at the Catholic University in Yaounde. When my application to teach at the Advanced School of Mass Communication was rejected, Chandon-Moët offered me a position as part time lecturer of sociology at the University.

I in turn introduced Séverin Cecil Abega to Chandon-Moët, who eventually recruited Abega as Maître de Conference, when I moved to take up a permanent position at the University of Buea in 1993. In 1999 when I left Buea for the University of Botswana because of administrative censorship of my scholarship by the Vice-Chancellor Dorothy Njeuma (Jua and Nyamnjoh 2002), Jean-Pierre Warnier assisted with letters of reference. During my tenure as Head of Publications at the Council for the Development of Social Science Research in Africa in Dakar, Senegal (2003-2009), we benefitted with gratitude from Abega's exceptional skills as a resource person in the workshops we organised on research and scholarly writing. I was pleasantly surprised in Ouagadougou, during a writing workshop when Abega invited me to take a look at his laptop. I was excited by a folder of ethnographic field notes he had made on Su-Bum, where he had been commissioned by some NGO to do a study on HIV/AIDS. Abega's approach to anthropology was not limited to narrow ideas of belonging and what was researchable. As Jean-Pierre Warnier never tired of emphasising in his lectures, the encounters and interconnections entertained by the researcher, know no bounds in their capacity to generate, maintain, and enhance social networks and intellectual curiosity.

As a scholar, I have come of age, and am able to share with my own students some of the attitudes towards research which Warnier taught me. It was thus with pride, that I shared with him recently the thesis and publications of one of my students, Walter Gam Nkwi (2010; 2011a&b), a much younger generation of scholars drawing on his tradition and practice of marrying ethnography and history to good effect, in the study of social processes in the Grassfields. It did not end at that. Jean-Pierre Warnier invests a significant amount of his time promoting social democracy, freedom, equity and justice in France, as well as in Cameroon. When he wrote to me recently asking for background information on an asylum case he had been requested to provide an expert report on, I could think of none better placed than Walter Gam Nkwi to render such a service. So I passed the address on. Warnier got satisfaction, and both have been involved in intellectual conversations and exchange of publications. This is how the world works, but somehow, not adequately accounted for when we discuss research.

Like everyone else, I move with my networks. In August 2009, I took up the position of Professor and Head of Department of Social Anthropology at the University of Cape Town (UCT). To me, that has meant sharing my networks with colleagues and students, through facilitation of new encounters. It is in this connection, that Jean-Pierre Warnier and Michael Rowlands, among others, have visited UCT. From August 31 to September 30 2011, Warnier honoured an invitation by my colleagues and me, thanks to the Mellon Visiting Fellowship programme. The purpose of the visit was to contribute to the research of the department related to the anthropology of the body, material culture, and technologies of power and to teach at the graduate level. Warnier presented his work at the departmental seminar series, and participated in the activities of the interdisciplinary archives and public culture programme headed by Professor Carolyn Hamilton. He delivered a keynote lecture at the Anthropology Southern Africa conference in Stellenbosch and made extensive contacts, including with Professors Kees van der Waal and Steven Robins of the Department of Sociology and Anthropology at the University of Stellenbosch. He also used the opportunity to establish contacts with the Kaplan Centre for Jewish studies (UCT) on the question of Jewish migrations, in the interest of his partner, Caroline Ulmann.

Warnier's Grassfields research is certain to impact the intellectual and research trajectories of colleagues and students here in South Africa, just as it has colleagues and students in Cameroon, France and elsewhere. The essays in this book are a further invitation by Warnier for us to perceive and relate to research more as a cultural enterprise, with collective and social dimensions, than merely as an individual pursuit. Like the Grassfielders who believe a child is one person's only in the womb, Jean-Pierre Warnier is of the conviction that encounters shape and direct research in fascinating ways. Warnier was one person's anthropologist only in the womb.

References

Fo ANGWAFO III, 2009, *Royalty and Politics: The Story of My Life*, Bamenda: Langaa.

KOPYTOFF, I., 1987, "The Internal African Frontier: The Making of African Political Culture," in: I. Kopytoff (ed.), *The African Frontier: The Reproduction of Traditional African Societies*. Bloomington: Indiana University Press, pp. 3-84.

NANTANG, B.J. and Nyamnjoh, F.B., 2002, "Scholarship Production in Cameroon: Interrogating a Recession" in: *African Studies Review*, Vol.45(2): 49-71.

NKWI, W.G., 2010, *Voicing the Voiceless. Contributions to Closing Gaps in Cameroon History, 1958-2009*, Bamenda: Langaa.

—, 2011a, *Kfaang and Its Technologies: Towards a Social History of Mobility in Kom, Cameroon, 1928-1998*, Leiden: African Studies Centre.

—, 2011b, *Sons and Daughters of the Soil: Land and Boundary Conflicts in North West Cameroon, 1955-2005*, Bamenda: Langaa.

NYAMNJOH, F.B., 2002, "'A Child Is One Person's Only in the Womb': Domestication, Agency and Subjectivity in the Cameroonian Grassfields," in: Richard Werbner (ed.), *Postcolonial Subjectivities in Africa*. Zed Books: London. (pp.: 111-138).

—, 2008, *Souls Forgotten*, Bamenda: Langaa.

WARNIER, J.-P., 2007, *The Pot-King: The Body and Technologies of Power*, Leiden: Brill.

Acknowledgments

The publication of this book gives me an opportunity to pay tribute to Langaa Research & Publishing CIG and to Francis Beng Nyamnjoh, its charismatic founder and manager. A Cameroonian publishing house located in Bamenda and essentially devoted to promoting Cameroonian and African literature and scholarship is a miracle only made possible by his acumen and competent use of the most sophisticated digital technologies. It breaks the monopoly of Western Publishing houses. It provides an unexpected and formidable freedom to publish many texts that would never find their way to the established publishers.

Francis is a friend if there is ever one. I take it as a privilege to publish the present book at Langaa thanks to him. He has put an order for this book sometime around 2008. It took me four years to respond. Producing a PDF document clean enough to be published is an achievement far beyond my competence although, in his typical manner, Francis had stressed the unfathomable easiness of the task. He did not want to scare me away right from the start. Fortunately, two persons made up for my total inaptitude at taming the softwares needed to produce the PDF document needed by the Publisher. The first one is Emmanuella, Francis' daughter who scanned the original published articles that provide the bulk of this book. The second one is Isabelle Le Quinio, whose quasi-shamanistic knowledge of the digital wilderness succeeded in turning a shapeless and disjointed typescript into a perfect PDF document complete with illustrations, maps, bibliography and the like. In addition to her technical expertise, she put her energy at enhancing the contents of the book, captions and titles to achieve better clarity and scholarship. To them my gratitude is beyond words.

The first, introductory, chapter to this book presents anthropological research as a series of personal encounters. In itself, it is an acknowledgment of sorts. However, amongst all the many encounters I made, I wish to make a special mention of Fo Angwafo III S.A.N. of Mankon, Elizabeth Chilver and Igor Kopytoff who have been my Mentors and benevolent guides in my Cameroonian *Wanderungen*.

Table of contents

Introduction

1. Forty years of research in the making

Take a human subject. Put him in contact with other subjects in a given situation. If he plays the interactive game, something will happen. What kind of thing? No one can predict. It is said that one of Napoleon's generals asked him how to win a battle. As usual, the Emperor gave a curt reply: "Get involved and see what happens." In principle, an anthropologist stands at the opposite of the military. However, they have one thing in common: if they get involved in a situation, something is bound to happen. In the case of the anthropologist, he will get to meet people, interact and observe. Then he will construct what happens as an anthropological topic. Except that, in the particular case, the observer and the observed are to some extent one and the same person. The anthropologist does not analyse a given people. He analyses his interactions with given subjects and groups.

This is, it seems to me, how anthropology constituted itself as a particular academic endeavour, even if this is not the usual way to put it. If I am right, anthropology has been a haphazard and unpredictable venture because the scenario of the encounter has never been written in advance. Since anthropology defined itself as a professional pursuit, and until recently, anthropologists have been prone to keeping fieldwork in the straight jacket of standard textbook methods. But this is just pretence. As D. Fassin (2000) suggests contra O. Mannoni (1950) and J. Carothers (1954), there is nothing pre-determined in the encounter of different subjectivities that will dictate the patterns it will assume. This is true of the anthropological encounter. In other words, the notions of field of enquiry and fieldwork cannot be disconnected from the personal engagement of the researcher. This is, in my view, one of the basic differences between the sociological tradition and the anthropological one in Western countries, even if their ambitions are the same, that is, to produce some kind of educated, if not scientific, discourse on society and social processes.

In this introduction, I propose to explain what it is that took place once I engaged into the local Grassfields situation. I do not entertain much illusion concerning the accuracy of such a belated reconstruction. However, what seems important in my view is not so much the autobiographical exactitude (however commendable) of such an endeavour, than the conclusions that may be drawn from this sort of experience, namely that the ethnologist is in possession of a multipurpose research tool upon which he may adjust all kinds of extensions or contraptions for more specialised purposes. This single, versatile, tool is nothing less that his own subjectivity. This point was made clear as early as the mid-1960s by Georges Devereux (1967), a psychoanalyst and anthropologist. His contribution has been a major turning point in the methodology and the epistemology of the social sciences, laying the foundations for a reflexive approach in anthropology. I endorse it wholeheartedly. In other words, this introduction constitutes a re-interpretation or a deciphering of the forty years of research I have so far spent in or around the Cameroon Grassfields.

In May 1971, I set foot for the first time in Cameroon and, for that matter, in Africa. I was coming from Philadelphia in the United-States where I was reading anthropology at the graduate school of the University of Pennsylvania. The air temperature was about the same on both sides of the Atlantic. As far as all the rest was concerned, the contrast was utterly striking. What I remember is a feeling of confusion. This feeling became an enduring dimension of my life in Cameroon. It has never disappeared to this day although I tried hard to contain it by implementing all the methodological trappings of standard field research one may find in textbooks such as the most useful Notes and Queries in Anthropology. So much so that my successive enquiries in the field appear to me as so many, more or less successful or unsuccessful, attempts to find some kind of order, some kind of criteria to sort out and arrange the huge mass of new perceptions. At face value, I seldom knew if I should consider them as relevant to my research and therefore as worthy of my scholarly attention. Some of them, like the gesture of spraying raffia wine, accomplished by the King, have been lying dormant in my notebooks and in my memory for more than two decades before they migrated to the forefront of my research.

Before 1971, I knew nothing about Africa, except from the books I had read, the films I had seen and the lectures I had attended. When I set foot in Douala, I was overwhelmed by an inordinate mixture of strong feelings: the pungent smell of 'miondo', palm oil and grilled fish, the cramps I experienced when folding my large frame to fit into crowded bush taxis, the five days of investigation on my case by the Special Branch in Buea, the unbelievable splendour of the tropical storms in the mountains. As it turned out, I found myself incapable of mobilizing on the spot any grid of criteria that would help me to decode and find any kind of order and meaning in such a huge mass of new and powerful impressions. This state of confusion pushed me to move forward. Everything was new to me. There was a wealth of knowledge to be won. There was no sadness for me under those tropics. I was just hit and saturated by the perceptive and sensory experience of any empirical research in an unfamiliar, exotic and foreign society.

If I mention this confusing experience right from the start, it is because it became the daily weft of my enquiries, and that it inscribes the latter in a time span measured in decades – the time needed for the dust to fall down before I begin to guess at the main features of the socio-cultural landscape, before a new event puts me at the heart of a sandstorm, with nothing to be seen and guessed at, although I was trying hard to cling to the methodological and theoretical tools I had learned at college as so many branches to cling on and keep me above the dust cloud. Thus, from one encounter to the next, from one confusing experience to its clarification, my experience in the field developed together with my understanding of the local royal hierarchies of the Grassfields. Everything, said Aristotle, is perceived according to the idiosyncrasies of the perceiving subject. My own subjectivity provided a frame to the ethnological encounter I was directed to experience, not from my own will, but due to various circumstances.

The Grassfields: an object I did not chose

I became attracted to anthropology by its potential for social and scientific critique. This took place in the mid-sixties, at a time of intense socio-cultural turbulence in Western countries. When I filed an application at the Graduate school of the University of Pennsylvania, I meant to kill two birds with one stone: get acquainted with the United-States where I had never set foot, whereas my late father, who was bilingual, had been intimately acquainted with Great-Britain and the United-States, and, second, studying anthropology. When in Philadelphia, I was told that one had to conduct fieldwork. I was asked to select a culture area, however reluctant I was to wet my shirt under some distant tropics. So far, in my view, this obligation only concerned the ethnographers, whereas an anthropologist could spend his lifetime in his study after a short and redundant trip in a faraway wilderness, more or less as Claude Lévi-Strauss had done. So, that was it. I had to do field work. Given my scanty financial means, Oceania and Asia were out of my reach. The Americas were the preserve of North American anthropologists – some of them being instrumental in intelligence monitored by the CIA as it appeared when the Camelot operation was blown up in the late 1960s. Remained Africa that was easily accessible from France and that allowed me to put to good use my knowledge of French and English.

Since it was Africa, I was told, my supervisor would be Professor Igor Kopytoff. The latter turned down the project I had devised on Ivory-Coast. I had chosen that country after enquiring about low cost flights. This criterion is as good as any other. Instead, Igor Kopytoff directed me to Cameroon where Ngwa'fo, king of Mankon, had informed Elizabeth Chilver, a historian from Oxford, of his wish to have an anthropologist conduct some research in his kingdom. At least, I was welcome, and it saved me the trouble and the anxiety of having to make a choice and to explain to the local people what the White man proposed to do and why. Accordingly, I did not choose my field situation, nor the kingdom of Mankon, or the kind of society I wished to study. I consider this as a favour. Constraints provide a structure. May I confess that I was no more of a Marxist than most students at the time, nor a revolutionary or a radical activist in those years (the late 1960s) of ideological and cultural turmoil, even if I had spent a full week in the basements and on the roofs of the Sorbonne in May 1968 where I was completing my BA in philosophy. My departure to the United-States saved me the trouble of having to provide an answer to the question "where do you speak from?" that is, where do you stand in the class struggle? This question was the lot of most French anthropologists at the time, except those who had made their allegiance to the structuralist obedience and were considered as lost souls by the Marxist school.

I completed my graduate studies and went to Mankon in May and June 1971. I returned to Paris for one year to read African linguistics at the University of Paris III. I returned to Mankon for two years of fieldwork in July 1972. Bit by bit I got to learn what an ancient social hierarchy was all about: a king (at the time, the word 'king' had been dismissed by the colonizer and the independent State in favour of the less prestigious 'chief'). He lived with his fifty odd wives in a large traditional household lacking the basic amenities that became so desirable in the last decades of the 20th century. Below him stood a number of palace and descent group notables imbued with their intrinsic worthiness, and down below, battalions of male cadets promised to urban migrations. I found it almost impossible to bridge the gap between the Mankon royal hierarchy on the one hand and my own experience as a subject of a Western so-called democracy. My subjectivity was still heavily informed by my feelings and the categories of the colonial situation. I still had to deconstruct it.

At the time, I experienced the African continent as an open frontier in which, all of a sudden, I could construct an new trajectory for myself, far away from the constraints of my family, my social class, the university syllabus, while getting confronted on a daily basis to a society completely different from the one I was coming from. But all this was extremely unclear in my mind. First and foremost, I felt the urgency to learn, to understand, to introduce some kind of order in the data, to mumble a few words in the vernacular without getting mixed up with other languages.

It seemed strange to me that Ngwa'fo had wished to attract an ethnologist into his kingdom. At first, I did not find any adequate explanation. Once the first year had passed and I was getting more familiar with the kingdom, I fitted myself into one of the categories of American anthropology that was current at the time. I thought I numbered among the 'prestige goods' of the monarchy. After all, the kingdom of Bali-Nyonga had had its white literati in the person of Eugen Zintgraff (1895) who had published a book, followed by Hutter (1902) and the historian Elizabeth Chilver (1967). Bafut, to the north of Mankon, had been the object of a publication by the anthropologists Robert & Pat Ritzenthaler (1962) and by the zoologist Gerald Durell (1958). It befitted Mankon to have an ethnographer and his associated publications, focused on the palace and the information kept by the entourage of Ngwa'fo. It is only in later years that I discovered how wrong and prejudiced I was in that respect. After two years in Mankon, Ngwa'fo gave me the title of *Sang-Nto'* ('courtyard of the palace'). This gave me a position in the palace hierarchy. I felt deeply honoured. At the same time, I was at a loss to understand what it implied and what I could do with it.

Various disappointments around my dissertation

In the 1960s and 1970s, Western social anthropology provided a well established recipe for the analysis of any African kingdom: take down genealogies, descent groups, clans and lineages, marriage alliance rules and practices, rules of descent and succession; warm up while stirring. Add up the palace institutions, the king and his regulatory societies, the social dynamics of conflict and conflict resolution procedures, especially through the colonial situation. Put everything in a regional perspective. Implementing the recipe allowed one to produce a Ph.D. dissertation in less than three years: two for the field enquiry, plus six months devoted to writing down the chapters. It was edible. With the help of Igor Kopytoff to whom I am indebted for his constant supervision and for the heavy copy-editing he had to do, I got my Ph.D. in the spring of 1975 (Warnier 1975).

As soon as it was available, I sent a copy to Ngwa'fo who handed it over to an educated member of his entourage to be assessed. The latter remonstrated on a number of points that did not conform to the narrative of the palace. He said I had to alter these points in the dissertation. Alas, it was too late. But, more importantly, it pointed out the gap between a scholarly and critical piece of research on the one hand, and the cultural requirements of the host society on the other hand. I promised to take those points into consideration in my subsequent work. This is one more occurrence of the state of confusion I have already mentioned. In that particular case, it came from the conflicting expectations of the kingdom and the academia. In subsequent years, I tried to wind a path between the two.

What happened next was no less confusing. I had gone to the United-States with a French scholarship of the Ministry of Foreign Affairs assorted with a promise not to feed the brain drain to America, and to come back to France once I had obtained my diploma. Fair enough. As soon as I obtained my Ph.D., I applied for a teaching position in France, just to be told by the Ministry of Higher Education that it did not recognize foreign degrees. My application was turned down on those grounds. This is typical of any bureaucracy the world over. Each sector of the administration follows up its own logics. They seldom coordinate. I was *de facto* an exile, pushed out of my own country by the very means it had provided for my education. I found employment in Nigeria, on a local contract at Ahmadu Bello University for two years followed by one more year of research in Mankon financed by my personal savings, by research money allocated to Jacqueline Leroy, a linguist and my wife at the time, plus various odds and bits. After one year in Cameroon (1977-78), the two of us returned to Nigeria where we found two teaching positions at the University of Jos: migrations and precariousness – the lot of most young researchers in the humanities.

This is when the two of us came across an unexpected piece of good luck. At the time, the much regretted Professor Martin Njeuma was the Dean at the Faculty of Letters and Human Sciences at the University of Yaoundé. I had met him previously though we had not had time to get properly acquainted. However, he was quick to see that he could have Jacqueline Leroy and I recruited as technical assistants by the French *Coopération* programme. To say the least, Martin Njeuma was disappointed by the University lecturers who were sent to him by the French Ministry of Cooperation. They were incapable of speaking a word of English for the benefit of Anglophone students. He needed reasonably bilingual lecturers with a good background in African studies. This unexpected piece of luck meant academic salvation for Jacqueline Leroy and myself. And also, it was crucial in changing my approach to the Grassfields and to the Mankon kingdom. I will always cherish the memory of Martin who soon became an intimate friend.

An accounting sheet of the 1971-1978 years

Let me summarize briefly the various issues I had tackled so far. In 1971-1974, I focused on a very standard monograph of the Mankon kingdom cast into the theoretical mould provided by British social anthropology. At the same time, I planted some seeds that were to germinate and to grow up in later years. As regards the history of the Cameroon Grassfields, the accepted wisdom in the 1970s was that they were almost empty of population until the 17th century when migrants came from Widekum, Tikar, Munshi and other areas to establish the local chiefdoms. I had my doubts regarding such a scenario. My impression was that the Grassfields had been settled very early in human history and that there had been a potent demographic growth as early as the beginning of the Neolithic, still to be dated at the time. In 1973, a CNRS conference was held in Paris on the contribution of ethnological research to the history of Cameroon civilizations. The proceedings were later published under the direction of Claude Tardits (1981). Nicolas David, who had been my archaeology lecturer at the University of Pennsylvania, attended the conference. I asked him to brief me on the ways of finding stratified archaeological sites in the Grassfields that would provide a chrono-stratigraphy of the area. Following his indications, Jacqueline Leroy and I found several rock shelters of great archaeological potential during the dry season of 1973-74, that is, Abeke, Shum Laka, Fiye Nkwi and Mbi Crater. Bassey Andah, a Nigerian archaeologist, succeeded in raising funds to do some excavations, but was denied a research permit by the Cameroonian authorities. It turned out that the latter did not wish Cameroonian history to be put into the hands of a Nigerian. I did not find any archaeologist to do the digs until Pierre de Maret and Raymond Asombang started to do the work as from 1978. This was the inception of the archaeological extension of my research program.

Also in the period 1971-1974, I found two important things. First, the Grassfields were an area of local economic specialization and trade. Marketplaces, currencies, porterage, trading friendships surfaced time and again in my enquiries. I also sensed the importance of long-distance trading, including the slave trade with the coastal areas. But it was not until 1976, when I met Mike Rowlands who was travelling through Zaria that I acquired a clear view of the research issues pertaining to the economic history of the area. Mike Rowlands was to become my tutor in that respect. In 1977-78, I spent one more year in Mankon and I devoted it to exploring the trading networks of the Bamenda plateau. I had taken over from Mike who had spent the year 1976-77 in Mankon. Second, it appeared quite clearly that Mankon, like most, if not all, surrounding kingdoms, was a composite one. 30% of the women married in Mankon around the turn of the 20th century came from another local community, and quite a few descent groups came from various neighbouring regions. I had the impression that this was a key feature in the social and political organisation of the kingdom. It deserved a thorough investigation. It also seemed to be logically articulated to the rise and history of the local kingdoms. When I returned to Nigeria (in Jos) in 1978-79, I started working in the Jos Museum, in the Kaduna archives and in several other places to collect material on the economic history of the whole subcontinental area surrounding the Grassfields.

Hence my interest in two aspects of Grassfields civilization: its *longue durée* history, to be grasped through archaeology, historical linguistics, the landscapes and agricultural systems, etc., and second, its economic history insofar as it could be reached from various kinds of evidence for the last three centuries (from 1700 to 2000).

1979-1985: My research is taking shape

For one thing, I moved from Jos to Yaoundé in 1979 thanks to Martin Njeuma. Once in Yaoundé, I could get easy access to Mankon, and pursue my enquiries. Most importantly as well, I started teaching at the History Department under Professors Martin Njeuma and Engelberg Mveng. The next year, I shared my time between the Department of History and that of Sociology under Professor Jean Mfoulou. This was a time when there was a high density of competent scholars and researchers in Cameroon. In addition to the staff at the Faculty of Letters and Human Sciences (with Bongfen Chem Langhëë, Lovett Elango, Verkijika Fanso, Joseph-Marie Essomba, Jean-Louis Dongmo, etc.) there were the researchers of ORSTOM (later to become IRD – Institut de Recherche pour le Développement), CNRS, and other expatriate research institutions. A couple of years after I had arrived, the Institute of Human Sciences received sizable financial, administrative and logistical means. It became a key operator in the years to follow. During those six years in Cameroon (1979-1985), I had the unique opportunity to meet many researchers with a vast array of scientific qualifications – historians, anthropologists, archaeologists, linguists, but also geo-morphologists, geologists, geographers, hydrologists, etc. Consequently, I had an opportunity to discuss many questions raised by Grassfields history and anthropology.

Their number was such as to exceed what can be accommodated in a short introduction. I will content myself with mentioning the dead to whom I am most in debt. Father Engelberg Mveng was not only an inspiration by his vast and authoritative knowledge of Cameroon history. Until he was tragically and cruelly murdered, he had a clear understanding of my position. It was paradoxically a weak one, since the accepted wisdom in Yaoundé was that if a 'coopérant' was employed in Cameroon, it meant that he was not qualified enough to find a decent job in Europe. Consequently our position, as 'coopérants' was being undermined by scholars who were permanently employed in Europe and came to Cameroon on short visits. They were certainly very knowledgeable in their field, but did not necessarily know much about Cameroon, and more than that: they never stayed long enough to built up something that would stay behind them once they had gone away. Yet, they were entitled to the red carpet while we were pushed aside. Professor Mveng knew better. He was sharp and quick in his judgments. He came as a constant support and expressed his appreciation in what Jacqueline Leroy and I contributed to the Faculty. So were Martin Njeuma and Jean Mfoulou who became very close friends. In later years, they experienced acts of terrible violence meted upon them. They were left broken down and depressed for several years.

I now wish to mention the key contributions of Dieudonné Miaffo and Séverin Abega. They wrote their doctoral dissertations under the supervision of Jean Mfoulou seconded by myself. From the position of students, they soon assumed that of tutors as far as my research was concerned.

But, to begin with, let me go back to the general theme of this introduction. I pretend that doing research is perhaps not primarily a matter of designing a research project and the relevant methodology needed to conducting it successfully. It consists in taking a person, that is, a human subject, in putting this subject in a given situation, and then in looking at what happens. In other words, encounters with other subjects provide the impetus and the orientation of the research. Sally Chilver had met Ngwa'fo. She had met Igor Kopytoff who became my supervisor and who sent me to Ngwa'fo whom I met, the first one of scores of Mankon people. I met

Nic David and discussed with him. I met Mike Rowlands and, when travelling through Yaoundé, a number of people including Martin Njeuma. All such encounters ended up in my being recruited as a 'coopérant' in Yaoundé and in meeting other people, including Dieudonné Miaffo, Séverin Abega, and Francis Nyamnjoh.

Teaching is one of the best ways of learning. A University lecturer has to work hard to get to understand an academic domain at such a level of competence that s/he is in a position to transmit his/her knowledge to the students and to answer their questions and queries. However, as far as I was concerned, teaching in Yaoundé added a considerable surplus value to this process since the students, especially at the graduate and doctoral levels, had a first-hand knowledge of their own society and were doing research on topics related to mine. It turned out that, in such a context, the input coming from my friends, from the students and colleagues in Yaoundé far exceeded what I could feed to them in return. It became of immense benefit to me. It was under such circumstances that Francis Beng Nyamnjoh became my mentor concerning many issues pertaining to Grassfields kingdoms. In the later years, his achievements in the social sciences and, very importantly, in literature, were a source of enlightenment concerning many topics that escaped the usual tools of anthropological enquiries and yet were crucial for a proper understanding of contemporary Cameroon societies.

As regards Dieudonné Miaffo, he produced his dissertation on labour among the Bulu. It was a contribution in economic anthropology. In the meantime, Paul Biya had succeeded Ahmadu Ahidjo as the Head of State. This was in 1982. Soon after that, Jean-François Bayart came to Yaoundé. He had published *L'État au Cameroun* (1979) that won him the status of persona non grata in the country. His ban was waved in 1982 when Paul Biya succeeded Ahmadu Ahidjo. He came back to Yaoundé. I was quite eager to meet him and I did. We kept in touch. I became more and more interested in his work and impressed by his intellectual acumen and intimate knowledge of the anthropological literature. Much later, in 1988, he invited me to participate in an international conference in Leiden on the local trajectories of accumulation in Cameroon (see Geschiere & Konings 1993). I was to link up what I had done on the economic history of the Grassfields with the practice of contemporary Grassfields entrepreneurs (both Anglophone and francophone). Miaffo had already collected a number of life histories of prominent businessmen and women. We pooled our data and ideas, and published them (Miaffo & Warnier 1993). We planned to write a book together. But Dieudonné passed away before we had started writing. I published the book alone, in memoriam of Miaffo (Warnier 1993).

In the meantime, I had written my Doctorat d'État (1983) and published it (1985a). It concerned the local and regional hierarchies on the Bamenda plateau. I had also been recruited as a Professor of ethnology at the University René-Descartes (Paris V) in 1985. I was compelled to leave Yaoundé and take office in Paris although I kept making short trips to Cameroon quite frequently.

New research perspectives

Dieudonné Miaffo shifted my research interests in a way that was to turn upside down and transform my overall approach to the kingdom of Mankon and to anthropology altogether. Enquiring about capital accumulation in the Grassfields and about businessmen and women, we noticed how many of them combined capital accumulation and status building in their kingdom of origin. There was something to be investigated and understood about the ways these individuals put their assets into bank accounts, shops, workshops, houses in town and in the hamlet they built in the village. In other words, they accumulated financial, productive, symbolic and social capital in one movement with a heavy emphasis on being present in their chiefdom of origin and on acquiring 'traditional' titles, and, as we noticed more recently, on being buried at home. There was a definite pattern to be analysed and understood regarding the way they used to safe-keep and store things, or else, give them out. So much so that, one day, Dieudonné Miaffo came to our meeting with a pamphlet written by two Bamileke Catholic priests, Father Tchouanga-Tiegoum & Ngangoum (1975:33) who meant to explain to the Catholic hierarchy and to the believers that practicing the ancestral cult was not repugnant to the basic tenets of their faith. The gist of their argument was that any human being owes his life to his forefathers and cannot possibly severe such a link with the source of his life because, they had written, the family head "is a vital piggy-bank for the whole family: in him can be found the plenitude of the blood received from the origins through a whole line of ancestors" (my translation). Once they had received their life from their forefathers and acknowledged it by making offerings to them, the Christians could address the Church to gain the salvation they sought, through receiving the sacraments.

It was the first time that I read or heard, expressed in so many words, the fact that a notable, the head of a descent group or, for that matter, a king is a vital piggy-bank, that is, a container. This is not a metaphor. The notable or the king is not to be likened to a container. His body is a container that safe-keeps and stores ancestral substances: breath, speech, saliva, semen, and associated substances: raffia wine, palm oil, camwood powder, medicines. Such is the king: a 'pot-king', corpulent, filled up, sitting at the top of the social hierarchy, whose principal function consists in anointing, spraying, speaking, blowing, smearing camwood, ejaculating so as to bestow the life essence and reproductive principles on his subjects, his spouses, the land, the crops and livestock to insure their health and reproduction.

There were powerful echoes between the work of Jean-François Bayart and that of Dieudonné Miaffo on the one hand, and what I had seen in the field on the other. They turned my attention away from the paradigms obtaining in social anthropology. They directed my attention to a historical sociology of politics, taking into consideration the production of subjectivities through the study of bodily and material cultures. The king incorporates many material substances and containers in his bodily schema. Marcel Mauss and his article on "The techniques of the body" (1936) provided a basic reference. At the time, material objects were not considered as a legitimate research topic in the social sciences, except in semiotics and consumption studies. The Anthroplogy Department at University College London, and Mike Rowlands in this Department, contributed greatly to the development of material culture studies at the crossroad between archaeology, symbolic anthropology, consumption studies and semiotics. I tapped this resource, but it was not enough to tackle the issue of the 'Pot-King'.

Several other encounters were crucial in providing elements of a new tool kit to study such matters. I gave a course on material culture at the University René-Descartes. Céline Rosselin was one of the students who read the course. She wrote an MA dissertation and eventually a doctoral thesis. She brought the 'dynamic sociology'of Georges Balandier and the Manchester School into the picture. What mattered, she said, was the dynamics of the bodily/material system: how it is on the move. Motricity was the key issue and we needed to improve on the tool kit needed to study the way human bodies move together with objects in a material world.

As time went on, several people got together to form a research group that Céline Rosselin and Marie-Pierre Julien christened 'Matière à Penser', that is, 'matter (or food) for thoughts' – since materiality was at the core of our endeavour. After a while, it became clear that 'Matière à penser' lent itself to some kind of declension and could yield *Matter for politics* (an edited volume under the direction of Bayart & Warnier, 2004), and *Matter for religion* (still in project). During the years 1990-2010, the group read and discussed a vast selection of authors and publications. Pierre Parlebas, himself a colleague at the University Paris-Descartes, helped us with his praxeological approach to games and sports (Parlebas 1999). We also read Schilder, Jannerod, Berthoz, etc. We learned about the theory of situated action and distributed cognition. In the end, it became clear that the bodily motions of the human subject can be seen and analyzed as being propped against a man-made and embodied material culture to such an extent that we began talking about 'bodily and material culture' rather than just 'material culture'.

Back to Mankon and the Grassfields

In 1985, when I was recruited in Paris, I had to leave Yaoundé. The next year, the Structural Adjustment plans pressed upon Africa by the neoliberal package of the IMF and the World Bank hit the country, to precipitate it into a politico-economic crisis that culminated in 1992 with the Ghost Towns operation. I paid a last visit to Mankon in 1989, to return only in 2000 for a short visit. It was then that I decided to catch up by staying four months in 2002, during which I meant to test my interpretations of the Mankon hierarchy in terms of bodily and material culture of the king and his subjects.

Since the early 1980s, African kings had made an unexpected come back in the forefront of national politics. In 2000, a conference held in Paris by several dozens social scientists studied this remarkable phenomenon. Their findings were published in an edited volume (Perrot & Fauvelle-Aymar 2003). These scholars were fairly unanimous in considering that the hopes raised by the construction of independent modern African States had not been satisfied. The crisis or relative failure of African States began to show in the early 1980s. In such a context, African kings provided a source of legitimacy that could be tapped for the benefit of the State.

They also provided 'civil society' partners who could be recruited into the 'good governance' advocated by the International agencies to substitute for 'failed' States seen as inefficient and corrupt. By the end of the 1980s, it became clear that Paul Biya was taking the kings on board in the composite alliance needed to establish a hegemony sustaining the power structure ruling Cameroon. The Fon (or king) of Mankon was clearly part of the scheme. The kingdom was still operating along the logic of the 'vital piggy-bank' of the ancestors. At the same time, it became a stakeholder in the Cameroonian hegemonic alliance. In 2002, both aspects needed to be investigated anew and this is one of the many reasons why I went back to the field for four months.

Other encounters were crucial in feeding my thoughts. Let me mention just a few. When I came back to Paris in 1985, Jean-François Bayart was running a seminar dubbed 'Trajepo' for 'trajectoires du politique'. I attended and participated in it inasmuch as the heavy workload at the University permitted. As the years passed, Max Weber and Michel Foucault took place among the major references in this effort to construct a historical sociology of politics. The Foucauldian theme of the microphysics of power and their technologies addressed to the body came in handy in the late 1990s and early 2000s to analyze the technologies of the 'pot-king'. The sensori-motor conducts of opening up, closing down, pouring, storing, spraying, anointing, crossing over thresholds, transforming, swallowing, expelling bad things and people as so many excreta, etc. could be seen as micro-technologies of power. Moreover, they were propped against an elaborate embodied material culture: drinking horns, bags, calabashes, *azo'* bowls, drums, houses, doors, raphia wine, palm oil, camwood powder, medicines, the ditch around the city, etc. It now sounds fairly clear, explicit and easily understandable. However, at the time, exploring all the intricacies of such an elaborate bodily and material culture was extremely messy and confusing.

At some point, this gave me a clue to the reasons of my presence in Mankon. It should be remembered that the king had asked Sally Chilver to send someone to do research in the kingdom. In so doing, the Fon complied with one of the main functions of a monarch, that is, to pick up anything or anyone roaming at large outside the envelope of the kingdom and to bring it inside, should it be good enough to be absorbed and eaten. Such adopted strangers are called *ankyeni* in Mankon. This is the name of an edible grasshopper that appears at the end of the rainy season and that is considered as a delicacy. When applied to human beings, it designates a social category that has its place in this composite kingdom. It meant that I had been deemed good enough to be eaten, kept in the kingdom, and given a title. At the time, it put me under an obligation to provide something edible and valuable to the Mankon people in terms of publications, archival documents, financial support to various programs and events such as the equipment of a dispensary, the Jubilee held in 2009, or the MACUDA association. Also, when teaching in Yaoundé, I endeavoured to help Mankon students by way of more or less informal tutorial and counselling.

A couple of years before I left the University of Yaoundé, Séverin Abega had presented his doctoral dissertation on the Esana among the Beti under the direction of Jean Mfoulou, with myself as a tutor (published in 1987). At first, his research did not seem to converge with mine and to provide useful grounds for relevant debates. The Beti did not have kings, and, at first, Abega was more interested in a structuralist approach to Beti civilisation than to political sociology. However, as the years passed, it turned out that Abega was becoming an outstanding anthropologist and a prolific writer of novels, essays, short stories and theatre plays. From the mid 1980s to his untimely and sudden death in 2008, he volunteered sharp and insightful critical comments on my findings and on many related topics such as sex, since it became clear that, in Grassfields kingdoms, high polygamy and the control exercised on the sexuality of women and unmarried cadets put sex at the heart of politics until the 1960s and 1970s, when urban migrations and the reformulation of the kingdom hierarchy transformed the politics of sex.

Let me give just one example of the way Abega shifted the way I analyzed the kingdom hierarchy. Around 2000, I gave a public lecture in the 'Amphithéâtre 1500' at the University of Yaoundé. In my lecture, I mentioned the fact that the subjects of the kingdom brought to the king what they deemed to be the produce of the ancestral substances bestowed on them by the king. Consequently, they brought girls as spouses, boys as retainers, crops, money, livestock. They were paid back, said I, by the king spraying on them the contents of his mouth, that is, with nothing more than wind. Abega pointed out that I was wrong. What the king gives out to his subjects with his breath and saliva is priceless, since it is the principle of all life, reproduction and wealth, whereas what the subjects bring to the palace fetches a certain, limited, price, on the market. This is why, said Abega, the subjects consider that they have not been cheated. They genuinely believe that they are the winners in the bargain. He was right. This brought to my attention a number of issues pertaining to the construction and the politics of value that I put to good use much later.

At the Catholic University in Central Africa, Yaoundé, Abega had built a research team and was highly successful both in obtaining research funds for his team and in providing intellectual leadership. His demise was catastrophic for his colleagues and for the future of anthropological research in Cameroon, not to speak of the grief of his family and friends, including myself.

Research programs as series of encounters

Textbooks in the social sciences usually provide a chapter on research designs, protocols and methods. The standard procedure consists in identifying a puzzle to be elucidated, in formulating hypotheses, in devising a hypothetico-deductive methodology, and in selecting the means – interviews, questionnaires, observation, etc. – most suitable to collect the relevant data and to test the hypotheses. I am not saying that this is wrong or useless. I made extensive use of methodology textbooks on interviews, life histories, genealogies, kinship terminology, a herbarium, and the like. No beginner can dispense with this kind of research techniques.

However, I fully agree with what George Devereux (1967) expressed in his seminal book on anxiety and field research methods. Doing fieldwork, he says, generates anxiety. Why is it so? Mainly for two reasons: The first one is that the researcher has to establish a contact with other subjects. This generates some amount of anxiety since there is much uncertainty about such encounters. Most people the researcher will meet are unknown to him at first. This puts some strain on his emotional responses. Besides, he does not know if s/he will be able to establish a rewarding relationship or be rejected or mislead. The second cause of anxiety comes from the fact that the researcher does not know if s/he will be able to collect relevant data. S/he does not know if s/he will have enough data to fulfil the research program, to write a dissertation, a book or an article, and to meet the expectations of the funding agency. Usually, beginners collect vast amounts of data. They find themselves with so much matter that their dissertation expands out of any reasonable proportion. This is compounded by the fact that they do not want to sacrifice large quantities of hard won data and to cut short. In film-making, one learns that twenty of fifty hours of footage are needed to cut a 20 or 53mn documentary film and that all the rest of the footage will never be put to use. In the social sciences, beginners are so anxious that they want to collect huge amounts of data, and when this is done, they are obsessed with putting everything to good use.

When doing fieldwork, the temptation, for the anxious researcher, says Devereux, is to cope with his own anxiety. S/he does it by keeping people at arm's length and by clinging to objectifying methodologies: collecting statistics and kinship terminologies generates less anxiety than real and unpredictable human relationships and interactions. Research programs and methods become a shield behind which the researcher takes refuge, instead of being a valuable adjunct to an inter-subjective relationship with the people the researcher happens to meet. The result, says Devereux, is an objectifying and disappointing social science that misses the sociological point. The only way out of this dead-end is to get to meet other subjects, see what happens, let oneself be emotionally involved, questioned, directed, and informed. What will happen in the course of the encounters will become the stuff of the enquiry, instead of what has been outlined beforehand by the textbook. Then, provided the contact is established, using the proper methods of field research may be of immense benefit.

If this is true – and I believe it is – an account of the way I built up my research must be an account of my encounters with the people I happened to meet. In such encounters, I, as a subject, have engaged my subjectivity. The latter became the tool that allowed me to establish a relationship with other subjects. They, in turn, orientated me towards various people, places, situations and questions that altered the way I perceived the research situation. Accordingly, I made use of specific methodological tools to construct the relevant data and elaborate some kind of scholarly discourse on Mankon as a kingdom and on the Grassfelds situation and history as a whole. This is why, in this introduction, I focus on the encounters that have shaped the research I conducted in the Grassfelds. Over the last four decades, this has produced various publications some of which have been selected to provide the substance of this book.

Outline of the book

The first part of the present book reflects my interest in the 'longue durée' history of the Grassfields once I had rejected the historiography that was current in the early 1970s. In other words, and in Braudelian parlance, it concerns the civilization of the Grassfields, and it provides the title of the present volume. The historiography of the Cameroon highlands that I challenged was based mostly on oral traditions and on the trope of migrations. I shifted away from this kind of approach. The first part of this book now reflects the outcome of my discussions with Nic David in 1973 and the subsequent 'invention' of several archaeological sites of first magnitude, tested in 1977 by Pierre de Maret and myself, and subsequently excavated by R. Asombang, P. De Maret and his team. The second chapter on the Ndop Plain iron industry was the result of my encounter with Ian Fowler, then a student of Mike Rowlands. We worked together in 1976-77 with an aim at mapping, quantifying, and hopefully 14C dating the Ndop Plain iron industry. We expected that it would provide the backbone of the economic history of the Western Grassfields over several centuries. The 14C dating did not yield much significant result. By contrast, the rest of the agenda was successfully conducted by Ian Fowler (1989 and 2011). The third chapter is the result of a common venture with Jacqueline Leroy, a linguist, and my wife at the time. Thanks to her, who was (and still is in 2012) studying the Mankon language, I met all the linguists of the Grassfields Bantu Working Group (GBWG), namely Ian Voorhoeve, Maurice Tadadjeu, Larry Hyman, Jean-Marie Hombert, and others, who initiated me to the intricacies of Grassfields language classifications, and the contribution of linguistic history to the 'longue durée' history of the highlands.

This first part of the book provides the general historical framework of the second and third parts. In my view, the arguments it develops, together with other publications I have not included for want of space, and because they are more easily accessible (for example Warnier 1992), establish the fact that the Grassfields have been densely and continuously settled since the Neolithic, six thousand years ago. Linguistic differentiation, the construction of elaborate systems of economic specialization and trade, and the emergence of kingdoms are mostly endogenous phenomena rooted in a Neolithic and Iron Age civilization of great sophistication.

The second part reflects my interest in the political economy of the Grassfields. It took shape very early in my research. When discussing with elderly Mankon men such as Avwontom, Tse Ndi, Markus Njoya, Tawa and many others, I found out that trading and market organization (trading households, trade friendships, currencies, measuring and accounting systems, rotating credit associations) were key issues in the Mankon kingdom. My encounter with Mike Rowlands helped me to upgrade my approach at a time when I started working on the history of agrosystems in the Grassfields. Chapter five is the result of my meeting with Karin Luke, a German veterinary doctor involved in various programs of pig production. We also met several Peace Corps and NGO volunteers (such as those of the Heifer project) who were dismayed by the gap between the glossy paper flyers of the organization they belonged to and the perfect political correctness of their agenda on the one hand, and the inadequacy, hidden agenda and failures of the same organizations in the field. We had lengthy and disillusioned discussions on the topic, reflected in a very soft and muted way in this fourth chapter on 'improved' pig production in the Grassfields.

One of the ways to reconstruct the economic history of the Grassfields is to probe into the distribution of significant items. Guns definitely qualify in that respect. They still loom large in funerals, annual festivals, and material culture. Chapter six addresses their history and trade. Some of those guns were (and still are) manufactured in Africa. Igbo blacksmiths had a reputation in such matters right from the end of the 19th century (and probably much earlier). Grassfields gunsmiths learned their trade with Igbo masters in the first decades of the 20th century. However, the first guns to be introduced in the area were traded from Europe. Many of the earliest ones are still in use. Sampling them could provide useful historical and economic information. Second, guns were said to be a key item in the slave trade. Accordingly, they could provide some quantitative and historical data that could be matched with other sources on the slave trade. In that respect, I approached Mr. H.L. Blackmore, then the curator of the small firearms collection at the Tower of London. He welcomed my initiative and pushed my research somewhat ahead of what I had expected by giving me private tutorial on proof and view marks, bores, gun-maker houses, the organization of trade and manufacture in Great Britain in the 18th and 19th centuries. He also identified the most popular flintlock still in use in the Grassfields from the photographs I had brought to him.

Hence the seventh chapter on the slave trade. Contrary to accepted wisdom, the flintlock is a very inefficient weapon unless used in significant numbers by trained soldiers, following strictly coded tactics. It would have been next to useless in slave raiding. This fact, and many others, induced me to enquire more deeply into the mechanics of slave procurement. The trade played a key role in long distance exchange in luxury goods that was the preserve of kings and high-ranking notables.

Ancient published sources such as the *Polyglotta Africana* of the missionary Koelle (1854), specific entries in *Goldie's Efic Dictionnary* (1862), and archival sources in the Foreign Office on the harbours of the Bight of Benin provide significant information on Grassfields slaves, generally known under the name of Mbudikum in coastal areas in the 19th century. When I met Ute Röschenthaler, Nicolas Argenti and Stephan Palmié, we decided to tackle the question of possible cultural transfers sustained by the slave trade along the ways from the Grassfields to the coastal areas of Cameroon and to the New World. This piece of research provided the substance of the eighth chapter – the last one in the second part of the book. This second part very much reflects the impact of the encounters I made in the 1970s and early 1980s. To make a long story short, it combines a very classical sort of social anthropology with a number of themes in economic, political and cultural history along the lines developed by the Annales historical school, and some adjuncts such as a systemic approach to the Grassfields as an internally diversified ensemble or civilization.

By contrast, the third part of the book reflects more recent concerns with a Foucauldian and a praxeological approach to the technologies of power, bodily and material culture, and the techniques of the self. Chapter 9 is an English translation of an article originally published in French in the journal *Le Portique*. It underscores the importance of the boundaries and the processes of territorialisation in Grassfields kingdoms, in connection with material culture and the outgoing and ingoing flows of people and things through the apertures of the kingdom.

Chapter 10 provides theoretical insights into the praxeology of containment and the assorted issues of material or bodily containers, surfaces, openings and transits as technologies of power in the Grassfields. First published in 2006, it summarizes the contents of a book that I was to publish in its English version in 2007 and in the French one in 2009 (Warnier, 2006, 2007, 2009a). It explains in what ways the king's body may be considered as a receptacle of substances imbued with the life essence given out by the ancestors. He is a 'Pot-King'. Such bodily substances (breath, speech, saliva, semen) are in limited supply. They have to be expanded upon and multiplied by such substances as palm oil, raffia wine and camwood powder. The burden of kingship consists in acquiring them, storing them in bodily and material containers, and giving them out to the subjects of the kingdom in order to insure the fertility and multiplication of people, livestock, crops and wealth. The embodiment of power in the king and his bodily substances implies that the material culture of containers and contents is part and parcel of the king's bodily schema. A complete analysis of the African sacred kingship should therefore rest on a theory of bodily and material culture. This is the object of chapter 10 on surfaces and containers.

The eleventh chapter dates back to an earlier period but it can be read anew in the light of the previous two chapters. As I have just said, in Mankon, as in most Grassfields kingdoms, the king and the descent group heads are used, so to speak, as containers of the reproductive substances of the corporate group under their care. High polygamy, and the large number of their wives is the logical implication of such practices and representations. As a result, in the past, a large proportion of the male population did not have access to genital sex and to marriage. Given the fact that the body of unmarried cadets was not considered as a container worthy of storing ancestral substances, inegalitarian and hierarchical societies such as the Grassfields ones faced a permanent problem. They had to do something with those people who were, as it were, in excess or redundant. The condition of the unmarried male cadets is therefore a key issue when analyzing the governemtality of containers suggested in the tenth chapter of the present volume, and fully developed in my book on *The Pot-King* (2007).

As the years passed, I ended up considering that the king has three bodies: his own, the palace and the city. They all share a similar structure: an envelope and apertures. They share the same contents: the ancestral substances and what they produce – people, livestock, crops and wealth. They have the same functions of containment, communication between inside and outside, and of transformation of the contents. The palace of the king, in that context, deserves much attention. The twelve and last chapter concerning the Mankon palace is a much earlier piece of work written at a time I had not yet engaged in the analysis of the 'Pot-King'.

However, being quite ethnographic in overtone, it can be easily recycled in the context of the governmentality of containers.

The conclusion of the book (chapter 13) addresses three issues that came to the fore around 2010 and lie therefore beyond the scope of the articles collected in the present volume. The first one concerns a reassessment of Grassfields history within the paradigm of global history. There are more and more indications that, for the last couple of millennia, the Grassfields have been a centre of accumulation of people, power and wealth. In those respects, they enjoyed a high degree of self-reliance and autonomy although they were part of a much larger, encompassing, African frontier. If this is the case, then a crucial issue in the history of the Grassfields would be their possible connexion to other centres of wealth accumulation in the larger world system, and especially to the most ancient and enduring one that included the Nile valley, the Horn of Africa and most of southern Asia all the way to China since the middle of the first millennium BC.

The second issue to be tackled as regards the history of the Grassfields relates to the antiquity of kingdom formation and the processes that induced it. This issue is closely related to the one that has just been mentioned. The most reasonable hypothesis is that kingdom formation started much earlier and in a more endogenous manner (e.g. not under the impact of Tikar migrations or the Atlantic slave trade) than has been assumed so far. However, if kingdom formation may be seen as a regional process encompassing large numbers of kingdoms rather than any single one, it does not follow that all the kingdoms share a common, standard, pattern. There is much internal diversification. The issue of the internal diversity of the Grassfields kingdoms will be addressed in this part of the conclusion.

The third issue concerns the impact of modernity on the kingdoms of the Grassfields and the major historical dynamics that affect them in the early 21st century.

Part I

The historical background

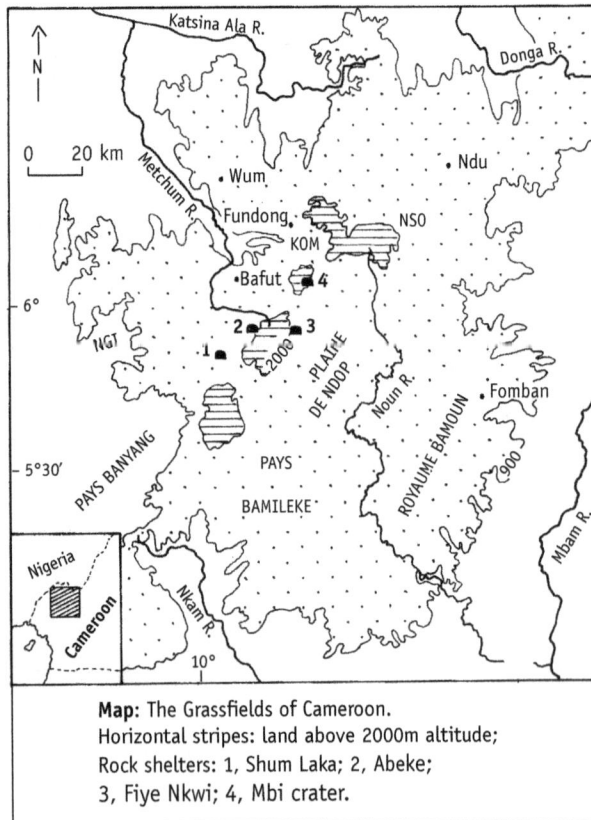

Map: The Grassfields of Cameroon.
Horizontal stripes: land above 2000m altitude;
Rock shelters: 1, Shum Laka; 2, Abeke;
3, Fiye Nkwi; 4, Mbi crater.

The history of the peopling of Western Cameroon and the genesis of its landscapes

Not so long ago, in the 1970s, the generally accepted opinion, summarized by Ghomsi (1972: 65), was that the high plateaux or Grassfields of Western Cameroon had been peopled, in succession, by a very ancient stock whose presence was evidenced by archaeological finds, then by a less ancient stock, composed of more or less scattered populations speaking languages akin to those spoken nowadays and finally by a recent stock (dated to about the 17[h] century) of migrants, arriving in successive waves from the north-east ('Ndobo-Tikari' country), the West ('Widekum' country), or, for the Aghem, from the north-west ('Munshi' country). The largest group of these supposed migrants, that is the so-called 'Tikar', were said to be the founders of the Bamileke, Bamum, Nso', Kom and Bafut chiefdoms. In the absence of reliable evidence about the history of the peopling of the region, there were various conjectures current about the creation of its landscapes, concerning which it was agreed that they were derived from the original forest cover by clearance at a period difficult to put a date to.

At that time archaeological data hardly existed, but were not wholly absent. Jeffreys (1951: 1203; 1970: 3-11; 1972: 114-18), following Migeod, had collected numerous basalt stone implements in the Bamenda region and suspected the existence of an ancient 'Neolithic agricultural' population which he mentioned in several publications, following which the British archaeologist Hartle (1969: 35-9) made a reconnaissance which confirmed Jeffreys' opinion; it was confirmed anew by Marliac (1981, I: 27-77) and David (1980: V, III: 618-19). Linguistic data, and in particular the genetic classification of languages, which can supply population historians with valuable clues, were also barely in existence, though not entirely absent. Richardson had published some in 1957, to which Voorhoeve (1971: 1-12) and Williamson (1971: 245-306) had added further information. The view summarized by Ghomsi was a considerable advance over those presented in earlier publications – principally in works by colonial administrators such as Delaroziere – which one can find graphically condensed in Champaud's Atlas (1973: 36-41), in which successive 'waves' of migrants are depicted as moving to the assault of the mountains – then supposedly sparsely peopled or not peopled at all – in about the 17th century.

The synthesis proposed by Tardits in 1973 (published in 1981) on the occasion of a conference on the history of Cameroon civilizations, gave an account of the uncertainties that marred current opinions on the history of population groups. These rested on weak sources, namely oral traditions, and not any or all of them at that. Those in question had been almost exclusively collected from royal lineages and not from all sections of the population, commoner lineages in particular. Moreover these traditions had not been compared, either, with the data of archaeology or those of historical linguistics, sparse as these then were. Tardits, supported by the opinions expressed by Kaberry and Chilver and by phytogeographical, archaeological and linguistic data, stressed the contribution of ancient settlement and played down the historical value of oral traditions of migration in favour of the political meanings they conveyed.

By 1984 the situation had become quite different. One could then state categorically that the Grassfields have been peopled for several millennia, very probably continuously, and that the beginnings of the humanized landscapes familiar to us today are very ancient. These conclusions are the necessary consequence of the linguistic and archaeological data accumulated in the late 1970s and early 1980s.

Grassfields languages as evidence of an ancient and continuous human settlement

In 1973 some fifteen linguists of different nationalities formed themselves into a Grassfields Bantu Working Group (the GBWG) under the direction of Larry Hyman and Jan Voorhoeve. A strong impetus was given to their work in 1977 by a conference, financed by the CNRS and conducted by the GBWG, which took the expansion of the Bantu as its theme and which published its proceedings, edited by Hyman, Voorhoeve and Bouquiaux, in 1980 (Hyman et al., 1980). In the following years the work of the group concentrated upon about fifty Grassfields idioms, selected from the highlands as a whole, with the aim of proposing a genetic classification for them, reconstructing the 'proto-languages' of the groups they fell into and establishing their degree of relationship to common Bantu. For what follows I rely on a report by Hombert (1979), a publication by Stallcup (1980), and personal communications from J. Leroy. All the Grassfields languages are genetically related to one another and share between 55 and 100 percent of their basic vocabulary. Four groups can be distinguished among them: Mbam-Nkam (e.g. Bamileke, Bamum and Ngemba), Momo (e.g. Assaka, Ambele, Ngwo, Mogamo, Menemo), Ring (e.g. Nso', Babungo, We, Kom) and the Metchum group.

Furthermore, these languages display a characteristic which is of importance to population historians: they are diversified and very numerous in relation to the land area in which they are spoken. In other words, the density and the diversity of the Grassfields languages is high – indeed the highest on the African continent. Now, according to the linguists, this situation can only be the result of a long history of diversification on the spot. If you press linguists to give figures, they tell you that the time-depth is to be measured in millennia, but refuse to say how many.

The studies made by the GBWG satisfy the requirements of Greenberg's method of genetic classification, save in one respect. The Grassfields, in fact, are criss-crossed by very active trade networks and have been so for a very long time, so that one cannot say that the languages were totally isolated from each other. The percentage of common roots could reflect a relexification of the basic vocabulary just as much as a common genetic linguistic stock. I have discussed the methodological and historical implications of this situation in a paper the interested reader can refer to (Warnier 1980). The hypothesis of a relexification of the basic vocabulary of Grassfields languages is reinforced by the fact that genetic classifications obtained from the basic vocabularies of Grassfields languages differ appreciably from those obtained by means of a comparison of grammatical characteristics; this raises historical problems which I have discussed in another paper (Warnier 1980). In short, this phenomenon can only be explained by an intermixture of populations within and around the Grassfields.

Suppose, now, that the percentages of common roots do adequately commemorate the degree of genetic relationship between them, could one calculate the length of time that would have been required to arrive at the linguistic diversity observable in the Grassfields? This is the question that glottochronology attempts to answer. Swadesh and the Europeanists have relied on a rate of 80 percent of basic vocabulary retention per millennium – a rate that could be verified, more or less, from written documents. But Carnochan (1973) rightly observes that there is no good reason to suppose that retention rates are the same in African as in European languages. If they were the same one would have to estimate that some 3,000 years have passed to arrive at the situation in the Grassfields. But, as both Carnochan and David (1980:609) stress, nothing allows us to presume that retention rates are actually uniform.

Did the linguistic differentiation happen on the spot or in the course of migrations? In Greenberg's view (1966), the Bantu languages originated in the area stretching from the Benue to the Grassfields, an area which thus becomes an ancient cradle-land of peoples, for two reasons: (1) it is the area of maximum diversification of Bantu languages and of those closely related to Bantu; (2) it is the meeting-point between the Benue-Congo group (to which Bantu belongs) and other groups also belonging to the larger Niger-Congo-Kordofanian family. Grzymski (1981), however, has warned the historians of Africa against the blind application of the principle of maximum diversity. In the course of his plea for caution he cites, in particular, the hypothesis of the origins of

Bantu in Cameroon. In the Grassfields case, there is an argument in favour of a lengthy evolution on the spot. This is the remarkable correlation that exists between (a) the geographical limit of the plateaux, represented by the 900m contour line, (b) the boundary of related languages within the Grassfields languages which are closer to one another than to all neighbouring languages, and (c) the area in which one finds a specific socio-political organization— the chiefdom, more or less state-like, based on a lineage organization, centred on a fon or mfe, controlled by societies with custom-maintaining functions. This correlation suggests that the Grassfields, as a geographical unit, provided the frame for specific linguistic, economic and socio-cultural evolution, in a nutshell: a specific civilization. This is what makes me think that, without excluding some mixing of peoples, this evolution essentially concerned peoples in continuous occupation of the high plateaux.

Before proceeding to conclusions, let us note a last significant contribution from linguistic studies: Tikar and the languages of the Mbam-Nkam group (Bamileke, Bamum, Ngemba) only share 20 percent of their basic vocabulary. The closest relationships of the Grassfields languages are to the east (33 percent of Mbam-Nkam roots shared with Banen), to the south (46 percent shared with Bandem) and the southwest (30 percent with Ekoid). In any event the Grassfields languages are clearly Bantu in the case of Mbam-Nkam and gradually distance themselves from Bantu as one moves westwards.

So what conclusions can we draw from linguistic data? That the whole region between the Benue and the Atlantic coast was anciently settled, that its peopling is counted in terms of millennia, though how many is unknown; that, in general, this human occupation was continuous, especially on the high plateaux (though there is no proof that there were not empty zones at one period or another); that there was a significant mixing of peoples; that the latter took place in many directions; that the peoples of the high plateaux are linguistically closer to those settled between the Banen and the Ekoids to the south than they are to the Tikar, Mambila and Jukunoids. This is, at the same time, a lot and a little. A little, in the sense that these data do not convey any absolute certainty. But a lot, to the extent that these hypotheses are capable of some initial confirmation if they are set against oral tradition and the contributions of archaeology.

Oral traditions as indicators of political relations

Let us now return to oral traditions about migrations. And let us undertake a first exercise which consists of questioning the commoner lineages which, let us not forget, form the bulk of the population except in those cases where the dynastic lineage has ingested the whole polity (as was the case in Bamum, for example). And let us observe the rules of the ethnographic game in doing so by not asking informants the loaded question 'Where do you come from?' But instead by collecting genealogies and letting them speak for themselves. I undertook this exercise first in Mankon, then generally on the Bamenda plateau, as can be seen in two works of mine (Warnier 1975, 1983).

Here is the outcome: (1) the populations of the high plateau moved in every direction. Chiefdoms never ceased from exchanging their inhabitants. The majority of the genealogies harked back to a local origin or to one in a nearby chiefdom. The migrations they bear witness to are micro-migrations without any directional pattern. (2) On the other hand the genealogies of men of title and of dynastic lineages implied kinship links between them or referred to a common prestigious ancestor. Since lineages and ancestors are necessarily localized, these relationships, real or imagined, were translated into the terms of migratory movements. (3) All oral traditions concerning the migration of men of title have a political message: they connote either the legitimacy of a notable's powers within his lineage or that of a Fon within his fondom, or refer to external political relations. Faced with such oral traditions the ethno-historian is led to put forward the hypothesis that they do not necessarily refer to real migrations but that, rather, they express the local and regional distribution of power. This hypothesis, already advanced by Tardits (1981), is hard to verify in the present state of our knowledge, even though the linguistic evidence supplies a strong presumption in its favour. It is not impossible that, one day, archaeology may be able to deny or confirm it.

The archaeological data establish the antiquity of the population

Since 1973 I have carried out surveys with a view to finding stratified archaeological sites, rock-shelters in particular. These surveys resulted, successively, in the discovery of the rock shelters of Shum Laka in Bafotchu-Mbu' with a surface area of 800m², of Abeke at Akum, with a surface area of about 1,000m², of Fiye Nkwi at Babanki Tungo (surface area c. 7,000m^2) and at Mbi crater (surface area 700m^2). Morin (1982) has given a geomorphological description of the last three. In 1978 De Maret and Warnier dug a test-pit at Shum Laka. The radiocarbon dates from this dig, published by De Maret (1980), are stratigraphically coherent and indicate a human presence in this region between the beginning of the seventh and the end of the fourth millennium BC. In subsequent years De Maret (1982) continued his excavations at Shum Laka and the dates suggest a human presence at later though still uncertain periods.

Abeke shelters a stone-chipping workshop using rhyolite. The implement types run from the Mousterian-Levalloisian to early trials with microliths. An excavation by De Maret has provided a dating in the middle of the fourth millennium BC.

Fiye Nkwi, despite its huge size, is unpropitious to archaeological deposits. This rock-shelter has, however, been the object of a dig by Asombang (1988) that has yielded implements very similar to those at Abeke and Mbi crater.

By contrast the rock-shelter at Mbi crater, situated at an altitude of 2,080m on the western flank of the explosion crater of Mbi, is the most promising site. Since January 1982 Raymond Asombang (1988 and personal communication) has undertaken excavations there, opening a trench some 12m long, which has yielded abundant and well-stratified lithic and bone material. He has also discovered a burial which, to judge from the stratigraphic level and associated material, is probably contemporary with the oldest Shum Laka period. The burial is that of young female adult of normal proportions, but very short (about 130-140cm). The bone remains (in a very poor state of preservation) have not yet been studied. But at first glance they appear to be of an individual of negroid type. The upper levels include pottery. The material of this excavation thus covers a period which certainly runs from the upper palaeolithic to 'Neolithic', and even perhaps to the Iron Age. It is still being studied and will certainly revolutionize our knowledge of the region.

Let us also note the presence of megaliths at Sa, north of Nkambe, and the discovery of 18 polished stone axes at Fundong in the North-West Province, and of another such at Bapa, near Bafoussam.

What can we make of this? The linguistic data point to a continuous history, over several millennia, accompanied by some intermixture of peoples. But there is no proof that this took place entirely on the high plateaux. On the other hand, the archaeological data attest to the presence of a human population for at least nine millennia. But nothing in the archaeological record proves that this presence was continuous. Be that as it may, the two categories of data distinctly reinforce each other and offer support to the proposition of a very ancient, continuous, human occupation, accompanied by mixing of populations. But one must beware of regarding it as firmly established. And finally one must point out that while the archaeological data for the North-West Province are rapidly accumulating they are entirely lacking, so far, for the Western Province, a few surface finds apart.

The process of deforestation and the agrosystems

Hawkins and Brunt (1965, I: 205-6), Letouzey (1968: 265-74, 281-94, 336-40), and the geographers who have followed up their studies, such as Dongmo (1981, I: 36-38), consider that the vegetational cover of the high plateaux is derived from montane forest formations and the Biafran forest and that deforestation and reforestation with fruiting trees (*Dacryodes edulis, Canarium schweinfurthii, Cola nitida* and *C. acuminata* etc.) or with trees and bushes of economic interest, are due to human action. They base their views on the existence of some remaining fragments of primeval vegetation, on the nature of derived associations and on the zonal schemata of climate as modified by altitude. There have been no palynological or palaeozoological analyses to confirm their opinion. On the other hand, the find of a tooth of a gorilla (a forest species) at Shum Laka would seem to confirm this hypothesis. It is congruent with the climatic sequences of the last 20,000 years, which have been marked by maxima of temperature and rainfall about 10,000 years ago accompanied by the northward advance of the Biafran forest.

For the sake of the argument, let us assume that the Grassfields were deforested and that the present-day landscape is very largely the consequence of human activity. Could we then derive hypotheses concerning the chronology and impact of this activity? The factors we must take into consideration are as follows: the practice of slash-and-burn horticulture and the stages of agricultural development, demographic dynamics, regional economic specialization, the introduction of ironworking, and population movements.

Grassfields horticulture is grounded on the cultivation of an ancient stock of African cultigens: sorghum (*Sorghum bicolor*), bulrush millet (*Pennisetum americanum*), cowpea (*Vigna unguiculata*), bambara nut (*Voandzeia subterranea*), yams (*Dioscorea cayenensis* and *D. rotundata*), oil palm (*Elaeis guineensis*), kola (*Cola nitida, C. acuminata*), raffia (*Raphia farinifera*) and some vegetables – *Hibiscus esculentus* or okra, *Telfaria occidentalis*, a type of pumpkin, *Cucumeropsis edulis* or egusi, *Lagenaria siceraria* or gourd, *Aframomum malagueta* or malagueta pepper. We have at present no direct means of dating the introduction of this plant association to the Grassfields.

Thurstan Shaw (1976) has observed that the highest densities of population in sub-Saharan Africa are to be found where the cultivation of yams is associated with that of the oil palm which have complementary nutritional values. He sees in this association an indicator of a core of human settlement. This high-density zone is centred in Igbo country. It extends to the middle Benue, into Tiv and Idoma country, and includes the Grassfields where the consumption of palm oil is strongly rooted in the culture, and in ritual and eating habits. On the basis of indirect evidence (pottery, polished stone axes, and the tool-making industry of the Late Stone Age) Shaw dates the start of this complex to at least five millennia ago. According to De Maret (1982) pottery makes its appearance at Shum Laka a little after the sixth millennium ended. So I am tempted to adopt this broad dating by way of hypothesis as the terminus a quo of the introduction of horticulture into the Grassfields. A convergent pointer, provided by Williamson (1970: 156-67) and accepted by Shaw (1976: 138), comes to us from comparative linguistics, namely that the distribution of the roots for the words designating raffia, oil-palm, yams and kola is such that it suggests that their cultivation harks back to proto-Niger-Congo and thus points towards a time-lapse of four millennia at the very least. One notices that these species still play a central part in the Grassfields economy.

The next stage of agricultural development is marked by the introduction of cultigens from Southeast Asia, namely the plantain (*Musa sapientum var. paradisiaca*), the banana (*Musa sapientum*), the taro (*Colocasia esculentum*), and another variety of yam (*Dioscorea alata*). The introduction of this complex to Africa is dated to the early centuries of our era. We have no means of dating its introduction to the Grassfields, but it must be very long ago to judge from the importance of the banana tree in rituals and food habits.

The introduction of American cultigens, subsequent to 1500 AD, is easier to date. It looks as if the first two species to be adopted were the groundnut (*Arachis hypogaea*) and the tobacco plant (*Nicotiana tabacum*). The latter was certainly cultivated before the start of the 19th century since tobacco pipes are to be found on sites that, according to oral tradition, were abandoned under the impact of Chamba raids (c.1825-30). It is probable that, in coming years, it will become possible to arrive at a closer dating. Oral tradition and linguistic data allow us to date the introduction of maize to the middle of the 19th century for the north-western Grassfields: it came by two routes, via the valley of the Cross River and that of the Benue. The diffusion of manioc (cassava) can be quite precisely dated to 1918-20 as a consequence of the shortages of farm labour that accompanied colonization and the epidemic of Spanish influenza.

Groundnuts and maize must have played an important part in agricultural development and, consequentially, in population increase. Both of these species have a short growing season (of about three months) and thus enabled some weeks to be cut off the annual period of food shortage during the gap before the new harvests. Groundnuts, rich in lipids and proteins, had improved nutrition and, since they are leguminous plants, played an important part in crop rotation and the maintenance of soil fertility.

Throughout the plateau area food is grown nowadays, as it was in the 'Neolithic' and Iron Ages, by gardening over the tracks of forest and savannah clearance reduced to ashes by burning. During the Neolithic period cultivation was done with digging sticks and what seems to have been an agricultural tool chipped from basalt (a 'hoe' and pick), and later on with an iron hoe. As the forest was felled it gave way to mixed plots of cultivation alternating with grass fallow principally of *Hyparrhenia*, and spear grass *(Imperata)* on poorer soils. The annual bush fires, linked to both hunting and bush clearance, combined with long-term trend towards more arid conditions, interrupted by wetter periods over the last four millennia, have maintained the grassy cover except on southwest-facing hill slopes, which have a higher rainfall and are more wooded than others. Traditionally bush fires were spread out between December and March. Nowadays, since Fulani graziers want to burn the dry grass as soon as possible, the grass is burned before the end of January. The impact on the vegetational cover is bound to have different results in each case, since the effect of late dry-season fires was to eliminate shrubs and tree seedlings. In other words, early bush fires are conducive to forest extension since they do not destroy tree seedlings.

The effect of cultivation on the environment depends on population densities. These, at the end of the 19t[h] century, were very unequal – low in Bamum – 8 to 10 inhabitants per km² according to Tardits (1981, II: 401) – high in Bamileke country (30 to 40 per km²) and more or less the same on the average in what is now the North-West Province with the highest density of 80 per km² in Ngi country. There were also thinly populated areas, like the Metchum valley and some which, despite their fertility, are curiously under-populated, like the Wum plateau. Can one give a rough idea of population density and settlement patterns in the past? I agree with Caldwell (1982: 127) that extrapolations from contemporary figures, on the basis of likely demographic growth, are worthless. For such estimations one can only base oneself on (1) a map and periodisation of archaeological sites, and (2) a history of agricultural techniques and, in particular, a list, for each period, of the species cultivated.

No map of archaeological sites has yet been completed. But the following observations will at least enable us to raise precise questions. Firstly, one picks up, on the surface, basalt stone implements all over the North-West Province at every altitude up to over 2,000m, and in all districts, even those at present uninhabited. What is striking is the abundance of these implements. Jeffreys claims to have picked up over a thousand hand-axes. I personally scarcely ever made a day's journey without picking up two or three items. If these implements are indeed 'neolithic' as Jeffreys, Hartle, Marliac and David all think, one is driven to the conclusion that, from the beginnings of horticulture, the high plateau areas (or at least those in the North-West Province) were subjected to forest clearance. Boserup (1965) has already pointed out that cultivators, when population density does not compel them either to cultivate the fallow or practice rotation, prefer to clear the forests with their richer soil. It is only when the forests have been more or less felled that people turn to cultivating fallow lands. One can thus put forward the hypothesis, which remains to be verified, of a pretty extensive forest clearance, from the 'Neolithic' onwards, due to an itinerant horticulture on a slash-and-burn basis, followed by long-term settlement on some tracts with the adoption of a system of alternating fallow and cultivation. Morin (personal communication) thinks that this hypothesis seems to be confirmed to some degree since the river terraces in the North-West Province display a horizon of ash fossilized at an ancient soil level and thus bear witness to a period of forest clearance (it would be important to date this horizon). The factors which played a part in the choice of, as it were, 'permanent' habitats may be guessed at: the best agricultural soils were preferred, to wit, for the North-West Province the colluvial soils of the Ndop Plain, the humus-rich soils of the high lava plateau, and the volcanic soils of the Wum plateau. Habitats at high altitude were abandoned in favour of land situated at up to 1,500m, very occasionally higher. Finally the development of regional economic specialization (which we shall return to) may have induced the population to congregate in sites that favoured the development of production and exchange, around the main crossroads of commerce and centres of growth.

The introduction of the Asiatic complex of cultigens, which was certainly more or less coeval with the introduction of iron metallurgy, must have both responded to demographic increase and been instrumental in provoking further population growth. The sites I excavated at Fundong in 1982 are Iron Age sites (but eighteen polished stone axes were found 20m distant from one of them) but seem to belong to a period prior to the diffusion of American cultigens and to the corresponding technical and demographic history of this period. These sites suggest a substantial but dispersed population on the Fundong plateau in a region which, to judge by Kom oral tradition and Moisel's map (1913), was practically denuded of inhabitants at the end of the 19th century. The dates point to the practice of iron smelting in this area from the middle of the 1st millennium AD to the present.

The introduction of American cultigens, groundnuts in particular, no doubt contributed to a new spurt of demographic growth. Probably it first took place in the Bamileke region, linked to Duala by long-distance trade from the middle of the 17th century or even earlier, perhaps: this would help to explain the demographic and cultural lag between the Bamenda Grassfields and the rest of the high plateaux, namely the Bamileke area. In the Bamenda region, where oral tradition correspond in all respects with the material evidence of human occupation before the main Chamba raids (c.1825-30) one can reconstitute the map of a dense (20 to 40 inhabitants per km²) but dispersed settlement pattern, in opposition to what was observable in the 19th century. One could say the same for the Ndop Plain.

I had long been intrigued by groups of terrace habitats at 2,000m altitude in places difficult of access, and far away from sources of water supplies, around the Ndop Plain and up to Kom, where one can see several hundreds of them along the escarpment facing the Fon's palace at Laikom. A dig at one of these sites, in 1980 above the Sabga pass, convinced me, on account of the pottery we uncovered, that we had to do with sites datable to ca 1800, most probably refuge sites occupied at the start of the Chamba raids at the turn of the 19th century. This hypothesis receives some support from the accounts given by those slaves, as a result of these raids, who acted as the informants of the missionary linguist Koelle (1963/1854: 11-13 and 20-21). These accounts, like the oral traditions collected, describe the panic that took hold of the region's inhabitants and the dispersal and relocation of villages and hamlets. If this hypothesis could be verified, one could, by means of a simple totting-up of the terraces and by comparisons with recent traditional settlements, arrive at an approximate notion of the population of the Ndop Plain at the time of the raids. At first it seems to have been at least equal to that at the end of the 19th century. This second occupation of the higher land (second after their 'Neolithic' occupation) could have given occasion for a second felling of high montane forest.

Let us return now to the regional economic specialization mentioned earlier. In the 18th century, and to a certain extent in the nineteenth, the high plateaux were characterized by a developed regional economic specialization, accompanied by mercantile exchanges. Palm oil was produced in the lower lands on the periphery of the high plateau and exchanged there for root vegetables, grain and pulses, small livestock and craft products. The localization of production between the periphery and the centre took place broadly in the order mentioned above, as a function of increasing distance from the palm-belts and the weight/value ratios of the goods carried for the purposes of trade. This specialization apparently took place in accordance with Ricardo's law of comparative costs, as I tried to show in another work (Warnier 1983). Its importance in landscape formation has been considerable. The oil-palm belts are all peripheral to the Grassfields: in the valley of the Upper Nkam, between the Nkam and the Nun, in the Mbam valley, in that of the Donga, Katsina Ala and Metchum, in the lowlands of the Nggi, Mogamo, Bangwa and Banyang, in the Cross River basin. Elsewhere the oil-palm is rarely present in quantity, not because of ecological reasons in the main, but chiefly for economic ones. On the other hand, it is the rearing of small livestock and the cultivation of legumes and cereals (groundnuts, cowpeas, sorghum and maize) which have given the plateaux their typical appearance: open country as in parts of the Bamenda plateau, the Ndop Plain, the Nso' region, where small stock were freely pastured on fallow or tracts remote from cultivation; bocage country as in Bamileke or in the heavily settled areas of the Bamenda plateau, where small stock were freely pastured in the uncultivated uplands or in alternation with intensive cultivation in farmlands enclosed by live hedges or barriers of raffia midribs. Bocage here implies that stock rearing and intensive cultivation were undertaken with an eye to trade.

Economic specialization and regional trade in tandem with long-distance trade had another impact on the landscape through their combined influence on the localization of the population. This complex of commercial exchanges gave rise to centres of economic and demographic growth that were reinforced at the expense of their peripheries. For example, it was thus that the Metchum valley was partially emptied of inhabitants by the implosion of Bafut. The development of the Kingdom of Bamum and the depopulation of its borderlands at the start of the 19th century are perhaps to be explained by the same kind of process. The result was a local population concentration and a reshaping of the landscape, exemplified by the re-growth of forest in part of the Metchum valley, the shift of oil-palm stands into Bafut territory, and the abandonment of no man's lands in Bamum.

Ironworking was an important component of regional exchanges. David (1981, I: 84) considers that it was introduced into the Grassfields some two millennia ago, perhaps a little more. The recent excavations I made in Fundong show that it was already established in this area, and part of the regional economy, in the middle of the first millennium AD (see Warnier 1992). The sites at Fundong and the slag dispersed from Bambui to Bali, on the western flank of the range which separates the Bamenda plateau from the Ndop plain, suggest that there was a time when ironworking sites were situated closer to the palm-belts than they came to be in the eighteenth and nineteenth centuries. At that time the most active centres were at Esu and We and in the area surrounding the Ndop Plain. There was then a movement of geographical and industrial concentration in the course of these two centuries, to such a degree that one can today find more than 200,000m³ of slag in three Ndop Plain villages (Babungo, Bamessing and Bamenyam) with at least 250 smelting sites. What is in question, then, in the 18th and 19th centuries, is the presence of a sedentary industry of large capacity directed to export – and this in a savannah milieu. It has been described by Warnier and Fowler (1979, reproduced in this volume, see chapter 3).

It must have borne heavily on the environment. In a well-documented article, Goucher (1981) has tried to calculate the environmental effect of ironworking for all the West African metal-working industries. Basing herself on researches in Dapaa in Ghana, she calculates that 2,000m³ of slag requires the production of 2,000m³ of charcoal, or the felling of about 300,000 stems of Burkea Africana. On the basis of these estimates (which Goucher qualifies as conservative) the 200,000m³ of slag of Babungo, Bamessing and Bamenyam represent the felling of 30 million stems of savannah tree species.

The techniques used reflect a shortage of timber: the furnaces were massive constructions that stored heat within their inner walls and were used uninterruptedly day after day to conserve energy. An ample use of kaolin in their construction and inner lining gave refractory properties. Forced and preheated ventilation using tuyeres, and the prior drying of ore allowed high temperatures reached while consuming a minimum of energy and producing iron with good mechanical properties. The techniques used at the ironworking sites at Fundong are different. To judge by the size of the cakes of slag, the furnaces were much smaller than that of Ndop (see Warnier 1992). The fact that no trace of them has been found suggests that they were modest and perishable constructions. Being dated around the 5th to 10th c. AD, there was probably no energy crisis at that time such as the one to which the Ndop industry bears witness. One can perhaps hypothesize a first phase of ironworking when it was relatively dispersed and when combustible materials were sufficiently available to require no constraints in usage. The second phase was marked by the concentration of metallurgy at the centre of the plateaux, a considerable development of its production, followed by deforestation and the perfecting of smelting techniques designed to mitigate energy shortages, especially in the Ndop Plain where the climate is drier than elsewhere.

The iron goods of Oku and Nso' were exported to the middle Benue in exchange for cloth and salt. Towards the middle of the 19th century the trade in kola developed following the advance of the so-called 'Hausa' caravans. The chiefdoms of Kom, Nso', Oku and others, including in Bamileke the chiefdoms of Bangwa and Bangou entered into the kola export trade and planted thousands of trees. The replanting continued into the British colonial period in the Bamenda Grassfields. In Oku, kola vied with iron goods as an export while metallurgy went into decline: no doubt some forest regeneration followed (but latterly it has been destroyed).

The last factor to bear in mind is that of population movements. I have already mentioned those related to regional trade – the concentrations in areas of high production (the Ngi for the oil palm, the Ndop area for craft and metallurgical production), and in centres of economic growth (for example, the large chiefdoms of Bafut, and Bali on the Bamenda Plateau), and the depopulation of certain areas as a result of processes of implosion.

Superimposing themselves upon these movements, the Chamba raids also helped to alter the map. They induced concentrations of population in the Ndop Plain and on the Bamenda Plateau and no doubt contributed to the depopulation of the northern Grassfields in direct contact with the Takum region in which the Chamba had settled in considerable numbers. The story of these raids can be found in the works of Chilver (1981), Chilver and Kaberry (1968), and Fardon (1988 and 1990).

From 1840, and after the conquest of Adamawa by the Fulani, following the proclamation of the Jihad, the north-eastern Grassfields (the Ndop and the Ndu areas for example) suffered from repeated raids launched from Banyo and Gashaka. More detail on these raids is given in the sources dealing with the Chamba. Paradoxically these raids that depopulated certain areas in the northern Grassfields from Wum to the Mambila plateau will have doubtless also prevented replanting of anthropic origin. In fact, well-watered slopes apart, wooded areas are often (not always) made up of protected species (such as raffia, oil palm, and *Phoenix reclinata*) or deliberately planted ones (with *Dracaena arborea*, kola, *Ficus*, *Markhamia tomentosa*). One can take stock of this situation from aerial photographs, or more simply by looking down on the Ndop Plain or the Bamenda Plateau from a neighbouring cliff-top in clear weather: the most wooded regions are precisely those which are the most densely settled, leaving aside forest galleries and the remnants of primeval forest.

The last movement of population which has affected the landscape is the arrival of Fulani graziers, from 1916, the date of the settlement of Ardo Sabga. Champaud (1973: 55) tells us that from 10,000 in 1924, the bovine population increased to 244,000 in 1968 in the North-West province. The impact of cattle rearing on the environment has been threefold: it has supplanted the abundant natural fauna which inhabited the savannah; it has, at higher levels, replaced the *Hyparrhenia* by a *Sporobolus* grass cover; it has certainly contributed to the transformation of the former grassy to a shrubby savannah by reason of the practice of firing the bush at the start of the dry season.

Six millennia of Grassfields history

This synthesis is slightly less speculative than that proposed by Tardits in 1973 and published in 1981. It reinforces the trend in the historiography of the 1970s to 1990s by putting more and more emphasis on the ancient and continuous settlement of the high plateaux, at the expense of the contribution of recent migrations.

The hypotheses I have advanced on the basis of archaeological evidence, linguistic classification and regional economic history can be recapitulated as follows: under the late Stone Age, the high plateaux were already occupied by a population of negroid type. Some six millennia or so ago horticulture on a slash-and-burn basis was introduced, giving rise to the first deforestation, while a long-term tendency to more arid conditions and the practice of bush fires maintained a grass cover on fallow. This population of horticulturists spoke proto-Benue-Congo languages, doubtless close to proto-Bantu. Multidirectional mixing and several millennia of diversification produced the complex situation we have today. Some 2,500 years ago ironworking and, subsequently, Asiatic cultigens were introduced, giving rise to demographic growth and an intensification of forest clearance and, eventually, to a regional structuring of production and exchange.

The diffusion of American cultigens tended to reinforce demographic growth from the 17th century onwards, first in the Bamileke region, then in the rest of the high plateau area while specialized production (palm oil, cereals and pulses, small stock, crafts) imposed the characteristics we can still recognize in the regional landscapes, that is, open farmland, savannah, bocage, palm-belts, wooded areas around human habitations, forest galleries with raffia groves.

Population movements linked to regional trade, and to the Chamba and Fulani raids remodelled the settlement map by creating human concentrations contrasting with peripheral empty areas which eve either towards regenerated forest or to a shrubby or a grassy savannah in accordance with local ecological factors.

I would like to underscore the hypothetical nature of this reconstruction. It will have made its point if it does not lead to a new orthodoxy but rather to a different reading of the mountain landscapes of Western Cameroon, and away from the well-trodden paths of oral traditions, in order to confront them with further questions concerning languages, archaeological evidence, the environment and economic history. On the language side, a huge comparative task remains to be done, especially on the vocabulary. The archaeological evidence – it is now clear – is extremely abundant but still dramatically understudied. The study of the palaeo-environment – arrived at by palynological analysis and the identification of the fauna at different periods – should be able to give us a historical geography of the Grassfields landscapes. Finally, the history of production for exchange, reconstructed on the basis of oral tradition, material culture, contemporary economic organization and archaeological sites is capable of adding a good deal more information to the history of settlement.

To be complete, this study should mention the modifications to landscape which have taken place during the period of European colonial rule and since independence: further deforestation, the disintegration of the Bamileke bocage during the troubles linked to independence (since when it has been reconstituted here and there), the introduction of cash crops, of new cultigens, new tree species (*Eucalyptus* in particular), the introduction of cattle husbandry, an intense demographic pressure, leading to over-utilization of land and environmental degradation. I mention these factors only to draw attention to the differences between the 19th century landscape and the contemporary one. A study of the factors that have given rise to these differences is beyond the scope of this paper.

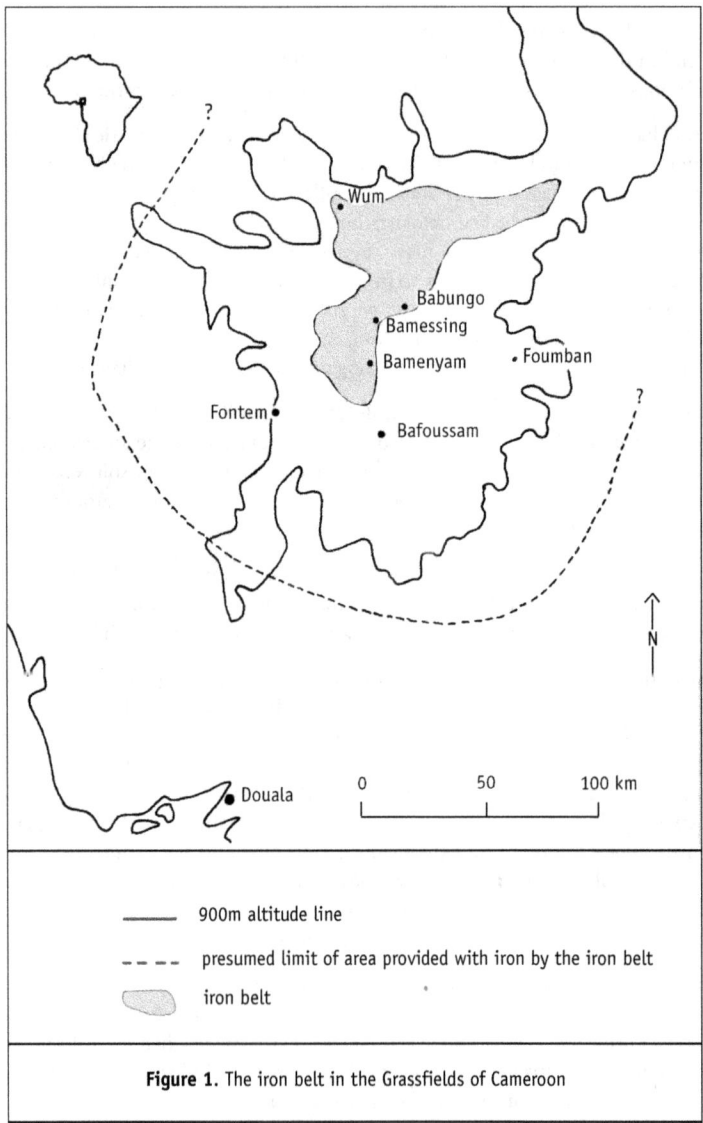

Figure 1. The iron belt in the Grassfields of Cameroon

A Nineteenth-century Ruhr in Central Africa
(with Ian Fowler) [1]

Over two hundred thousand cubic meters of slag and smelting debris, at least two hundred and seventy smelting sites, more than seven hundred recorded kaolin pits for building and lining furnaces, and probably half as many again not visited by us – these are a few figures that establish three villages of the Ndop Plain, in the highlands of Western Cameroon, as a 'Nineteenth-century Ruhr in Central Africa'. To this day, this all Sub-Saharan African record leaves Meroe, 'the Birmingham of Africa' well behind. Perhaps the record remains unbroken, however, just because scholars interested in African iron industries seem to have been unconcerned with the overall output of these industries

Productivity figures on ore, charcoal, and labor inputs, compared to the output of iron, may be found in Cline (1937), and many others: Jeffreys (1942a & b), Tylecote (1965), Pole (1974) for example. However, none of these give any idea of the overall volume of production of given industries, and we have found no indication in the literature of this statistic. Even Meroe is poorly documented from a quantitative point of view. An investigation of the vast literature about Meroe and related sites yielded only the scantiest of data: six mounds of slag inside the town of Meroe, plus a dozen around the outskirts-each about twelve feet high (Wainwright 1945: 23).[2]

This article will have achieved its goal if it gives a yardstick – the first of its kind as far as we know – by which the importance of other iron industries can be compared, for a better understanding of the history and economics of the Iron Age in Africa. This we intend to do by discussing (1) the general setting of the Ndop Plain iron industry, (2) the industry itself, with emphasis on the chiefdom of Babungo, and (3) the case of the chiefdom of Bamessing. In Bamunkumbit and Babadjou, the slag was often scattered over the ground, making it almost impossible to obtain figures that would compare in accuracy to those of Babungo and Bamessing. Since 1968, the Highways Department of the North West Province of Cameroon has taken away more than 100 lorry-loads of debris every year, to put on dirt roads on the Ndop Plain. Five heaps in Babungo and two in Bamessing were thus taken away, totaling five to seven thousand cubic meters in volume. These are included in the count given in Table 1 (see on page 26).

Our concern is definitely quantitative: just how big was the Ndop Plain iron industry in terms of number of furnaces in operation, number of people employed, volume of output, and areas supplied with iron? These are the questions that we would like to discuss. Further, we are not concerned here with smithing, but only with iron production. Suffice it to say that iron was seldom traded in its raw form. The basic trade item was the hoe, and in all smelting centers large numbers of smiths were turning out hoes for export and a considerable assortment of ironware for the domestic market.

The setting

The Ndop Plain iron industry is part of a much more widespread one located in what Warnier (1975) called the 'iron belt' of the Grassfields of Cameroon (see Figure 1 on page 24). The Grassfields are a high plateau averaging 1,000 meters in altitude, roughly circular in shape, which extends between the 5th and 7th degrees north of the Equator, and lies between the Cross and Mungo river basins to the south, and the Adamawa plateau to the north. In pre-colonial times, the iron belt was part of a network of commercial exchanges between areas that each specialized in the production of one or several commodities. The main commodities that were traded were iron, palm oil, small livestock, foodstuffs, pots, and a dozen other products of local handicrafts.

In the present state of our knowledge, it seems that the nearest sources of readymade iron were the Atlantic coast at Calabar (Latham 1973: 24-5) and Douala that took in European iron, and a small area near Fontem (Wilhelm 1981). According to Barbier (1981), no iron was smelted in what is known as the Bamileke country of the Grassfields. We do not know how far the iron produced in the iron belt was being traded. According to Latham (1973: 7), there are indications that iron from the Cameroon hinterland reached the Calabar area before the importing of European iron that began in the 17th century. Yet, we may safely assume that the iron belt was supplying all of the densely populated Grassfields (perhaps some 500,000 people circa 1900), and perhaps many people beyond, with all the iron they needed throughout the 19th century. For how long before that, we do not know for sure. Nevertheless, the linguistic data, and what scanty archaeological evidence we have, point to an ancient and continuous occupation of the Grassfields. The languages of the Grassfields are closely related to the Bantu family and belong to the area where Greenberg (1966) locates the original homeland of Bantu speakers. (Archaeological research conducted in the 1980s indicates that iron production dates back to the middle of the first millennium B.C.)

The earliest well documented events in the Grassfields are raids by Chamba mounted warriors who came from southern Adamawa around 1825-30 (Chilver 1967 and 1981; Chilver and Kaberry 1968: 20, 22, 26, 28, 29, 32; Fardon 1988, 1990). Presumably, they were following the long-distance commercial routes that supplied them with slaves, ivory and perhaps iron and kola nuts. They swept through the Grassfields, were defeated near Dschang, and split up into raiding bands that became the nuclei of a number of local chiefdoms. Bali-Kumbat, one of these intrusive chiefdoms, was established in the Ndop Plain on top of a large hill. From this stronghold, it raided the neighboring villages and forced them into reorganizing their economies on new bases, creating the situation that we shall now describe.

The Ndop Plain iron industry and the chiefdom of Babungo

Though smelting debris is ubiquitous in the Ndop Plain, and in the hills overlooking it, it is found in much greater quantities in three chiefdoms than anywhere else. These are Babungo, Bamessing and Bamenyam (see Table 1 and Figure 2). The data summarized in Table 1 were obtained in a one by one count and measurement of slag heaps in Babungo (by Fowler), Bafanji, and Bamessing (by Warnier). In Bamenyam, the volume of 10,000 cubic meters is a very conservative estimate obtained by a one by one count and rough assessment of 46 slag heaps by Warnier. To these, 25 other heaps must be added, which Warnier did not see, but which were brought to his attention. The actual quantity of debris may be two or three times larger – in which case the production in Bamenyam and Bamessing would have been of comparable volume.

Table I: Volume of smelting debris, and number of sites in seven chiefdoms. Ndop Plain and vicinity		
Chiefdom	Volume (in m³)	Number of sites
Babungo	163,000	125
Bamessing	40,000	54
Bafanji	1,500+	25
Bamunkumbit	traces	?
Bamenyam	10,000	70 +
Bagam	?	?
Babadjou	traces	?
Total	214,500 +	274 +

Of course, slag and smelting debris have accumulated over a long time – probably several centuries – and these figures do not tell us anything about the average yearly output of a given smelting centre at a given time. However, the history of the Ndop Plain and some clues given by technological changes may provide us with some rough estimates. Before the Chamba raids of c. 1825, the settlement pattern was one of dispersed homesteads and hamlets allied within single chiefdoms. The raids, and the situation of violence that followed up until the

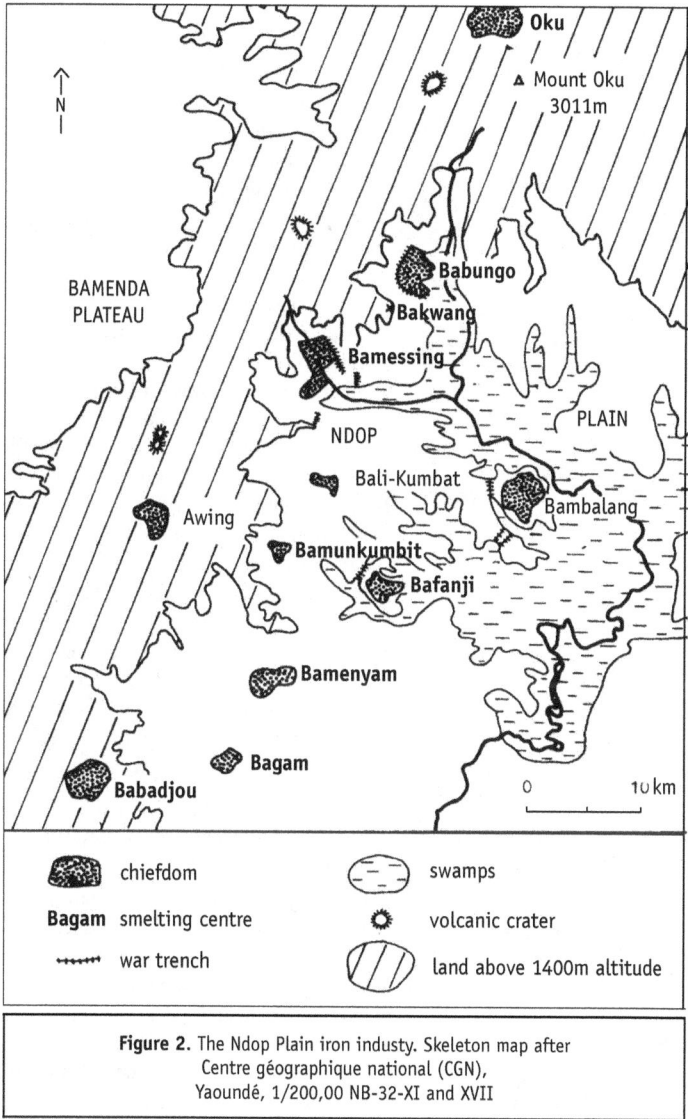

Figure 2. The Ndop Plain iron industy. Skeleton map after
Centre géographique national (CGN),
Yaoundé, 1/200,00 NB-32-XI and XVII

colonial era, compelled the peoples of the Ndop Plain to congregate in dense settlements, always protected by natural obstacles (cliffs, swamps and rivers) and by man-made moats and defenses. These settlements were continuously occupied until the Pax Britannica allowed people to settle outside the defensive perimeter of the village. Thus pre-Chamba smelting sites tend to be more scattered than later ones. Plotted on the map, they would depict a kind of 'Milky Way' that extends from Oku to Bagam, with denser clusters around the core settlements of the pre-Chamba chiefdoms. Some of these sites were located on the land that was to be enclosed within a defensive perimeter after the Chamba raids. Thus, we cannot assume that the smelting sites found within the post-Chamba settlements are all 19th-century sites.

Yet, we have other indications as to their dates. In Babungo, two types of furnace are found: an old one (that we shall call 'old Babungo' or 'Bakwang') and a more recent one (that we shall call the 'Babungo clump furnace' – see Figure 3). The Babungo clump furnace is found only within the limits of the 19th-century settlement (see Figure 4). Whereas the distribution pattern of old Babungo furnaces consists of a dense concentration of sites within an area that may have been the core settlement of the pre-Chamba chiefdom, smaller clusters of sites overlap the war trench (in fact, one site is cut through by the trench) and extend into the surrounding hills where a few isolated sites are found. This pattern ties up neatly with Babungo oral traditions that recall an earlier, more widely dispersed settlement pattern that was abandoned in the face of a series of severe slave raids and rapidly increasing levels of violence and insecurity that reached a peak in the first half of the 19th century. The smaller chiefdoms and other dispersed pockets of settlement were decimated by mounted Chamba raiders and the scattered remnants were absorbed into the surviving chiefdoms. Babungo traditions state that it was just such a group of refugees that brought the idea for the new clump furnace. The Ndop Plain was further disrupted by the settlement of the chiefdom of Bali-Kumbat and its attempts to carve out an empire from the weakened chiefdoms of the plain and harassed groups such as Baba and Bangolan crossing the River Noun to escape Bamoum pressure in the second half of the 19th century. In response to these events a war trench was dug enclosing both the compacted centre of population and adjacent tracts of cultivated land of the Babungo chiefdom.

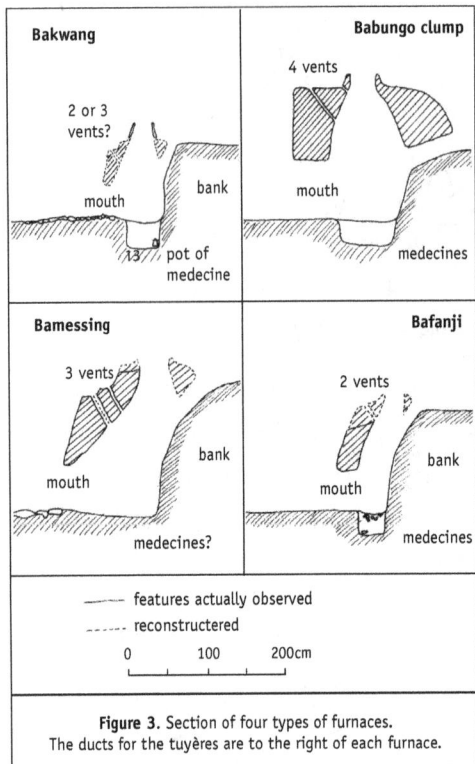

Figure 3. Section of four types of furnaces. The ducts for the tuyères are to the right of each furnace.

It seems that the technology of iron-production in Babungo underwent a transformation marked by the adoption of the developed clump furnace that occurred shortly after the compaction of settlement in response to slave raiding. The 'old Babungo' furnace and other similar types (Bamessing, Bafanji, and Bakwang) were built to be embedded in a natural or artificial bank (see Figure 3). The clump furnace is a transformation of such types of furnace produced by disembedding the furnace and erecting it as a partially free-standing structure. Such a change may have been induced by the need to produce thick-walled furnaces in a flat area (the village of Babungo) where there are few natural slopes which could be used for building the old-style furnaces. An alternative solution would have been to dig a large depression on one side of which the furnace would have been embedded. This labor consuming technique which was used in Bamessing and Bafanji does not seem to have been retained in Babungo. Changing patterns of access to labor and raw materials and transportation costs may also have been major factors in this technological transformation. Since the clump furnace is found only within the area of compacted settlement we may assume that it post-dates that compaction and hence that the clump furnace did not come into use in Babungo until after 1830 and probably did not fully displace the old furnace until a decade after that, c. 1840.

It was not possible to excavate old Babungo furnaces located within the area of 19th-century settlement since these are associated with taboos that make such investigations impossible. However, four sites outside the defensive perimeter were examined, debris was cleared from the interior of the furnaces and the remaining structure determined. These were found to be identical to the 'Bakwang' furnace (cf. Figure3) named after an abandoned pre-Chamba smelting site that the two authors excavated jointly. Bakwang is located very close to Babungo, on the lower hills that overlook the 19th-century settlement (see Figures2 & 4). In the Bakwang site, we found five furnaces associated with a total volume of c.1000 cubic meters of slag and smelting debris.

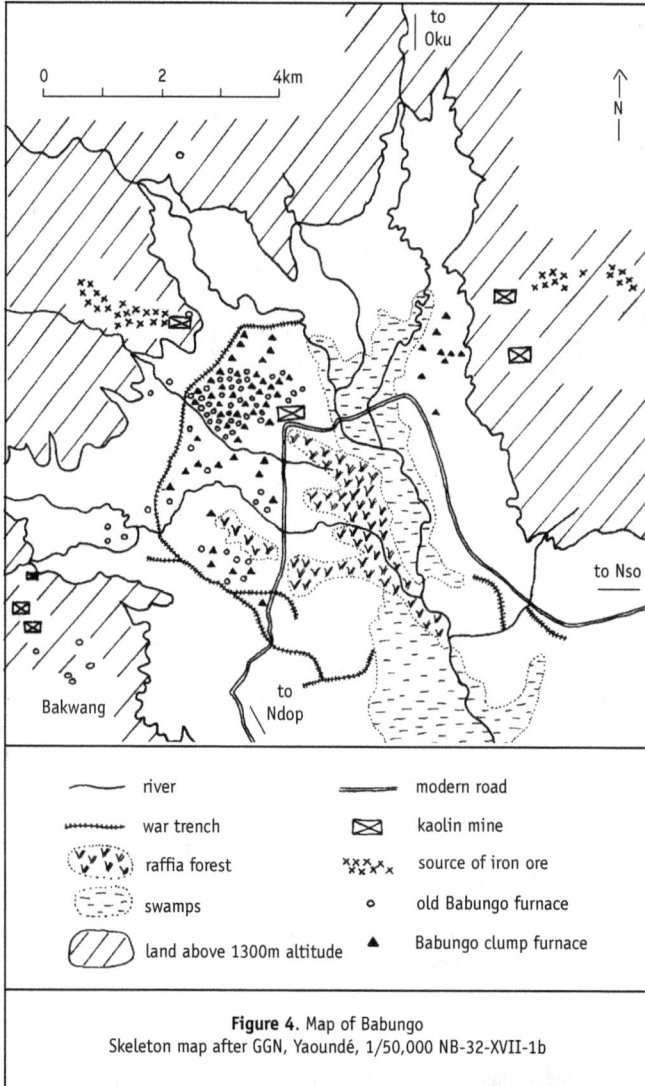

Figure 4. Map of Babungo
Skeleton map after GGN, Yaoundé, 1/50,000 NB-32-XVII-1b

If we are to attempt to quantify 19th-century levels of Babungo iron production in terms of the volume of debris associated with the clump furnace type we must take care not to include debris that derives from the earlier furnace type. This may seem no easy task given the dense concentration of both furnace types in the central parts of the village. However, heaps of smelting debris associated with the old Babungo furnace are typically low (two meters on average instead of four) and more widely scattered in relation to their total volume, whereas those associated with the clump furnace are high and compact (average ground area covered: 480 m² instead of 1,040; average volume in cubic meters: 2,220 m³ instead of 440). It seems likely that, as the population became concentrated within the defensive perimeter, pressure on land increased so that it became necessary to pile debris as high as possible in order to maximize the available arable land within the secure confines of the war trench. Female cultivators farming outside the trench risked capture and being sold as slaves by small bands of raiders and so it was necessary for the women farming to be guarded by parties of young men. We may assume that the heaps associated with clump furnaces post-date c. 1830. It may be objected that a clump furnace might have been built to replace an old Babungo furnace at the same location, in which case the lower strata of the heap would date from before 1830. This is possible, but unlikely in view of the taboos associated with the old furnace, and the fact that old furnaces seem to have been preserved, and not replaced. In Babungo, the smelting industry continued until the 1920s when it began to suffer from competition from European iron. The last smelts took place shortly after World War II, at a time when the war had created a shortage of iron in Africa (Jeffrey's 1942a & b).

In Bamessing, large scale iron production seems to have come to an end by 1860-80. Around 1840, Bali-Kumbat was set up immediately south of Bamessing (see Figure 2), and raided the neighboring villages for slaves, foodstuffs and all sorts of commodities. The predatory activities of Bali-Kumbat disorganized the Bamessing economy, forced the village to shrink into a smaller settlement, and more importantly, cut it off from its southern markets where it must previously have sold a good proportion of its output. At the same time, according to oral traditions, Bamessing was experiencing economic and military pressure from Kom, its northern neighbor. Though Bamessing seems to have attained some kind of modus vivendi with Bali-Kumbat, the latter did not make any effort to re-vitalize the Bamessing economy by re-opening the southern trade routes after they had closed in the initial violence. Traders who attempted to link up the chiefdoms separated by Bali-Kumbat were harassed and taxed. Contemporary informants compare them with smugglers. Meanwhile, the southern part of the Ndop Plain was facing a shortage of iron and had to develop its own metallurgy. The iron industry in Bafanji and Bamenyam is probably older than the Chamba raids, but it expanded considerably throughout the 19th-century, spread south, and went out of operation only in the late 1920s. The smelters of Babadjou, whom Warnier met, had learned their trade from Bamenyam people only a few years before the arrival of the Germans (c. 1900). This shows that by 1900, the iron industry was still expanding in that area.

The Bamessing iron industry received a second blow around 1880. Until then, the main currency used on the Bamenda Plateau, west of Bamessing, was the iron hoe. This was used for bridewealth payments and all monetary transactions of any importance. Between 1860 and 1870, the brass rods of the Calabar trade reached the Grassfields through the Cross River basin. At first, they trickled in, but by 1880, for reasons that need not be discussed here, they had entirely replaced the iron hoes as a currency on the Bamenda Plateau. This did not affect the Babungo area, which already had a cowry currency, nor the Bamenyam-Babadjou area that belonged to a 'beads' monetary zone. Bamessing, however, was seriously hit: not only did it lose its markets on the Bamenda Plateau, but one may speculate there was a slump in the iron market created by the sudden de-monetization, as it were, of large quantities of iron that became available for other purposes. By 1880, the large-scale iron industry of Bamessing was completely out of operation. However, small-scale iron production was carried out until the 20th century, by puddling old slag in open-hearth furnaces, to meet the reduced demand. The very large old Bamessing shaft furnace had been abandoned. This is not surprising: with the large furnace, the smelters could make significant economies of scale but a minimum output was required. The furnace was worked continuously for as long as the furnace lining did not need repair, which saved a lot of fuel, as the furnace was not allowed to cool down too much between smelts. But the output had to be sold, and when it could no longer find a sufficient market, the smelters had to discontinue this method of production, and meet the reduced demand with the less efficient, yet more flexible technique of puddling old slag on an open hearth.

The chronology may be summarized as in Table 2 (page 31). Thus the 200,000m³ of slag and debris found in the Ndop Plain represent centuries of smelting. However, it is possible to identify the 19th century sites by their location, the type of furnace, and the shape of the heaps of debris. From this, it is possible to make a rough assessment of the average yearly production of iron, in the 19th century, for a given chiefdom.

The most clear-cut case for such an assessment can be made for Babungo. In Babungo, the heaps of slag and smelting debris associated with the 19th century clump furnace represent a total volume of 133,000 m³. The yearly output for that century in Babungo therefore may be computed as averaging some 100 tons of pure iron[3]. This figure may sound unbelievable, in view of the clichés about African pre-industrial standards of production. Yet, it can be substantiated from other considerations. The Bamoum kingdom (some 60,000 population c. 1900), to the east of the Ndop Plain, relied entirely upon the outside for its supply of iron. Njoya, the Bamoum king

TABLE 2 Chronology of smelting	
Before 1830	Dispersed smelting sites from Oku to Bamenyam.
	Around Babungo, the 'Bakwang' furnace. Babungo and Bamessing are the main smelting centers.
c. 1830	Chamba raids.
	Concentration of the population in dense settlements.
	Babungo adopts the clump furnace.
c. 1840	Bali-Kumbat settles south of Bamessing.
	First decline of Bamessing iron production.
	Development of smelting south of Bali-Kumbat, Bamenyam becomes the main producer south of Bali-Kumbat.
c. 1880	End of large-scale production in Bamessing.
	Bamessing smelters shift to open hearth furnace.
	Babungo and the Bamenyam area carry on large-scale production.
c. 1920-40	Cheap scrap-iron from imported European goods puts the Ndop Plain smelting industry out of operation.

who reigned for 40 years around the turn of the century, was determined to reduce this dependency and had one furnace built near his palace (Tardits 1980: 315, 349). But what is one furnace compared to the 60 plus that were in operation in Babungo alone? Every Bamoum woman had a hoe (cultivation was done by women), and according to Jeffreys (1942a: 37) the average life time of an Ndop Plain hoe was three to four years. Old hoes were not welded into new ones; they were used as scrap to manufacture other implements. Thus the Bamoum kingdom needed some eight tons of iron every year to replenish its stock of hoes, not to speak of other implements. This iron came from Babungo via Bangolan, Baba and Babessi (Fowler 1989, see Tardits 1981) and from Oku and Banso (Tardits 1980: 349). Given the dense population of the Grassfields, and the concentration of iron production in a few centers, the reader, we believe, will be convinced that the figures presented here may not be far from the truth.

A few more figures: sixty clump furnaces can still be seen in Babungo, in association with heaps of debris. If our figure of 8,000 smelts per year in Babungo is correct (see note 4), it means that each of the sixty furnaces was successfully used an average of 133 days per year. Apart from certain predetermined occasions, such as the funeral of a chief, each foundry could potentially be in use each day of the eight day week. Three days were customarily set aside for the owner of the foundry to produce his own iron. Each of these three fixed days was followed by one of the three weekly local market days in Babungo, so that the foundry owner was always able to take his iron bright and fresh from the furnace to sell it at a good price in the market. The bloom is said to have become less attractive due to surface oxidization when stored. The remaining five days of the week were given over to anyone who had gathered the necessary materials and requested the foundry owner for the use of the foundry on a particular day. Such people would usually have already rendered assistance to the owner in repairs to the foundry and furnace, helping him to collect fuels and ores, and pumping the bellows for him on the days set-aside. Normally, the foundry owner took no part in the work on the five days when others were using the foundry. He would receive a part of the bloom and perhaps, a small basket of charcoal or iron ore as payment for its use. The foundry owner did, however, employ a permanent representative in the foundry, a celibate expert in smelting, who remained sleeping and working in the foundry for a period of four to six months, and who daily assisted and supervised the work. This expert, usually a son or male slave of the foundry owner, was fed by him and received gifts from him and also had small payments in cowries or bloom from the people using the foundry. Also present would be a number of youths, sons of the foundry owner and children from nearby compounds, who assisted with minor tasks of fetching and carrying in return for the chance to pick up small pieces of bloom from the foundry floor that were left over from the smelt.

From census and genealogical data collected from elderly informants an attempt to list all compound heads, with their titles and principal occupations, was made for the final decade of the 19th-century in Babungo. This gives us an approximate total of three hundred remembered compounds out of which a minimum of two hundred were intermittently active in smelting iron. Now, if our figure of 8,000 smelts as an average yearly total for the 19th-century is not too far from the truth and if each of these 200 compounds was able to provide the nucleus, at least, for a smelting group, this means that each compound made an average of forty smelts per year. This does not seem an excessive workload. If we take into account the heavy labor costs of preparing materials (ore, fuels, tuyères, etc.) for the smelt and also the potentially numerous occasions, such as certain death celebrations, Tifwan (the regulatory society) excursions, annual celebrations for the chief's ancestors, etc., when foundry work was forbidden, it seems a reasonable estimate.

The Bamessing smelting industry

In order to illustrate some aspects of the above, we would like to describe in more detail the Bamessing smelting industry. In Bamessing, there are 54 smelting sites. They are indicated by the presence of slag and smelting debris such as broken tuyeres, ash, and pieces of furnace lining (see Photograph 1). The volume of debris on a site may range from a few cubic meters scattered on the ground, to large heaps of up to 3,000 cubic meters (see Photograph 2). In most cases it was difficult to find any remains of the furnace. Eighteen of the sites however, show an almost identical pattern. Typically, the furnace is built in a hollow dug into the ground, some five meters across. The mouth of the furnace is oriented in a general southerly direction. The debris from the smelting process was piled up all around the furnace, leaving a passageway in front of its mouth. The accumulated debris would form a horseshoe shaped mound, with the workshop enclosed within it, at the centre of a big crater up to eight meters deep (see Figure 5 and Photograph 2). When the heap had become too large, another heap was started outside the passageway, or the branches of the horseshoe were extended. The furnaces associated with such configurations of slag heaps are easy to locate, even if no remains of them can be seen. Some of them are in a good state of preservation, and their structure is clearly apparent (Photograph 3).

As we have shown, the Bamessing iron industry was out of operation by 1880, and it is now impossible to collect any account of it from oral tradition. However, from oral tradition collected in chiefdoms that had very similar techniques, and carried on the work well into the 20th-century, and from the material evidence in Bamessing, we may reconstruct a reliable picture of the industry.

Photograph 1. Close-up of a heap of debris, Bameesing, showing glazed tuyère tips, one tuyère opening (to the side of the bellows), and pieces of slag.

The furnaces were massive structures (see Figure 3, and Photograph 3). They were made as follows: a large circular hollow was dug in the lateritic red soil, some five meters across, and more than waist deep. Part of the loose lateritic clay was put back into the hole, together with the same volume of kaolin dug in the hills. The mixture was watered and pounded under foot by a gang of men. When the clay was ready, it was piled up around a big bundle of grass, and two plantain stems, so as to leave open a space roughly the shape of the hearth, the chimney, the mouth and the two ducts for the tuyeres. This was done along the northern bank of the circular hollow, so that the body of the furnace was not standing free, but leant against the bank. Three pieces of used tuyeres were embedded in the furnace wall, above the mouth. According to Bamenyam and Bafanji information, these were for the proper ventilation of the furnace. When the mud had hardened, the bundle of grass and the plantain stems were removed. According to Babungo information, the structure was allowed to dry for one complete dry season. Then, a rectangular shed was built over it, a stone pavement put in front of the mouth of the furnace, with fine-grain mixture of kaolin and lateritic soil. These were left to dry, then pounded, sifted, and mixed in equal parts. The mixture was watered, pounded wet, and used to cover the inside walls, chimney and ducts of the furnace with a plaster some 3 to 5cm thick. This refractory mixture seems to have withstood the heat and erosion fairly well, while keeping the furnace free from cracks.

Photograph 2. A Bamessing slag heap. The heap is on flat and level ground. The man on top of it shows the scale. The second half of the horseshoe-shaped heap is to the right, out of the picture. In the background are the hills to the southwest of the village.

Photograph 3. Bamessing furnace (front view). The upper part of the furnace, with the chimney, has been destroyed, but the three vents, still intact, can be seen in front of the furnace. Near the mouth are pieces of broken tuyères. Scale : 1 metre.

When the furnace was ready for use, the mouth was blocked with potsherds and broken tuyeres packed together with fresh mud. Wood and charcoal were sent down to the bottom through the chimney with burning embers, newly made tuyeres were thrust through the two ad hoc ducts, and the bellows were pumped. More charcoal was added, and subsequently, throughout the smelt, iron ore and charcoal were continuously added through the chimney. The smelt started in mid-morning and lasted till dark. The mouth remained closed throughout the smelt, and slag was not tapped. The furnace was left until sunrise, when the mouth was broken open, and the hard cake of slag and iron dragged out. If the furnace did not need repair, the mouth was immediately re-locked and a new smelt started so as to take advantage of the heat accumulated by the thick clay walls. The smelting would go on day in and day out, without allowing the furnace to cool down until it needed repair, or the smelters wanted a rest. A normal smelting team would include the owner of the furnace and seven senior smelters, plus a number of aides and apprentices. Each of the eight senior smelters would provide the inputs for each day of the eight days week, and collect the output. Presumably, a gift was given to the owner of the foundry. Smelters were exempt from the sabbatical obligations associated with the two holydays of the eight days week.

When a smelt had been completed, the cake of slag and iron was dragged out of the furnace, broken, and the pieces of slag thrown away together with the two used tuyeres, on the heap of debris (see Figure 5). The blooms – according to Bafanji information, there were two, one at the extremity of each tuyere – were then processed. This involved crushing the bloom so that the small nodules of iron were freed from any slag. The bloom was put on a large stone and pounded to pieces with heavy stone hammers. Bits of bloom were then

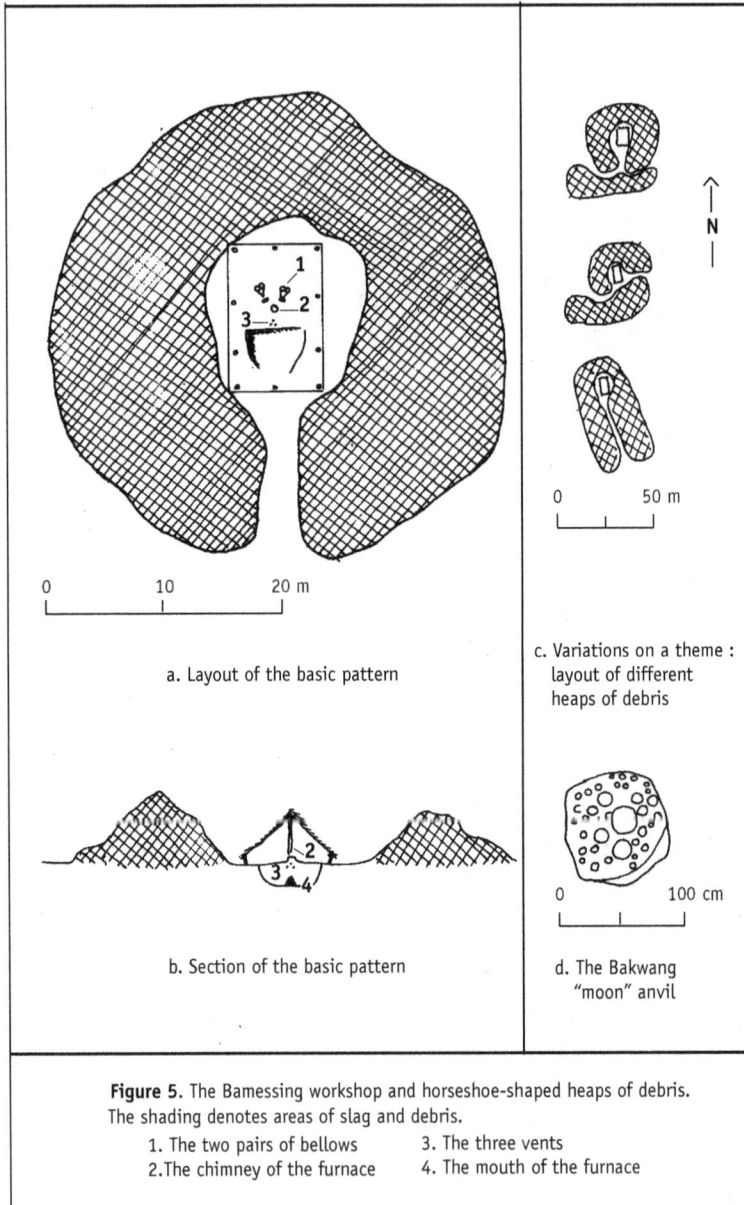

0   10   20 m

a. Layout of the basic pattern

b. Section of the basic pattern

c. Variations on a theme :
layout of different
heaps of debris

0   50 m

N

0   100 cm

d. The Bakwang
"moon" anvil

Figure 5. The Bamessing workshop and horseshoe-shaped heaps of debris.
The shading denotes areas of slag and debris.
1. The two pairs of bellows   3. The three vents
2. The chimney of the furnace   4. The mouth of the furnace

picked up by the workers and further crushed with smaller stone hammers. In the process, the iron would wear down the granite anvil and hammers, digging craters in them. The big stone anvil looked like the moon, pitted with many craters from the repeated hammering of the bloom (see Figure 5d). The craters were put to use as they prevented the iron from scattering all over the foundry when it was being hit with the hammers.

Lumps of bloom were put in a crater, wrapped in a ring of grass, and then hammered. When the bloom had been crushed to pieces the size of a small pea, it was sifted. The slag, reduced to powder, went through the sieve and the iron that remained in the sieve was wrapped in bundles and sent to the smith.

Many Bamessing foundries seem to have lacked a 'moon' anvil. Besides, in Bamessing, the smelting sites are far more numerous than the smiting sites (the latter are easily recognizable by their flat anvils raised to 40 to 50 cm above ground level). This suggests that Bamessing specialized in smelting, and that another chiefdom – perhaps Bafanji – and a couple of chiefdoms of the Bamenda Plateau bought the raw iron to turn out hoes. A similar division of labor existed between Bamenyam (smelting) and Bafanji (smiting) for at least a century before smelting came to an end. In such cases, the bloom was broken into big lumps by the smelter. The fine-grain crushing was done by the smith himself. In Babungo the block of slag was removed from the furnace and broken open and two large lumps of bloom removed. Any slag or dirt adhering was cleaned off with a stick and the bloom was sold in this form to the smiths. However, a type of 'moon' stone was found in the Babungo foundry and this was used by youths and casual helpers in the foundry to break up and crush small lumps of slag in order to extract small quantities of bloom that were collected in baskets and sold. It appears that isolated pockets of bloom were found to be in the slag formed close to the two central lumps of bloom.

After a number of smelts, the lining of the furnace started to melt or to come away in bits. Cracks might also develop in the furnace walls so that repair was needed. The furnace was allowed to cool down, and the entire lining was knocked off the inside of the furnace and a new one put in. The debris of the old lining was dumped on the slag heap. Thus, the heap contained ash, slag, broken tuyeres, and bits of furnace lining, and odds and ends such as broken pots and worn down and cracked stone hammers. In Bamessing, we made no attempt to assess the proportion of these various items in heaps of debris. But in Bakwang, where very similar techniques were used, the proportions are as indicated in Table 3.

TABLE 3 Composition of a Bakwang slag heap (in % of the total volume of the heap)	
Pieces of tuyere	5
Slag	60
Debris of furnace lining, ashes, organic material from vegetation growing on the heap, discarded hammers, miscellanea	35
Total	100

NB: It may seem surprising that pieces of tuyeres represent only 5% of the total volume of debris. It must be remembered that part of the tuyere was fused and incorporated into the slag. Most of the rest (except the last 30-40cm near the tip) remained unbaked and was dissolved by the rains, to be incorporated into the debris or washed away.

The raw materials needed for smelting were lateritic mud and kaolin to build and line the furnace, clay to manufacture the two new tuyeres needed at each smelt, iron ore, and charcoal. All these were found in the neighborhood of Bamessing. Lateritic soil is found everywhere. It was dug on the spot where the furnace was built and turned into mud by adding water.

The kaolin was mined in the hills surrounding the village (see Figure 6 on page 36). Shallow trenches were dug, and wherever a good vein of kaolin was found, it was dug deep, and tunnels were extended on both sides, following the direction of the surface trench. At intervals of three to ten meters, new pits were dug to reach the tunnel from the surface. The pits average 3 meters in depth, but some are up to 7 meters deep. The tunnels average 70 cm in width, and are very irregular in height (see Photograph 4 on page 37). They largely follow the veins of kaolin between the decaying granite rocks. Five such mines can still be seen around Bamessing. Two are on the hill west of the village, one with ten pits, the other with three surface trenches, running down the slope.

In this one, the pits were filled up by soil carried down the trenches by erosion. A third mine, of seven trenches with 80 pits and connecting tunnels lies southwest of the village. It is by far the largest one. A fourth one, fairly small, lies in the hills, to the northwest of the village. A final one, which we did not visit, was indicated to us south of Bamessing. Such kaolin mines are found in association with all the smelting sites of the Ndop Plain. Their number and their volume indicate that large quantities of kaolin were used in making furnaces and lining

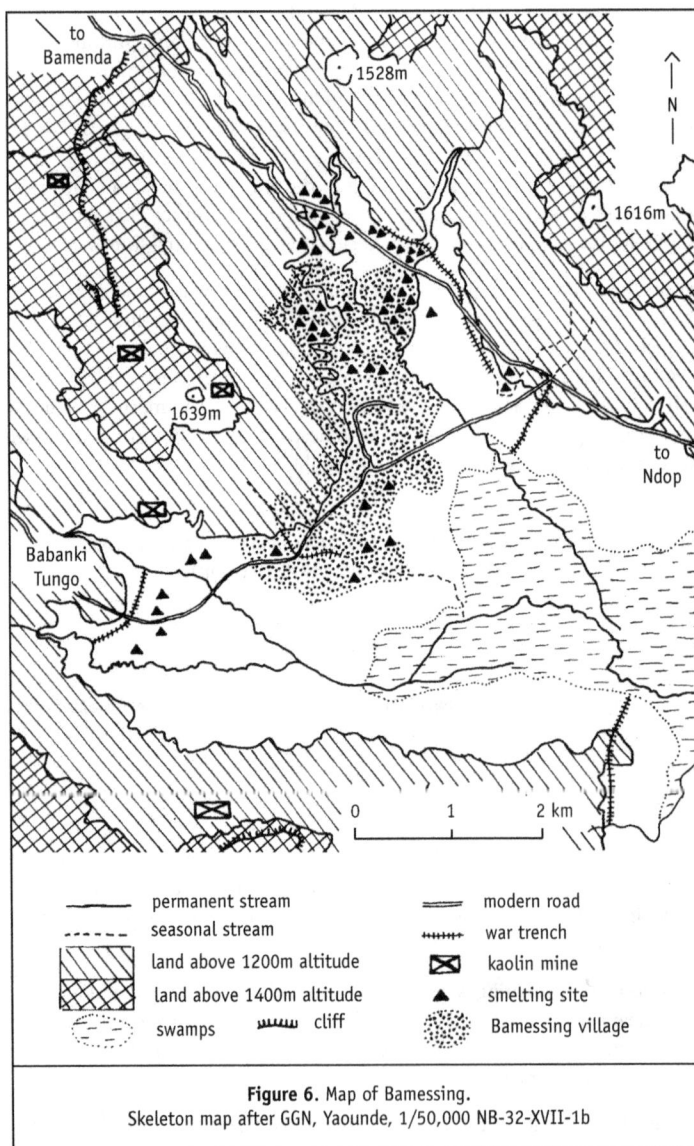

Figure 6. Map of Bamessing.
Skeleton map after GGN, Yaounde, 1/50,000 NB-32-XVII-1b

them. The total number of furnaces that can still be seen (some 150 at most) is probably a small fraction of the total number that have ever been built in the area. Presumably, new furnaces were built to replace old ones of the same type, on the same spot, as these cracked beyond repair. Besides, large quantities of kaolin must have been consumed to maintain the furnaces by entirely re-lining them every now and then. Judging from the quantity of broken pieces of hard baked lining in the slag heaps, this must have been done fairly often, perhaps every twenty or thirty smelts.

The ore that was used was lateritic gravel found everywhere in the hills, and in the streambeds at the bottom of the hills. It must have been dug out from right under the topsoil, and no trace is left of such mining nowadays.

Photograph 4. A kaolin pit, above Bamessing. The picture is taken in the shaft of the pit. In the background is the tunnel connecting with the next pit. Scale : 1 metre.

The charcoal was made from two hardwood species, burnt in shallow pits, and quenched with water. The trees are fire-resistant species that are found in sufficient supply (given the technology) all over the grassy hills around the village.

Clay for tuyeres is abundant in Bamessing. It was dug along streams in various parts of the village, by potters as well as smelters. Two tuyeres were used at each smelt. They were about two meters long and had to be thick enough not to break because of their sheer length. Each of them, dried, weighed some 10 to 15 kg.

Thus, running a foundry raised transportation problems. Kaolin had to be fetched from at least 3 km away, on average, and if in the hills, had to be brought down 300 meters in altitude along steep paths. Iron ore and charcoal had to be fetched from about the same distance, and some 30 or 40 kg of wet clay for tuyeres brought for every smelt. It is hard to tell the quantity of iron ore and charcoal used up for every smelt, but it is not difficult to guess that the staff of a foundry must have included a number of men working outside the foundry mostly to obtain and transport the raw materials. In the 1920s, the District Officer of Ndop assessed at 16% of the total male population the number of men engaged in trades related to the iron industry (Drummond-Hay 1925). At that time, people had almost entirely given up smelting. When both smelting and smiting were done, perhaps one third of the total male populations were engaged in some trade related to the iron industry.

Conclusion: the economic and technological impact

In view of the figures given in this article, one may speculate about the economic and technological impact of iron production in pre-colonial African societies. It is clear from oral tradition and from the material record that Grassfields people were well equipped with iron tools and weapons. Each woman had a hoe, a knife for weeding her farm, a kitchen knife and an iron axe to split her wood. Girls were provided with similar implements reduced in size to suit their strength. Men had cutlasses, knives, various tools to tap raffia wine, spears, war machetes, bells for their hunting dogs, iron gongs, ornate cutlasses and spears for dancing on festive occasions. Specialized craftsmen such as potters and wood-carvers all used iron tools. Iron was comparatively commonplace and cheap. Correspondingly, the smelter and the smith were ordinary people. Their position in the society offered nothing to be compared with the caste system and the numerous taboos and ritual prescriptions that characterize the smelters and smiths of the Western Sudan. In societies that, unlike those of the Grassfields, did not have a large-scale iron industry, iron may have remained, until recently, a luxury, mostly used for weapons, regalia, and a small number of important tools. Agricultural activities and craft production may have been carried out with other kinds of tools. Bohannan (1968: 117), for example, reports that according to Tiv oral traditions, wooden 'hoes' were in use along with iron ones in the past. In the forest belt, the digging stick was still in common use in the 19th century. The Iron Age was not solely an age of iron in all parts of Africa.

The data we present suggests that iron production, though widespread in West and Central Africa, may have been concentrated in centers producing on a very large scale. We may expect that iron was traded far away from such centers as part of the long-distance trade. Plotting such centers on a series of maps taking account of chronology would provide the skeleton of the economic structure of many areas of the African hinterland for which there are no other quantitative data available. For a proper assessment of the economic importance of each of those centers, however, we would need to know the quantity of marketable iron each of them is likely to have produced over a given period of time. In this article we have tried to do this for one particular village of the Ndop Plain (Babungo), by assessing the volume of production from the volume of smelting debris, matched to a chronology based on a typology of the sites, the heaps of debris and the furnaces. We have no doubt that our method could be extended to other villages, and greatly refined by using various means of absolute dating, by submitting the material remains to physical and chemical tests for a better understanding of the technology, and by reconstructing the smelting process with the various types of furnaces. But this is beyond our reach at the moment.

In our opinion, the extension of our enquiry to other large-scale sub-Saharan smelting centers would raise the following questions to be answered in each particular instance: Is the volume of slag a reliable index of the volume of production? Was slag used as ore, with the result that evidence of earlier smelting was destroyed? How does one assess the productivity of a given technique and the output of pure iron? How and where was the iron traded? How does one assess the iron needs of a given population? Were there shortages of iron at certain periods? Were other kinds of tools and weapons available in case there was a shortage of iron?

Such an assessment may not, however, be feasible in some instances. The case of Babungo (and other Ndop Plain chiefdoms) is a particularly favorable one, because the conditions were such that a sedentary industry could operate on a large scale over several centuries. The material remains are concentrated to such an extent that they cannot go unnoticed, and they provide good material for a quantitative assessment. At the less easily investigated end of the spectrum, there may have been large-scale iron industries of an itinerant type, due to the lack of sufficient timber. Such may have been the case in the Western Sudan where furnaces were usually built and worked until the supply of timber had diminished to such an extent that the furnaces had to be abandoned and new ones built in an unexploited area. The material remains of such slash and burn industries would be scattered over immense areas and most of the evidence would remain unnoticed.

Endnotes

1. This article, under a slightly different form, was first published in *Africa* (Journal of the IAI), 1979, 49 (4): 395-410. It is based on research conducted by J.-P. Warnier in 1972-74 with the financial support of the Department of Anthropology of the University of Pennsylvania and again in 1977-78; by M. Rowlands in 1976-77 with the financial support of the Social Science Research Council (SSRC) of the United Kingdom; and by I. Fowler in 1975-76 with the financial support of SSRC, and again in 1977-78. The authors would like to express thanks to Murray Last for his valuable critiques and suggestions.

2. The volume was assessed by equating the slag heap to a prismatic or a conical volume depending on its shape. For a conical volume, we applied $V = \pi r2 \times h/3$, and for a prism, $V = (1/2bxh)xl$, where V=volume, r=radius, h=height, b=base; l=length. In Babungo and Bamessing, the land is fairly flat and horizontal, and the debris highly concentrated in big heaps of regular shape. The error should not

be more than 10% of the total volume of the slag heaps surveyed. The number of heaps that are likely to have escaped our attention is very small. In Bafanji, Bamenyam, Bamunkumbit and Babadjou, the slag was often scattered over the ground, making it almost impossible to obtain figures that would compare in accuracy to those of Babungo and Bamessing. Since 1968, the Highways Department of the North-West Province (now Region) has taken away more than 100 lorry-loads of debris every year, to put on dirt roads on the Ndop Plain. Five heaps in Babungo and two in Bamessing had thus been taken away by 1978, totalling five to seven thousand cubic metres in volume. These are included in the count given in Table 1.

3. The average yearly output of pure iron for the 19th century can be worked out as follows: 133,000 m^3 of debris at 60% slag (see Table 2) = 80,000 m^3 of slag. One smelt represents 0.1 m^3 of slag; so 1 m^3 of slag represents the outcome. 19th-century smelts therefore numbered 80,000 x 10 = 800,000. Average number of smelts per year = 8,000. At 10-15kg of pure iron per smelt = 80-120 metric tons on average per year.

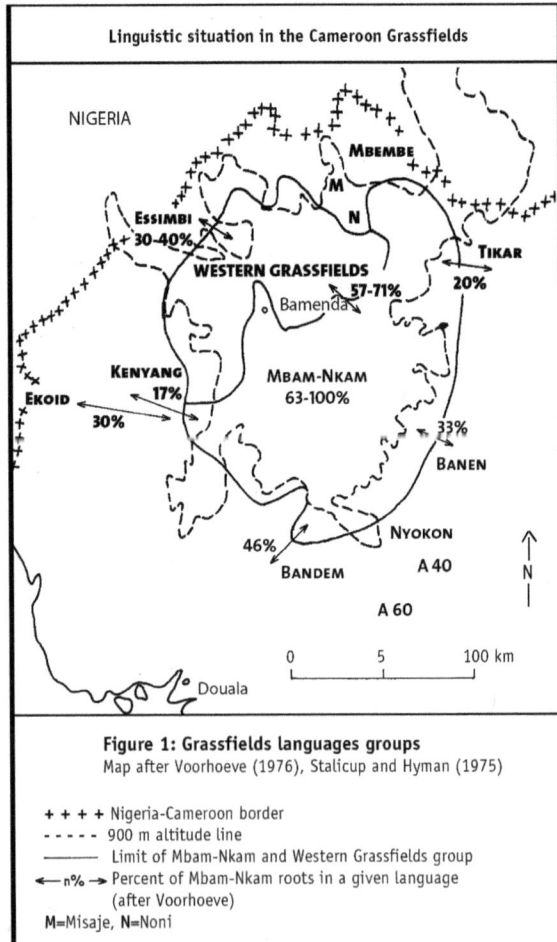

Figure 1: Grassfields languages groups
Map after Voorhoeve (1976), Stalicup and Hyman (1975)

++++ Nigeria-Cameroon border
----- 900 m altitude line
——— Limit of Mbam-Nkam and Western Grassfields group
←—n%—→ Percent of Mbam-Nkam roots in a given language
       (after Voorhoeve)
M=Misaje, N=Noni

The linguistic situation and the history of the Grassfields[1]

The linguistic situation in the Grassfields of Cameroon poses a problem, indeed a challenge. Basic vocabulary counts and shared lexical innovations point to one language classification and historical interpretation; but innovations in noun classes do not agree and point to another (Voorhoeve 1976). To reconcile these findings in a consistent historical explanation, one must have recourse to some hypothesis as to the past relationships among the speakers of the languages. Such a hypothesis must be controlled by whatever can be known about the sociolinguistic history, as it were, of the area. In recent ethno-historical research, I have been able to reconstruct a 19th-century pattern of multilingualism as an essential part of the social and political fabric of the Grassfields. Of the three hypotheses that might be advanced to explain the present language situation, the third is best supported by this reconstruction and other evidence. The case shows the necessity of sociolinguistic as well as narrowly linguistic reconstruction in explanation of actual cases of change.

Multilingualism in the 19th-century Grassfields

The contact situation in the nineteenth-century Grassfields

The Grassfields of Western Cameroon are an intermediate plateau about 1000 meters in altitude, with volcanic mountain ranges rising up to 2500 and even 3000 meters. It is surrounded on its western and southern sides by lowland rain forest. The topography had two important consequences: first, it created much ecological diversity over a rather restricted area, resulting in different regional factor endowments. The oil palm grows best on the southern and western fringes of the plateau. The plateau is well suited for the raising of small livestock (pigs, goats, sheep, dwarf cows, fowls), and for an agricultural production based on both forest and savannah crops. The central part of the plateau specialized in the production of iron that was traded towards the oil-producing areas. Local specialization in the production of tobacco, hides, raffia bags, wooden carvings, earthen wares, etc., depended on locally available resources but seems to have gone far beyond what could be predicted on such a basis. In the 19th century, the peoples inhabiting the Grassfields and their fringes depended heavily upon each other's production and formed a self-contained symbiotic community. The intense internal trade of which we have evidence from the early German and English travel accounts and administrative documents, from oral tradition, and from what is left of it nowadays, was described by Chilver (1961), Wilhelm (1981) and Warnier (1975).

The second consequence of the topography was that it channeled internal trade along well-defined routes, on which a number of chiefdoms acted as middlemen. In the 19th century, the Grassfields internal trade was linked by long distance trade to Calabar, the coast of Cameroon, and the Fulani Emirates to the north (Chilver 1961; Wilhelm 1981; Warnier 1975, 1985).

The Grassfields were (and still are) densely populated. The mountainous setting favored the fragmentation of the population in numerous independent communities, except in open, flat plateau areas that tended to promote the constitution of rather large chiefdoms and confederacies. Altogether there were a couple of hundred independent communities ranging from 1000 to some 60,000 people each. The types of political organization ranged from segmentary societies to centralized states, all of them combining in various patterns some fundamental elements such as patri- and matrilineages, sacred leadership, and men's regulatory societies.

Research by the Grassfields Bantu Working Group (summarized by Stallcup and Hyman 1975) shows the existence in the Grassfields of two major linguistic groups; a group that Voorhoeve (1971) named Mbam-Nkam and that occupies the eastern and south-eastern part of the highlands, and the Western Grassfields group that occupies the rest (see Fig. 1 on page 40). The language density, within the Mbam-Nkam and the Western Grassfields groups, was and still is considerable, both in terms of the small geographical area for each variety and the relatively small numbers of speakers of each variety.

There was no lingua franca in the 19th-century Grassfields. The Bali language (or Munggaka) spread as a lingua franca in the Bamenda area only after the Germans had established Bali as the paramount authority over most of its neighbors, and after the Basel Mission had subsequently selected it as a teaching medium. Pidgin English started being spoken in Bali when Zintgraff, the first German to reach the Grassfields arrived in 1889 with carriers and interpreters from the coast[2]. Subsequently, it spread all over the Grassfields, especially when the men, recruited around the turn of the century to work in the coastal plantations, returned home. Hausa never achieved the role of lingua franca in the Grassfields. In the absence of any lingua franca in the 19th century Grassfields, inter-chiefdom communications took place by means of the local languages.

A striking feature of the Grassfields of Cameroon is that their geographical, linguistic, cultural, and socio-political boundaries coincide for the region as a whole. This suggests that the Grassfields peoples have lived in relative isolation from the outside for a long period of time. In the 19th century, the highlands formed a well-defined regional unit quite distinct from the surrounding areas – or, in other words, a civilization on its own rights. Intense communication took place among the peoples inhabiting them, and whatever relations the Grassfields peoples had with the outside was linked to long distance trade connections.

The composite chiefdom and the multilingual household in the restricted Bamenda area

Now that the larger setting has been introduced, I shall focus on the surroundings of the modern town of Bamenda, within a radius of about forty kilometers, with which I am more familiar.

The area under consideration comprises languages belonging to both Mbam-Nkam and the Western Grassfields groups. To give an idea of the language density, the eighteen chiefdoms speaking Ngemba languages belonging to the Mbam-Nkam group can be classified into six linguistic communities whose languages are not readily mutually intelligible (Leroy 1977, 1980, 2003, 2007). One must consider that within a radius of forty kilometers around Bamenda more than twenty mutually unintelligible languages were spoken. Yet intense communications linked to trade, diplomatic activities, and inter-chiefdom marriages took place between chiefdoms. In the absence of any lingua franca, communications were carried out by means of the local languages, and multilingualism was widespread.

Multilingualism was geared to two regional processes: population movement and trade. The population of the Bamenda area was constantly in the process of being re-distributed among chiefdoms. Conflicts within chiefdom were often solved by the departure of one party. Such exiles were an expected feature of any succession to the position of chief. The unsuccessful contender would vacate the chiefdom with his wives, children, and followers, and seek adoption in another one. Each chiefdom was dominated by a number of lineages that provided its backbone and integrated all the newcomers by means expressed in the idiom of kinship. Occasionally, competition or open warfare dislodged a group from its niche and forced it into seeking either a different location or shelter with another group. Thus, at any time, each chiefdom represented a particular blend of all other surrounding chiefdoms. Several chiefdoms could associate into a confederacy, and not necessarily on the basis of common linguistic affinities. Thus, in the 19th century, the Mankon confederacy included five chiefdoms into a compact settlement. Four of these chiefdoms spoke Ngemba (Mbam-Nkam) languages of various descriptions and one chiefdom spoke a Western Grassfields language. The composite structure of each chiefdom can easily be ascertained from genealogies, cross-checked with evidence provided by names of lineage segments or individuals, and oral traditions. Thus, chiefdoms and confederacies were linguistically composite communities that, besides using minority languages, had an official language, so to speak, which was that of the leading elements of the chiefdom. Daily communications within the chiefdom, depending on its degree of linguistic heterogeneity, implied a corresponding degree of multilingualism.

The patterns of population movements in the Bamenda area explain the composite nature of the chiefdoms and some amount of multilingualism. Another factor – trade – played a critical role in promoting multilingualism.

Trade was carried on by series of short-link connections. Anyone was free to engage in it, and it was by no means the monopoly of a social category or a specialized ethnic group.

Trading was an enterprise conducted by household heads with the help of the male members of the household. It involved the maintenance of formal trade friendships, for purposes of security, food and shelter, marketing, credit, and the supply of trade goods, in a number of chiefdoms within a two or three day walking radius. In the absence of any trade language, it also involved a practical knowledge of the languages spoken in these various chiefdoms.[3]

Part of the success of a trading household relied on its capacity to maintain and increase its linguistic competence. Multilingualism was actually promoted and considered as an asset of critical importance. It was achieved by inter-chiefdom marriages and adoption.

A genealogical inquiry in most Ngemba-speaking chiefdoms showed that, at the end of the 19th century, from 20% (in Mankon) to 50% (in Akum) of the women married in a given chiefdom came from another one. This feature was explicitly connected to trade by all my informants. The most frequent pattern was for a man to give his daughter as a wife to his foreign trade partner or to his partner's son. The woman would join her husband (residence was virilocal) together with a young relative of hers who would help her with household chores and with the rearing and education of the children. The children were encouraged to speak the language of their mother. A small foreign-speaking community, constituted by the wife, her young relative, and the children, would thus form within the household. The children would also learn the local language and achieve fluency in both. Is it an indication? In the Mbam-Nkam language word for 'foreigner' is the same as for 'the newcomer among the wives'. In Mankon: /ngunge/. Establishing a trading household was not a short-term undertaking. It was usually handed over from father to son, following a principle of positional succession. Multilingualism, a large trade network, formal friendships, and marriages with foreign women built up together over several generations.

The second means by which a household could recruit foreign members was by adoption. Here, I use the term adoption to denote situations in which a person or a group of persons was – permanently or temporarily – put under the authority of a household head in a position of classificatory son or daughter. A frequent occurrence was for a trader to send one of his sons to live so to speak 'as a son' in the household of his foreign trade partner. The son would thus improve his knowledge of the foreign language, establish connections, and possibly initiate a matrimonial alliance. Another occurrence was the adoption of refugee groups or individuals who had vacated a neighboring chiefdom, following a conflict over a succession, accusations of witchcraft, serious conflicts within a descent group, and the like. Such refugees were adopted 'as sons' by ambitious household or chiefs, and given land.

In addition to the requirements of trade, those of diplomatic relations between chiefdoms made it a duty for the chiefs to marry wives from the chiefdoms with which they maintained constant relations. In the case of fairly large chiefdom such as Bali, Mankon, and Bafut, this meant marrying wives from most neighboring chiefdoms or at least from each linguistic community. Besides, the chiefs recruited and maintained important retainerdoms able to keep trade and diplomatic relations in foreign communities. Chiefs' compounds thus tended to assume the shape of small Babels.

It is now impossible to ascertain precisely which proportion of the 19th century population was actually multilingual, and in how many languages. This cannot be assessed by extrapolating from the present situation. The languages of larger diffusion that spread since the early 20th century – Bali, Pidgin English, German,

English, and French – replaced the short-range, local, 19th-century multilingualism. Nowadays, though local multilingualism has not disappeared – especially among elderly people – two people belonging to neighboring chiefdoms, speaking slightly different languages, may rather communicate through Pidgin English, English, or even French. This obtains for example among the younger generation of such closely related chiefdoms as Nkwen and Mankon.

However, genealogies collected around Bamenda, cross-checked by other types of evidence, show that, among the chiefdoms that acted as middlemen in the trade, 25% of the adult male population engaged in regular trading ventures, and that from 20 to 50% of the women married in any chiefdom were born in another one. Besides, most of the elderly informants whom I met were fluent in at least two of the local language. In view of this, my guess would be that, in the 19th century, between one-third and one-half of the Bamenda area population was fluent in at least two mutually unintelligible, if related, languages[4].

The proportion of multilingualism is an important factor, but so is the directionality of multilingualism. It followed political and matrimonial alliances, and trade activities. Peoples such as the Ngie, who were at the periphery of the main trading routes, spoke almost exclusively Mogamo, the language of their middlemen neighbors, as a second language, whereas such middlemen, as Mankon and Bafut had a more cosmopolitan multilingualism.

Multilingualism in space and time perspective

Would the sociolinguistic phenomena described above for a restricted area be found all over the Grassfields? This should be ascertained by empirical studies, but – given (1) the linguistic diversity of the Grassfields, (2) the absence of a lingua franca, (3) the omnipresence of trade, and (4) the widespread patterns of population movements from chiefdom to chiefdom – it is reasonable to assume that multilingualism was a common phenomenon all over the Grassfields in the 19th century.[4]

What about the situation before the 19th century? Hardly any archaeological research has been done in the Grassfields, and the early history of the area is inferred from oral traditions, cross-checked by linguistic evidence, and evidence taken from the social and political organization in the 19th century (this is no longer the case in 2012, see chapter 2). Available evidence points to the following conclusions: (1) the Grassfields seem to have been anciently and continuously populated; (2) the long distance trade in slaves, guns, gunpowder, and items of European manufacture is not very old. It dates back to the early 18th century at most, more likely to the beginning of the 19th century. It must have broken the relative isolation of the Grassfields only at a fairly recent date (this should be qualified; see chapter 13 in the present volume). The northern trade towards the Fulani Emirates is of rather recent origin, since it arose from the Fulani advance into Bornu and Adamawa; (3) on the contrary, the internal trade in palm-oil, iron, foodstuffs, livestock and a number of other locally produced commodities must be as old as iron production in the Grassfields. It must have made for intense internal relations over a long period of time; and (4) the political organization in independent chiefdoms seems to be as old as internal trade in the Grassfields. One can therefore assume that multilingualism, geared to internal patterns of population movements and diplomatic relations, is a fairly old phenomenon, perhaps an Iron Age one.

The Grassfields linguistic puzzle

Let us now turn to the linguistic map of the Grassfields (Figure 1 on page 40). It exhibits the following features: (a) the linguistic boundary that encompasses the two groups of Grassfields languages – that is, the Western Grassfields and Mbam-Nkam groups - fits very closely the limits of the highlands (the 900m altitude contour line on Figure1); (b) The said linguistic boundary, that separates Grassfields languages from all neighboring ones, is, as far as the vocabulary is concerned, a strong one. Voorhoeve (1976) shows that, on the basis of common lexical innovations, the Mbam-Nkam and the Western Grassfields groups should be considered as being closer to each other than to any of the neighboring groups. Further, basic vocabulary counts done by Voorhoeve (1971) reinforce the evidence provided by shared lexical innovations. Whereas Mbam-Nkam and Western Grassfields languages share between 57% and 71% of the basic Mbam-Nkam roots, they share only 20% of them with the Tikar, 33% with Banen, 46% with the Bandem, 17% with Kenyang (see Figure 1); (c) On the contrary, evidence taken from innovations in noun-classes gives a different picture (see Figure 2). The evidence raises here the question, famous in the history of linguistic inquiry in Africa, as whether the languages of the north-western Bantu borderland are to be considered members of Bantu family or not. On the basis of the Greenberg-Crabb criteria of Bantu languages (Williamson 1971) and subsequent additions by Stallcup and Voorhoeve (Voorhoeve 1976), to wit, the addition of a nasal to all of the nominal prefixes which had no other consonant, including classes 9/10, the near corollary of the merger of 6 and 6a, and the leveling of tone in 9/10, Mbam-Nkam would undoubtedly be included in Bantu. However, the genetic position of its closest relative (according to basic vocabulary counts and shared lexical innovations) – that is, Western Grassfields – would be ambiguous. Voorhoeve (1976) suggests that, according to grammatical (noun-class) evidence, Western Grassfields could be put together with the Bandem, Nyokon, and some of the languages belonging to the A60 and A40 language groups, to the south-east of Mbam-Nkam, and with Misaje and Noni to the north. Though, with respect to the intersection of the different nasal criteria, we have the following situation:

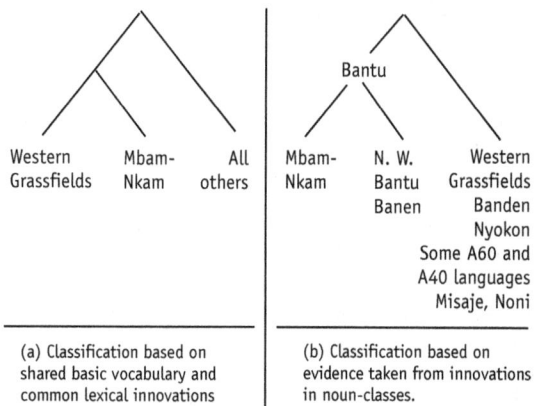

"One has to conclude, writes Voorhoeve (1976: 7-8), that a surprising contrast exists between the lexical and grammatical (noun-class) evidence, which asks for an explanation." This contrast is expressed in Figure 2.

Though it is nearly impossible – in the present state of our knowledge – to solve the puzzle, I believe it is worth speculating about the possible explanations so as to raise questions in the fields of historical linguistics and history. Three hypotheses can be put forward to account for this contrast between lexical and grammatical evidence: according to the first hypothesis, the Grassfields might have been occupied at one point by populations speaking languages sharing some north-western Bantu noun-class characteristics and proto-Grassfields basic vocabulary. Later on, the western part of the Grassfields might have lost some of its Bantu noun-class characteristics while retaining its basic vocabulary. Later on, the western part of the Grassfields might have lost some of its Bantu noun-class characteristics while retaining its basic vocabulary. However, the Western Grassfields group shares some noun-class characteristics with Nyokon, and some languages belonging to the A40 and A60 language groups, from which it is cut off on the ground by the Mbam-Nkam group. Huge migratory movements that might have brought Nyokon and some A40 and A60 speakers into contact with Western Grassfields – thus promoting the diffusion of noun-class characteristics among them – are most unlikely. It seems far more simple to admit either that we have here a case of independent and somewhat parallel changes in Western Grassfields, Noni, Misaje, Nyokon, and some A40 and A60 languages (hypothesis 1), or that these languages were once contiguous and were split off by the Mbam-Nkam group (hypotheses 2 and 3).

We still lack the evidence to test hypothesis 1. Features that have been borrowed or independently evolved obscure genetic relationships, and until we have much more detailed comparative data (a 200-word count among other things), it will be difficult to test this first hypothesis. However, this hypothesis meets with one serious difficulty: it postulates a situation where once upon a time all Grassfields languages shared common noun-class characteristics and a good proportion of their core vocabulary. Given the intense contact situation within the Grassfields, how could the Western Grassfields languages have lost some of their noun-class features, whereas Mbam-Nkam languages did not, and why did the boundary settle where it is now – a boundary that does not fit any other, geographical, ecological, or political? It is difficult to account for such a situation

Figure 2. Contrast between lexical and grammatical evidence

			Bantu		
Western Grassfields	Mbam-Nkam	All others	Mbam-Nkam	N. W. Bantu Banen	Western Grassfields Banden Nyokon Some A60 and A40 languages Misaje, Noni
(a) Classification based on shared basic vocabulary and common lexical innovations			(b) Classification based on evidence taken from innovations in noun-classes.		

of differentiation of areas in close contact with each other without resorting to an exogenous factor of differentiation (hypotheses 2 and 3).

The second hypothesis, then, runs like this: at one point in the past, the Grassfields might have been occupied by peoples speaking languages characterized by Western Grassfields-like noun-class features, related to those of Misaje, Noni, Nyokon, some A40 and A60 languages, and a basic vocabulary close to that of the same. Then, features of northwestern Bantu noun-classes might have been borrowed by the highlanders from the adjacent Bantu-speaking peoples immediately east of the Grassfields, generating the Mbam-Nkam languages in the process. Thus, the Western Grassfields languages might have been geographically cut off from their closest relatives grammar-wise. The implication in this hypothesis is that there has been little or no population movements: Bantu noun-class features – as against Bantu speakers – would have moved into the Grassfields.

We now come to the third hypothesis: once upon a time, the Grassfields might have been occupied by populations speaking languages characterized by proto-Western Grassfields, Nyokon, A40 and A60 noun-classes and vocabulary. Then Bantu speakers – as against Bantu noun-class characteristics – might have moved from the east up onto the highlands, and spread in such a way that they split off the Western Grassfields group from the Nyokon, A40 and A60 groups. Following this, intense communications within the densely settled Grassfields would have resulted in a relexification of both Western Grassfields and Mbam-Nkam languages, generating the puzzling linguistic situation that we know.

The means of testing hypotheses 2 and 3 are, I must admit, rather scanty. We do not have any positive evidence of borrowing of basic vocabulary within the Grassfields in the past. The only way to decide which hypothesis is the best one is therefore by assessing which one is the most unlikely.

The two hypotheses are based on the assumption of two different contact situations. In the second hypothesis, contacts might have taken place between the eastern part of the Grassfields and the Bantu-speaking populations living outside the Grassfields on their eastern fringe. This contact situation might have resulted in the spread of Bantu noun-class characteristics in a non-Bantu speaking population. This hypothesis implies that: (1) sufficient contact might have taken place between the eastern part of the Grassfields and the lowlands lying to the east; (2) in this particular case, basic vocabulary might have been more conservative than grammatical (noun-class) features. This second implication is consonant with the fact that basic vocabulary is notoriously conservative. Further, the selective borrowing of grammatical features to the exclusion of basic vocabulary is not at all impossible. There is at least one known example of a population – the Cushitic Mbugu – who took all the grammatical morphemes of the neighboring Asu, while keeping the Cushitic roots. But one may object to the conservative nature of basic vocabulary by remarking that basic vocabulary is conservative as compared to non-basic vocabulary, but not necessarily as compared to grammatical structures, to wit all the Pidgin and Creole languages.

Further, the first implication of the second hypothesis meets with serious difficulties: as indicated in the first part of this article, all available evidence points to intensive contacts over a long period of time between peoples of the Grassfields among themselves, and to little contact between the Grassfields and the outside. The contact situation in the highlands is thus much more consonant with the third hypothesis rather than with the second one. If the second hypothesis was to be retained, one would have to account for the fact that, from all points of view (vocabulary, material and non-material culture, social and political organization, etc.) the eastern border of the Grassfields is a strong one, except for some noun-class characteristics.[5]

The third hypothesis implies that: (1) Bantu speakers might have moved into the Grassfields and lost most of their social and cultural characteristics to adopt Grassfields ones; (2) intensive contacts might have taken place within the Grassfields between the Bantu newcomers and the indigenous population; and (3) in this particular case, noun-class features might have been more conservative than basic vocabulary.

There is no positive evidence in support of the first implication. One can only remark that social and cultural characteristics of the peoples of the Grassfields, were evolved to some extent in response to the peculiar ecological setting, and that any people moving into the Grassfields would be under pressure to adjust to the setting and to adopt many features characteristic of the other Grassfields peoples – a familiar theme in contemporary anthropology – while losing contact to some extent with its former neighbors outside the

Grassfields. Further, the patterns of population movements described in the first part of this chapter would promote a certain amount of diffusion between groups within the highlands. Lastly, the Grassfields constitute a very attractive setting, and if the Bantu speakers living on the fringes of the Grassfields happened to have, at one point, a technological advantage over their neighbors, or if they wanted to take advantage of the economic opportunities offered by the highlands, their moving up onto the plateau would have been the most natural thing they could have done.

Regarding the second implication of the third hypothesis – that is, a more intensive contact situation within the Grassfields than between them and the outside – there is much evidence to be brought forward in its support, as pointed out in the first part of this article. Intensive contacts, including exchange of population and of women, trade, diplomatic relations, took place between the Western Grassfields and the Mbam-Nkam speakers. Multilingualism was widespread. On the contrary, contact between the Grassfields and the outside was connected with long distance trade that is far less intensive in terms of daily contacts. Besides close contact within the Grassfields, evidence for the lack of eastern contacts of Mbam-Nkam group is that the area of greatest internal diversity of Mbam-Nkam languages is found in the geographical center of the Grassfields as a whole.

As far as the third implication is concerned – namely that, in the Grassfields, noun-class features are more conservative than basic vocabulary – there is some evidence in its support. In terms of phonological change, the Ngemba of the Bamenda area have the most conservative noun-class system of the Mbam-Nkam group (Leroy & Voorhoeve 1975). Yet, the Ngemba share about 60% of their basic vocabulary with their immediate neighbors, that is, the Meta, Kom and Ndop speakers. If the phonological aspects of noun-classes (and if noun-classes) had been less conservative than basic vocabulary, such a situation could not have been found.

Conclusion: a history of internal diversification and contacts

In this article, three hypotheses have been put forward to account for the Grassfields linguistic puzzle. The first one is based on independent retentions or losses of noun-class characteristics by different language groups. The second one is based on the diffusion of Bantu noun-class characteristics in the highlands. The third one is based on the migration of Bantu speakers into the highlands, followed by an intense process of relexification of all the Grassfields languages.

The basic problem met in attempting to test these hypotheses is that the situation of intense contact among Grassfields peoples makes it very difficult to sort out which features (both in core vocabulary and noun-classes) are genetic and which are borrowed. In the present state of our knowledge it is impossible to give much positive linguistic evidence in support of any of these hypotheses. This failure reveals the need for more detailed studies of all the Grassfields languages, focusing on the diffusion of core vocabulary, semantic clusters, and grammatical features, and the direction of such diffusions.

Nevertheless, the linguistic and historical data seem to dovetail best in support of the third hypothesis expressed in the second part of this article. To summarize, this hypothesis runs as follows: Misaje, Noni, Western Grassfields, Bandem, Nyokon, and some A40 and A60 languages were, at one point in the past, contiguous. Later on, Bantu speakers might have intruded into this group of languages and split off Misaje, Noni and Western Grassfields languages on the one hand from Nyokon, A40 and A60 languages on the other hand. A number of factors, among which the ecological diversity of the Grassfields, made for (1) intensive trade relations between the peoples of the Grassfields, and (2) a socio-political organization characterized by the fragmentation of the population into numerous composite units. Patterns of population movements and internal trade resulted in a situation where – in the absence of any lingua franca – multilingualism was promoted as part of the social, political and economic fabric. Multilingualism and a situation of intense internal contact might have resulted in a relexification of the Western Grassfields and Bantu languages while their respective noun-class systems retained many of their characteristics, thus generating the Western Grassfields and Mbam-Nkam groups. Intense internal contacts and relative isolation from the outside over a long period of time might account for the coincidence between the geographical, lexical, cultural, and sociopolitical boundaries of the Grassfields. Their relative isolation was broken only at a fairly recent period by the development of long distance trade with the coast to the south and the Fulani Emirates to the north (however, in 2012, this statement should be qualified in view of more recent investigations. See chapter 13 in that respect).

It must be stressed, however, that in the absence of any positive evidence of relexification, one cannot consider this hypothesis as a definite conclusion. Besides, the role played by multilingualism in the process is all the same very likely but yet only speculative.

Such a conclusion would appear rather frustrating and hardly worth publishing if it did not reveal that the solution of a conflict between lines of linguistic evidence as to historical relationships between languages requires some hypothesis appealing to the historical patterns of linguistic contact and linguistic change. Whatever hypothesis is retained to account for the Grassfields linguistic situation, this very situation forces one to be explicit about the socio-cultural context implied in any attempt at classifying languages. It also stresses the difficulties involved in drawing historical conclusions from linguistic maps and genetic classifications of languages.

Endnotes

1. First published in *Language and Society*, 8: 409-423. This chapter is a revised version of a communication made at the 12th Congress of the West African Linguistic Society, at Ile-Ife, 14-20 March 1976. My thanks go to the late Professor Jan Voorhoeve, Professor Dell Hymes, Dr. J. Leroy, late P. M. Kaberry, Mrs. E. M. Chilver, and Ken Stallcup for valuable comments and critiques, and to the former for permission to quote and make extensive use of his data. The responsibility for the opinions expressed in this article, however, is mine.

2. Personal communication from E.M. Chilver who adds that on his first expedition, Zintgraff was accompanied by Liberian Vai, some Cameroon coast men, Manga Bell's slave Muyenga as an interpreter, and, according to oral reports, a Yoruba. Pidgin spread rapidly to Bali. This knowledge was reinforced by the later, trading, expedition (1891) in which the coast element was stronger. After Hutter's arrival (1891), the Balitruppe was drilled and trained in Pidgin.

3. E.M. Chilver (personal communication) mentions that in Bali, the need of interpretation and hostelling for foreign visitors was met by the institution of the tamanji, a chiefdom official whose function it was to cater for such visitors. Similar institutions existed in Nso, Bafut, and several other Grassfields chiefdoms.

4. Kaberry (personal communication) strongly supports this view as far as Nso area is concerned. Stallcup (personal written communication) writes: "bilingualism in this area (the Grassfields) runs conservatively at 50% (much higher if Pidgin and Standard English and French are taken into account). It may have been a bit lower in pre-colonial times but the necessary trade relations of this area have always necessitated a high degree of bilingualism".

5. The Mbugu case might be explained by a very peculiar contact situation. The most convincing hypothesis is given by Terrence Kaufman (Thomason & Kaufman n.d.) who thinks that a completely bilingual (Cushitic-Asu) population suddenly lost touch with the Asu.

Part II

The Grassfields regional economy

The internal consistency of the first (historical) part of this book was provided by the second chapter that underscored the contribution of economic history and of linguistics to the history of the Grassfields. The second part is devoted to the regional economy of the highlands. However, the linkages between its four chapters (respectively devoted to the domestic economy, guns and slaves as part of long-distance trade in valuables, and the working and economic ethos of Grassfields people) are far from obvious at face value. In order to introduce them, let me indicate where they would fit in the overall picture of the regional economy. During the last three centuries at least, but most probably for a much longer period of time, the political economy of the Grassfields was divided up between two different kinds of endeavours of different magnitude: regional and sub-continental. The regional trading networks were open to all, had a limited range (from Ngi to the Ndop Plain, as far as the Bamenda plateau was concerned), were deployed in the open on local or regional marketplaces, and concerned subsistence goods such as palm oil, foodstuffs, ironware and small livestock. By contrast, the long-distance trade involved only high-ranking kings and notables, had a far-reaching range, was practiced in the secluded space of the households of the kings and notables, and concerned goods of high value such as guns and slaves.

The present, second, part of this book only deals with a few, restricted, aspects of this very complex and highly developed economic organization. In the 1970s, some development programs aimed at improving pig breeding in the Grassfields. However, the way they went about it amounted to subjecting the domestic economy to the needs of the pig, instead of the reverse. The pig and the functions it fulfilled in the household economy provide only one among many other possible topics pertaining to the regional economic system. Other topics could have been iron production (considered in chapter 2), crafts, cereals and palm-oil production, currencies, marketplaces and traders. However, though limited in scope, the case of pig breeding allows one to analyze the changes that impinged on the local systems of production and exchange over the last couple of centuries. Guns and slaves (chapters 5 and 6) featured prominently at the core of long-distance trade in luxury goods. As such, they provide a vantage point from which one can consider this form of trade that was so characteristic of Grassfields political economy.

Chapter 7 deals with one aspect of the cultural and political history of the hinterland of the Bight of Biafra including the Grassfields, that is, the slave trade. It resulted in the forced migration of tens of thousands people, mostly young men, to the coastal areas. They brought along with them the cultural practices and habits of their regions of origin. Amongst other things, they migrated with their specific attitudes to economic activities including productive work and trading. There are unambiguous archival indications that this aspect of forced cultural contacts went hand in hand with long distance exchanges and the slave trade. It left a recognizable impact on the contemporary situation in Cameroon.

Of pigs and people[1]
(with Karin Luke)

The developed economy of the Northwest Province of Cameron in the nineteenth century

The economic history of the Northwest Province (NWP) of Cameroon

As it was reconstructed by Warnier (1975 and 1985) and Rowlands (1979), this history shows the existence of a complex system of production and distribution at three different levels at the end of the 19th century. (1) Large polygamous households produced foodstuffs, livestock and other goods for household consumption, without however achieving self-sufficiency in a number of commodities. (2) In line with the first point, the same households specialized in the production of certain commodities for the market in exchange for other commodities not produced locally. These economic specialisations were localised depending on the natural endowments of a diversified mountain environment, and also according to the Ricardian law of comparative advantage costs. The lowlands specialised in the production of palm-oil for export in exchange for most other commodities. The economic specialisations of the highlands were located in relation to the palm-oil producing areas depending on distance and transportation costs, which differed from commodity to commodity along with their value to weight ratio. Next to the palm-oil producing areas, the farmers produced root crops for exchange. Further away still, small livestock (sheep, goats and pigs) were raised, and about a hundred kilometres away from the palm-oil producing areas, high-quality craft products were turned out (iron wares, pottery, textiles, and wood carvings). (3) At a third level, notables and chiefs were engaged in long-distance trading with the middle Benue and the Atlantic Coast. The regional and long distance trades were carried out through elaborate institutions including professional traders, synchronized markets, currencies (cowries and brass-rods), savings associations and a credit system. Altogether, this was the contrary of an underdeveloped 'subsistence economy'.

A case study in livestock development

We are going to discuss the history of pig production in the NWP within the last eighty years. The place of the pig in the elaborate pattern of economic specialisation and trade as described above, was to absorb the ups and downs in the production of non-marketable foodstuffs in each household. The households produced for export on a regular basis, and they specialized for the market depending on the region: either in palm oil or in root crops, grains, livestock and crafts. But all of them were also engaged in the production of foodstuffs for house consumption. This production experienced more or less unpredictable seasonal ups and downs of foodstuffs, which varied from month to month and year to year, especially plantains and root crops of low value that were too heavy to be transported at a profit. Sometimes, marketable foodstuffs were produced in excess, did not find favourable market conditions and could not be sold. These had to be consumed on the spot. In order to meet this requirement, the areas specialising in livestock production bred piglets for export. In all areas, including the one specialising in livestock production, the farmers who found themselves with an agricultural surplus (which was the case more often than not) bought one or several piglets and fed them the surplus. They had however to complement the pigs' diet with household refuse, leftovers from the kitchen, fruits and occasionally vegetable proteins which was the price they had to pay in order not to waste the less valuable agricultural surplus. The pigs were slaughtered for home-consumption, irrespective of their size as soon as the surplus had been absorbed. Consequently, farmers engaged in pig rearing on a somewhat irregular basis, depending on the availability of foodstuffs. Pigs have always been used in such a way by peasant societies all over the world. This is why the pig occupies such a special place in the peasant household and why, in Western countries, the 'piggy bank' precisely assumes the shape of a pig.

It is well known that the pig competes with man for the same foods. This, far from being a disadvantage, can be put to use in order to regulate an agricultural economy. In this respect, in a non-industrialized rural economy, the pig has quite different functions from those of other species of domestic animals, such as goats, sheep and cows, that do not compete with humans. This was precisely the case in the Western highlands of Cameroon. However, this also implied the existence of farmers specializing in the production of piglets for export and a fairly developed network of regional exchange.

The collapse of the regional economy in the NWP of Cameroon, and the reversal of the food-pig relationship

The 19th century pattern of economic specialisation and trade was partially ruined by the changes that have occurred since the beginning of the 20th century. Livestock production decreased dramatically under the impact of a number of factors. (1) The authority of chiefdom and lineage leaders was undermined. As a result, the large polygamous households that formed the basis of the regional economy (both for subsistence and trade) were not any more in a position to effectively control the labour force (especially the male labour force) engaged in production, porterage, trading, and tending the livestock, making and maintenance of fences, etc. The draft of forced labour and, subsequently, the rural-urban migration of the young men also contributed to the decline of the local economy. At the same time, the women, who produced most of the foodstuffs, both for local consumption and for export, were overburdened with more children, and they even lost the help of their children as soon as these could attend school. (2) As the population quintupled between 1900 and 1980 in a already densely settled area, pressure on the arable land increased, and agricultural productivity decreased accordingly in such a way that semi-intensive livestock production could not be practised any longer. (3) The development of modern transports allowed many small holders to market their foodstuffs surpluses in urban centres. They were not any longer forced to consume them on the spot, i.e. by feeding them to pigs. In this new economic setting, people and pigs began to compete for scarce labour, scarce land, and scarce food.

The present situation of pig production in the NWP of Cameroon

Attempts at improving pig production in the NWP

As explained in the previous section, the rearing of livestock in the NWP has drastically decreased in this century. Thus, it is understandable that major efforts are being undertaken to re-popularise livestock production in this area.

Generally speaking, the improvement of animal husbandry in developing countries is attempted in three different ways or by a combination of these: (1) improvement of management procedures and environmental conditions, (2) upgrading of indigenous breeds, and (3) introduction of scientifically improved (i.e. exotic) breeds usually from industrial nations.

The improvement of pig production in Cameroon through foreign aid organisations, private institutions, and the Cameroonian government is primarily based on the introduction of improved breeds of pigs. The following considerations are decisive for this proceeding in the NWP: (a) pig production in the NWP is mainly limited by the lack of feedstuffs, i.e. the number of pigs kept can only be substantially increased when feeding them or at least supplementing their diet with commercial feeds. (b) Raising indigenous pigs with commercial feeds will not be economical. These breeds grow slowly, are not very fecund, and show a less desirable meet quality. (c) Improved breeds of pigs are easy to introduce in the NWP. Major health problems are not prevalent. Besides, they are easy to produce in special animal breeding stations.

The erroneous assumptions at the basis of pig production programmes

Most foreign aid programmes are orientated along the 'strategy of basic needs'. Within this concept the fight against starvation and malnutrition is of outstanding importance. Besides provision of sufficient food, its quality – especially its protein content – has to be improved. The non-commercial animal production schemes in developing countries are usually based on this idea and on the fact that animal protein is of a higher biological value than plant protein.

The introduction of exotic pigs in the NWP is principally in accordance with these ideas, i.e. the growing number of pigs is supposed to provide particularly the rural poor with more protein, and thus improve the quality of their diet. However, the practice of improving pig production in the NWP through the introduction of exotic pigs is based on false premises, and neglects the role of the pig within the rural economy.

(a) The introduction of exotic breeds turns the function of the pig within the rural society upside down. From a regulator of foodstuff the pig is turned into a competitor for foodstuffs. This way, the pig that was kept according to the needs of the rural family and primarily used for home-consumption now submits the rural family to its needs. Formerly even if pigs were raised for the regional market, the production of pig feed used to be an integral part within the farming scheme of the rural family. Now the increased production of exotic pigs and poultry (incentives to keep these species and breeds of domestic animals are frequently related to foreign aid programs) puts an additional stress on the already tight foodstuff market of the NWP, and feedstuff by-products with the exception of rice bran are not available.

(b) The conversion of plant into animal products leads to a substantial loss of the total nutritive value. Even under optimum conditions, the conversion of caloric values in pig production comes to approximately 3 to 1, i.e. three plant calories are needed to produce one pig calorie. These losses of total nutrients are actually of no importance in extensively kept ruminants which live on plants not usable by humans, but they definitely have to be taken into consideration in the production of pigs and poultry that compete with man for the same foods, and that are also dependent on a source of animal or plant protein of higher biological value. It seems more advisable to recommend the cultivation of protein-rich plant products like soybeans. These can, to a major extent, substitute animal protein in the diet of man. Actually, the growing of soybeans is propagated among local farmers in some areas of the NWP, as well as their use in feeding animals and the production of oil. Little is known however about their potential value for the nutrition of man.

(c) The distribution of exotic pigs to local farmers is limited by the fact that raising improved breeds is to some extent dependent on the provision of commercial feedstuff. This requires a regular source of cash income, i.e. a steady employment. Rural families in remote areas, lacking such a source of cash income as well as transport facilities for the feed supply, can hardly be integrated into this programme. On the contrary, it can be observed that middle-class Cameroonians, mainly civil servants, get increasingly involved in pig production, i.e. the original intention, that of improving the living standards of the rural poor, cannot be fulfilled.

(d) The raising of exotic pigs and the investment of cash income in commercial feedstuff results in the necessity of marketing the pigs after they have reached an acceptable slaughter weight. An exotic pig is practically never used for home-consumption. The money spent on the pig has to be regained in order to pay for necessary commitments like school fees or consumer goods, e.g. cloths, salt, palm oil, and paradoxically meat. Even if exotic pigs are raised by rural people and for their own benefit, it means that these pigs do not improve the quality of the local diet in any way. By contrast, the pigs produced in the NWP are mainly sold outside the province and consumed by middle and upper class Cameroonians and, of course, by expatriates in the urban centres.

(e) Raising pigs with commercial feedstuff also changes the role of the pig within the rural economy in another way. Formerly pigs were predominantly raised for consumption, whereas the exotic pigs are nowadays solely produced for the market. As modern ways of saving and investing money in bank accounts or as share capital are up to now not very popular in developing countries, the population has to rely on other possibilities of 'money storage'. Investment of cash income in animals like pigs or poultry is quite popular because animals can be easily sold whenever money is needed. In this way it is understandable that the economic considerations that accompany pig production in industrial countries cannot be applied to the NWP. For example, pigs are sold frequently not when they have reached the slaughter weight, i.e. when it is economically advisable to sell them, but when money is needed. This is one of the many reasons why the raising of exotic pigs by local farmers in the NWP ends with an economic loss, a result that is hardly desired by foreign organisations.

Conclusion: possible improvements

Because of the above-mentioned flaws in the logic of pig production as well as the neglect of the historical and socioeconomic background of pig production in the NWP, a programme attempting to improve it through the introduction of exotic breeds has to be and actually is a rather disillusioning undertaking.

Basic considerations for the improvement of pig production in the NWP

A programme that claims to be orientated towards the basic needs of the rural population should be based on the following considerations:

(a) If possible, it should attempt to re-establish the function of the pig as regulator of foodstuff supplies, that is, as a piggy bank of the rural household. In this way, the competition between pig and man for the same foods would be reduced. Besides, the economic pressure to market the pig would fall away, and it could be used for home consumption. This approach has to rely on the capacity of indigenous pigs. Exotic pigs kept under such circumstances cannot compete with the well-adapted local breeds. Their superior genetic potential (fast growth, greater productivity, and better meat quality) will only show up under optimum conditions.

(b) An improvement of pig keeping in the NWP has also to rely on the knowledge and on the co-operation of already successful pig breeders. Their experience will help to avoid future errors. At the moment, it is primarily those local farmers who are more open to modern ideas (or more easily impressed by Western products and technology) who are included in the programme. They frequently have no idea about pig keeping or animal husbandry in general, which is one of the reasons explaining the lack of success with such schemes.

(c) Foreign aid organisations should above all assist in the organisation of an efficient extension service and a research programme in household economy. Support in the form of exotic livestock and money is a doubtful aid for the local population, especially when not accompanied by introductory and follow-up programmes.

Possible improvements in pig production in the NWP

As explained in the previous sections, improvement of pig production in the NWP has mainly to be concerned with indigenous breeds, i.e. improvement of management procedures and environmental conditions are the essential goals. These goals can only be achieved with competent extension workers, and in cooperation with already experienced pig breeders. This also means that achieving a larger pig population in the NWP is not the aim. If the extension programme is successful, this actually has to be a natural consequence. Pig husbandry and pig production can be improved in many ways, a number of which can be exemplified in the following:

(1) Nutrition: farmers could be advised to prepare and feed products which are up to now not or only rarely used, e.g. coffee pulp, rumen contents, or blood meal.

(2) Housing: pigs are often kept under unsatisfactory housing conditions. The ground becomes extremely muddy in the rainy season, protection from sun and rain is lacking. Knowledge about the construction of suitable shelters and enclosures are highly important.

(3) Breeding: the bad habit of inbreeding is still widespread. Education of farmers and the implementation of simple breeding programmes is a necessary component of a successful improvement of the pig production. Upgrading of indigenous pigs with improved breeds should be investigated, and may accompany the breeding program. It has to be kept in mind, however, that upgrading may lower the adaptability of animals to their environment.

(4) Hygiene and health: farmers should be provided with some basic knowledge about prevention and control of some common diseases and pests (sanitation, control of endoparasites and exoparasites, etc.). Investigations about the possible use of local medicines should be considered. Veterinary drugs are very expensive and often not even available.

(5) Marketing: as the market for pigs in the NWP is fairly limited, the attention of farmers should be called on alternative marketing possibilities. Usually it is advantageous to sell weanlings when breeding pigs. They are very difficult to rear because they require a highly nutritive diet. Besides, more people are interested in buying young piglets they want to raise for home-consumption primarily on food wastage. Adult pigs could be slaughtered and sold in bits instead of marketing them alive. Attempts to establish simple cooperative structures may eventually increase marketing possibilities and they also may stabilise the extension programme.

Final remarks

In this article, the authors intend to draw attention to a fundamental mistake that is the main reason for the failure of many foreign aid programmes: the neglect of the historical and socioeconomic background of the society which is supposed to benefit from this aid.

Pig production is actually a striking example of an attitude that is found in a number of animal production schemes introduced in developing countries. Of course, improvement in the production of ruminants (goats, sheep and cows) would be preferable in the NWP. It has to be stated, however, that the same basic mistakes that can be observed in the pig programme, reappear in the other animal production schemes.

In our opinion, the attitude of foreign aid workers has to change drastically in order to eliminate these mistakes. Expatriates from industrial countries have to accept the fact that the societies in the so-called 'developing' or even 'under-developed' countries actually are 'developed' ones, only showing a development different from the industrial societies. Therefore, foreign aid programmes will usually fail in the attempt to transfer Western technology and knowledge. Improvement can only be achieved if such programmes are based on the already 'developed' structure in the 'developing' countries. If this basic idea is not understood and accepted, foreign aid programmes are more likely to create problems than to solve them, and will damage the 'developed' structures they are seeking to improve.

End note

1. First published in the Proceedings of the International Colloquium Tropical Animal Production for the Benefit of Man, Prince Leopold Institute of Tropical Medicine, Antwerp, Belgium, 1982, pp. 504-510.

The gun is something to be displayed. Here, during the war parade, Mankon, December 1973

Trade guns as a source in history[1]

Flintlock and percussion muzzleloaders known as 'dane guns' are a popular sight among peoples of the Grassfields of Cameroon[2]. At death celebrations and annual festivals, crowds of men brandish them, execute grotesque charges, and fire them off in great clouds of smoke. These guns bear witness to the pre-colonial coastal trade with European merchants who bought slaves and ivory until the mid 19th century, and palm oil from the end of the eighteenth, in exchange for salt, cloth, iron wares, guns and gunpowder.

In this chapter, I would like to discuss what can be learned from a collection of such guns from the Bamenda area of the highlands, or Grassfields, of Western Cameroon. Which guns were traded, where and when were they made, did they have any impact on local warfare and tactics, what was their importance in the local economy? These are the questions I would like to raise.

The data on which this paper is based were collected in Bamenda during the year 1977-78. I examined some one hundred guns in a number of compounds, recording their dimensions and marks, and had a more casual view of a couple of hundred more, at funerals and on public occasions. I discussed my findings with elderly informants in several chiefdoms of the Mezam Division, especially in the chiefdom of Mankon.

Types of Guns and Origins

Guns wear out fast, and are repaired by local blacksmiths who are quite adept at their trade. Old flintlocks are converted to percussion, worn down parts are replaced, new guns made with the parts of old ones. I shall ignore the many variations thus introduced in the guns that are actually in use, and, for the sake of clarity, I shall describe the original guns, before subsequent repairs and modifications, starting with the more recent ones. Locally made Guns Currently, local blacksmiths are producing large numbers of guns. These are percussion muzzleloaders of medium bore (about 24 gauge). The barrel is made out of the drive shaft of discarded cars (Land Rover, Volkswagen 'Beetle', Renault 4). The base of the barrel is hammered to imitate the hexagonal shape of old imported barrels. A hole is bored in its side, and fitted with a nipple which receives the cap. The lock is made entirely by the smith with very simple tools: a couple of hammers, files and a small kit to turn out screws. The lock reproduces the 18th-century flintlock, with the exception of the cock. Barrel and lock are fitted onto a stock shaped like that of a modern double-barrel shotgun. The 'furniture' of the gun (that is, the butt plate, the trigger guard, ramrod guides, etc.) is made of iron or brass worked by the smith himself, by casting into stone moulds and filing. The furniture is more or less decorated and reflects the wealth of the patron as well as artistic proficiency of the smith. The gun is half-stocked, the rod being kept in place in a compartment made out of a bent sheet of iron that runs underneath the barrel and is screwed onto it. The blacksmith is always able to turn out the whole gun – lock, stock, barrel, furniture and all – single handed, and from locally available raw materials. This activity is illegal and people do not advertize it, but it is fairly easy to make contacts with gun makers and to see them at work.[3]

Guns made from Imported Barrels

Many of these gun makers are the successors of local blacksmiths. Asked about the way they learned their trade as gunsmiths, they point to Igbo gun makers who have come up the Cross River valley into the Bamenda area over the last fifty years, and from whom their fathers or themselves learned their trade.

Photograph 1. Gun made in Calabar area or in the Grassfields from an imported barrel, by an Igbo gun maker. The mark, on the tail of the lock plate, is an attempted fake of a European one. The lock is of the French type. Mark the way the flint has pushed the frizzen forward, thus opening the priming pan.

Whereas African smiths have been able to turn out locks for quite a long time, they have always been dependent on imported barrels. Until drive shafts could be found in sufficient numbers, barrels were imported in large numbers through Calabar. Several informants said that Grassfielders who went to work on coastal plantations after the beginning of this century, usually went to Calabar before coming back to the Grassfields, to purchase a barrel at a good price and bring it to Bamenda to be fitted with a locally made lock, wood and furniture, by one of the Ibo gunsmiths until local people learned the craft. As a rule, these barrels do not bear any proof or view mark.[4]

These guns can easily be differentiated from the first type. The first type is half-stocked and the barrel has the same section all along. The second type is fully stocked (the wood goes all the way almost to the mouth of the barrel) and the section of the barrel is not the same all along. At the base, it has much thicker walls to withstand the pressure of the explosion, whereas the walls thin down towards the muzzle. The shape of the cock and of the brass attachments of the barrel are of the French type, and were perhaps imitated from the Belgian guns traded in Calabar in the second half of the 19th century.

There has been a change of attitude as regards locally made guns. Thirty years ago, the local gunsmiths attempted to fake imported guns. They tried to imitate the various marks that are usually found on imported guns: the proof and view marks on the barrel, and the inscriptions on the lock-plate. These smiths were illiterate, and their imitations of the marks do not make sense (see Photograph 1). Contemporary gunsmiths have acquired a pride in their work, and do not try to imitate imported guns. Their guns are unmistakably locally made and do not bear any fake mark.

Photograph 2. Tafanga (top) and afurukwang (bottom) guns. Note the proof and view marks on the barrel of the tafanga, their absence on, and the hexagonal barrel of the afurukwang.

These two types of guns receive a variety of names expressed in kinship terminology. However, the terminology is vague and not quite consistent from one informant to the next. Thus in the chiefdom of Mankon, they receive the names of *ndom* or *mu ngare* ('husband' or 'child of gun'), *ndom* or *mu ati* ('husband' or 'child of tree'). They are also sometimes called etsame, for which I could not obtain any consistent translation. These terms do not seem to have any currency out of the chiefdom of Mankon where other sets of terms are used. In Mankon, the generic term is *ngare*.

Afurukwang

Before the guns of the second type were made from imported barrels, that is, roughly before the beginning of the 20th century in Calabar, and perhaps the 1940s in the Cameroon highlands, the whole gun had to be imported. No doubt, many different types of guns were imported, but specimens of two types only may still be found in any large number in the Grassfields. The first one is locally named *afurukwang* (or *furukwa, afrikwa, afarakwa,* etc. in the different chiefdoms). This may be a pidginized form for the 'Africa' barrels manufactured in Birmingham and Belgium in the second half of the 19th century, and usually assembled in Belgium for the African trade (White 1971: 176). I could not find any specimen in a good state of preservation. It is a fairly rare gun, though everybody knows about it, and can recognize it at first sight. Consequently my information is not entirely reliable. It is a light flintlock gun, of medium bore (see Photograph 2). There were no proof and view marks on the specimens I saw. It must have been very similar to the 'Northwest gun' made for the North American fur trade in the 19th century, as described by Hanson (1955).

Tafanga (or tafang)

This second type of imported gun is, unlike the afurukwang, well documented. I saw many specimens in a good state of preservation, and bought one with all its original parts, including the walnut stock (Photograph 3). The barrel is an eleven or twelve gauge. The total length of the gun is 137cm approximately, with a barrel of

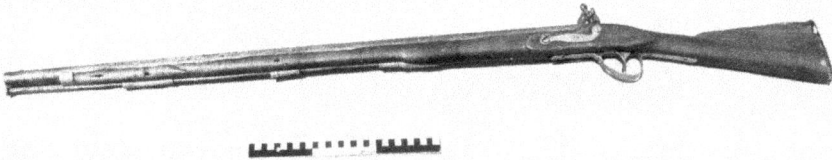

Photograph 3. The Birmingham 'India Pattern' trade gun. Scale: 30 cm

a maximum length of 102.5 cm. However, many guns are shorter by up to 15cm, because the muzzle corroded, started cracking, and had to be cut. Tafanga is a smoothbore flintlock, and the lock plate bears the inscriptions 'TOWER' or 'TOWER PROOF' on the tail. On a few guns, the name of the gun maker (e.g. 'WHEELER & SONS')

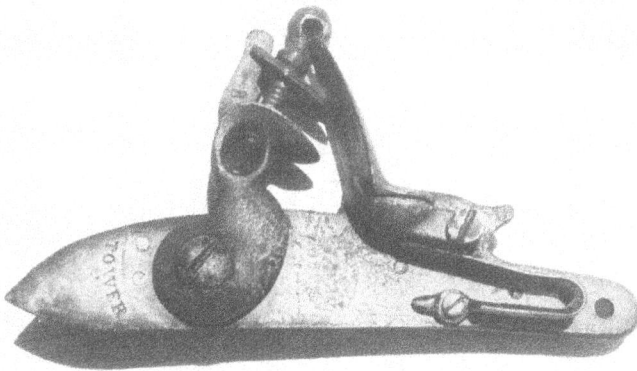

Photograph 4. The lock of the tafanga gun, with the 'TOWER' mark on the tail, and the king's crown on the plate. The spring, to the side of the plate, keeps the frizzen shut on the priming pan.

can be seen instead. In front of the cock, the cipher of the king (a crown above the initials 'GR') or simply a crown is engraved (Photograph 4). The gun is fully stocked and the barrel is fastened to the wood with three or four pins. These attachments were reinforced with leather or brass rings by Grassfields people. The furniture is all brass, and with no adornment. Altogether, the gun resembles the 'India Pattern' that was adopted by the British Army in 1797 (Wilkinson-Latham 1977: 74). However, though it is a good quality gun, its makers saved on raw material and labor. It incorporates less iron and brass than the British army musket. It also incorporates less labor: the furniture is purely functional, with little or no decoration. Of all the guns I saw, only one was a military gun. It bore a London proof mark on the barrel, a broad arrow mark as a view mark and the sign of government ownership (Blackmore 1961:265), and, on the lock plate, the royal cipher. The butt plate had regimental marks (1/V Lcs 56). All other guns were trade guns made especially for the African market as we shall see below.

The Trade of Guns to the Grassfields

My intention is not to deal with the trade in firearms with the African coastal areas. This has already been dealt with by White (1971) and Kea (1971). Rather, I would like to adopt a more parochial approach and focus on the trade in guns with the Bamenda highlands.

First, we may look at the dates of the trade. The proof and view marks of the guns give us an indication. Here, the reader will have to follow me through a number of technical details. In the eighteenth and nineteenth centuries British guns were manufactured mostly in Birmingham and London. There were many gun makers, and they obtained parts from an even greater number of sub-contractors. The lock and the barrel were sent to 'proof houses' where their quality was checked before finishing. Barrels were checked by viewing and firing with a bullet, using a quantity of powder equal to the weight of the ball that fitted the bore (Blackmore 1961:266). Once proved, they were marked with 'proof' and 'view' marks at the proof house and sent back to the gun maker who polished them and fitted them with wood, furniture and a proved lock. In 1813, an Act of Parliament allowed the Birmingham gun makers to have their own proof house. The proof and view marks that are found on Grassfields barrels of the type called

Photograph 5. The Birmingham proof and view marks on the barrel of the tafanga: a crown and cross scepter, with a 'v' for 'view' mark (to the right), 'B G' for 'Birmingham Gun makers' and 'P' for the proof mark (to the left). Between the two marks are the gauge of the barrel (12) and perhaps the initials of a merchant ('WFS').

tafanga are those of this Birmingham proof house (Photograph 5). This means that the guns were manufactured after 1813. How long after 1813? Some indications might have been obtained from the signature of the gun makers. However, these had taken to the habit of substituting the words 'TOWER' or 'TOWER PROOF' to their name on the lockplate of official and trade guns. These words do not indicate where the gun was made or proved. Army guns had such marks, and gun makers put them on trade guns as well, for, to the layman, they implied a reference to the proof house of the Tower of London that was prestigious on foreign markets. In fact these words did not mean anything, since they were neither a trade mark nor a proof mark. Some gun makers signed the parts they manufactured with their initials. But since few guns were entirely made by a single gun maker, several different initials may be found on different parts of the same gun. 'RW may stand for Robert Wheeler, a famous Birmingham gun maker, 'WG' for W. Greener or William Grice, and so on. Altogether, no information can be obtained from such marks for dating purposes.

Nor are the slight differences between individual guns an indication of their date of manufacture. Standardization did not exist at that time. The fact that many different workshops contributed to the manufacture, and that each gun was assembled by a worker who did not have any strict pattern to follow, explain that there are many slight variations in gauge, length, shape, position of the ramrod guides, number of pins to fasten the barrel to the wood, etc., from one gun to the next.

However, some information as to the dates may be obtained from what has been published on the trade in guns to the West African coast. Grassfields guns seem to have been obtained mostly from Calabar through the Cross River basin. Guns were not imported in Calabar until after 1713. But by 1767, they were a standard article of trade (Latham 1973: 24). Early guns were of two types, 'male' and 'female' – allegedly from their use in the slave trade, but more likely because of the shape of the stock (White 1971: 179-80). The 'male' guns were refurbished or assembled muskets of fair quality from London dealers. "The 'female' guns were cheap long barreled trade guns from the shops of Birmingham." (Hanson 1964: 322) If any of those guns reached the Grassfields, I doubt whether they would have been preserved until now. The African and North American trades created a specific demand, and British gun makers evolved models of guns purely for trade purposes. The gun sold in North America through various companies became known as the 'northwest gun' by`1777. Its description is found in Hanson (1955: 2). It was a light hunting musket usually 24 gauge, used mostly in the fur trade and secondarily for warfare and defense. The specifications of the tafanga musket indicate that the demand in Calabar and the Cameroon Grassfields was for a heavier gun that could be used in warfare, although warfare may not have been the primary concern of those who purchased it in the Grassfields (see below about the relative inefficiency of guns in warfare in an African context). The decline of the Atlantic slave trade did not put an end to the local demand for slaves, and to slave raiding. The inland trade carried on until the beginning of the 20th century mostly to provide oil-palm plantations with labor.

After about 1840 the quality of Birmingham muskets declined. In the early 1870s, Belgian gun makers entered the trade and turned out thousand of very low quality muskets for the Calabar trade (Latham 1973: 73-79), and other West African markets, often using Birmingham proof marks, or assembling guns from Birmingham-made barrels (White 1971: 176). The Belgian muskets may have reached the Grassfields, but I did not find any specimens. It may very well be that all of them went out of order even before reaching the highlands. The good quality of the tafanga on the other hand, can be gauged from the fact that many of them are still serviceable after more than one hundred years of permanent use and rough handling. In the Cameroon Grassfields, according to the oral tradition, the first guns appeared in the mid-19th century. The Grassfields were raided by Chamba mounted bowmen around 1830 (Chilver 1967; Chilver and Kaberry 1968: 20, 33, 26, 28, 29, 32, Fardon 1988, 1990). Grassfielders claim that their ancestors had no guns at that time to resist the raiders. By 1890, guns were part of the local armament in the southwestern part of the Grassfields, and German explorers and soldiers had to cope with them (Zintgraff 1895, Hutter 1902). However, they do not seem to have reached the northern and northeastern Grassfields in any great number by that time.

According to Tardits (1980: 139-40), the pa Ngirn, immediately south of the Bamoum kingdom, and their neighbors the Ndiki, had guns by the middle of the 19th century, to resist the attacks of the Bamourn king Mbombouo. Tardits (1980: 172) adds that the first firearms to be seen in the Bamoum kingdom arrived there at the end of the reign of Mbombuo's successor (around the middle of the century) but that the southern and eastern neighbors of the Bamoum always kept their advance in this respect (1980: 191-2, 208, 218, 365), which may help to explain why the Bamoum kingdom, though extremely powerful, could win no clear victory over them during the last three of four decades of the 19th century, and even suffered serious defeats at the hands of these chiefdoms.

To summarize: the tafanga gun was made in Birmingham between 1813 and 1840, especially for the African market. One may object to this conclusion that there was much counterfeiting throughout the 19th century (White 1971: 176) and that this constitutes a major problem in identifying African trade guns. However the consistency between proof and view marks on the barrels, the shape and marks on the lock, and the good quality of the gun all point to a Birmingham gun of the time when Birmingham gun makers were still turning out good-quality guns for the African market. The tafaga gun was probably the first that reached the Grassfields of Cameroon in any large number. It came mostly through Calabar, perhaps also through Douala, up the Mungo and the valleys of the upper Cross River, reaching the Grassfields probably not earlier than 1840. However, one cannot rule the possibility of quantities of guns reaching the Grassfields before the 1840s, for hundreds of thousands had been shipped to Africa long before, in connection with the slave trade. Considering the fact that a number of slaves caught in the Grassfields in the 1820s and '30s were among Koelle's informants, we may conclude that the slave trade between the Grassfields and the coast was already established at the beginning of the 19th century. How is it, then, that no gun older than the tafanga is found in the Grassfields? It may be that none of them actually reached the Grassfields. But it may also be that they were of such quality that they did not last long enough for the anthropologist doing research in 1970s to find. Before the establishment of the Birmingham proof house in 1813, immense numbers of guns were made in this town, "with the knowledge and certainty, that if were ever fired out of, they were certain to burst in the discharge. These guns were made for one market - that of the coast of Africa" (W. Greener, a Birmingham gun maker, quoted White 1971:180). White adds that the same Greener was of the opinion that the post-1813 gun made for the African market was "as sound and secure as the musket used by English soldier". This, however, did not last long, and by 1845 the barrels had again become "horribly dangerous" (White 1971: 180). Thus the tafanga gun may have been the only one strong enough to survive until now, creating the illusion that it was the earliest and nearly the only one traded to the Grassfields.

Guns and Warfare

How effective was the Birmingham gun as a weapon in the hands of a Grassfielder? Did it have any impact on local patterns of warfare? It goes without saying that, to be an effective weapon, a gun must be in working order. But this was far from always being the case, and again the reader will have to follow me into some technical details to see why. A gun is fired by releasing a firing mechanism. When the trigger is pulled, it releases the cock that holds the flint. A strong spring pushes the cock forward. The flint hits a steel plate – the 'frizzen' – that is part of the lid of a small pan located to the side of the barrel. The pan contains a small amount of powder called the 'priming powder'. The lid and the frizzen may pivot around a screw, but are kept in place by a spring. When the flint hits the frizzen, it pushes it forward, thus opening the pan and exposing the priming powder to a shower of sparks falling from the flint. The priming powder is ignited, and the fire is communicated to the main charge through a small hole – the touch-hole – bored into the barrel wall and opening in the pan. Throughout this process, a number of things may go wrong so that the gun misfires. Judging from what I witnessed in countless festivals and death celebrations, this happens at least two or three times out of four with flintlock guns still in use in the Grassfields. There is no reason to think it was much different in olden days, and informants agree that this was indeed the case. Due to lack of proper maintenance, the lock may not move very freely, and the cock does not hit the frizzen with sufficient strength to produce the shower of sparks needed to ignite the powder. In Europe, flints were manufactured especially for flintlocks. They exhibited a straight edge on the side of the frizzen. The flint was set in the cock so as to hit the frizzen squarely along all its width. Besides, it was discarded after twenty shots, fifty at most, and a new one put in its place. In the Grassfields, only locally made flints were used. They did not have a straight edge, and consequently were not as effective as European-made ones. They may not have been discarded and replaced as often as they should have been.

There does not seem to have been any trade in gun flints from the coast to the Grassfields, in exception to the general practice in Africa, where flints were not locally made (White 1971:175). In the Grassfields, to the best of my knowledge, flint-making is recorded only for the chiefdom of Big Babanki where it was (and still is) undertaken both for guns and domestic fire-making.

Care had to be taken that the flint hit the frizzen neither too high above the powder - in which case the sparks, when reaching the powder, would be cold – nor too low – in which case few sparks would be produced. During the rainy season, the powder could easily get damp or even soaked, despite the leather hood that most men put on the lock of their gun to cover it, and that could be pushed forward along the barrel when they needed to fire. In Europe, two misfiring out of thirteen rounds were considered a normal occurrence (Wilkinson-Latham 1977:75), with very good quality guns that were properly maintained and loaded. Among the Bamoum (Tardits 1980:804), one of the Grassfields peoples, misfiring seems to have been such a problem that the gunmen preferred to light the priming powder with a burning ember rather than with the firing mechanism.

Granting that the gun did not misfire, many things could happen to reduce its efficiency or even provoke an accident. Gunpowder was a mixture of saltpeter, sulphur and charcoal in various proportions. The quality of the powder could differ greatly from one consignment to the next. Moreover, in a single consignment, the different components of the powder could separate because of their different specific gravities. During transport, the saltpeter would congregate at the bottom of the container, underneath the lighter charcoal. The powder from the top of the container would hardly be effective at all, whereas that at the bottom, too rich in saltpeter, would burn too fast and cause the barrel to burst. As firearm technology improved in Europe, the proportion of saltpeter increased regularly. French powder increased from 62% saltpeter in 1800 to as much as 77% in 1850 (Kea 1971:204). Needless to say, guns that had been sold several decades before in Africa could not stand that kind of powder and burst in the hands of their users. Many an African must have paid for 'better' gunpowder with a limb or even their life. Stanley reports that the imprecation made in a blood pact with a chief called Mirambo went like this: "If either of you breaks the brotherhood now established between you, may the lion devour him, the serpent poison him, his gun burst in his hands and wound him, etc." (quoted by Brain 1977:78). Fisher and Rowland (1971:228) give an impressive report on dangerous firearms in Africa and quote Clapperton who, in 1826, "met some Dahomeyans returning from a campaign against the Fulani, with all their guns burst save two".

The projectiles too raised specific problems: in Africa, blacksmiths turned out round iron bullets that fitted the bore of the gun. These were the best bullets but were expensive as they incorporated much labor. Most of the time, the peoples of the Grassfields used small lumps of iron, stones, pieces of slag collected on iron-smelting sites, and, after their introduction in the area, bits of brass rods. These projectiles, being of irregular shape, did not follow a straight course, and may not have had much strength upon impact. Shots must have been highly inaccurate. Few gunmen took aim. Many informants claim that it was far too dangerous as the gunman could receive the burning priming powder on his right forearm or in his eyes. Most of them fired their gun holding it to their right side, at arm's length, at the level of the hip or chest, thus reducing even more the accuracy of the shot. Yet some men, whose guns were perhaps in better condition than others, did not hesitate to rest the butt on their shoulder and take aim.

The powder was corrosive, and the barrels tended to thin down, and the touch-hole to widen to such an extent that a significant part of the main charge was expended through the touch-hole instead of the barrel. Flintlocks had another shortcoming: the time that elapsed between the release of the trigger and the explosion of the main charge can be as long as one second. This is known as the 'hang fire'. This makes it almost impossible to shoot on a fast moving target by 'throwing' the shot, as is done with a modern shot-gun.

All these practicalities explain why the musket is best used in volley rather than individual fire, by a group of gunmen. In other words, the flintlock is useless as a weapon without implementing the appropriate tactics – a necessity stressed by all authors who wrote on old firearms (White 1971:173; Fisher and Rowland 1971:229-30; Wilkinson-Latham 1977:75). Did the Grassfielders have such tactics? The standard armament consisted of a handful of throwing spears, a shield and a cutlass carried to the side in a sheath. Bows and arrows were not in use in most of the Grassfields. The warriors fought in groups, moving backward and forward in quick leaps, waving one spear in their right hand above their head, ready to strike when they found the opportunity. When they had thrown all available spears, they tried to engage in short-range fighting with their cutlasses. The primary use of the cutlass, however, was to sever the head of a dead enemy and bring it back for display and to win the rewards bestowed on a good fighter. All informants stress that this armament and the corresponding tactics remained in use until the European conquest. They admit that the gun was an unreliable weapon, but they stress that it was by no means useless: first its range was much greater than that of the spear, and, in the absence of bows and arrows, it was the only effective means to keep spearmen at bay. It also gave a psychological advantage because of the noise it made and because of its range. The gun was put to best use as a defensive weapon, when warriors could congregate behind a natural or man-made defense and wait for the assailant. Even if many guns misfired, enough of them succeeded, to ward off the enemy with successive volleys. As an offensive weapon, the gun seems to have been more difficult to use. Accounts from other regions in Africa show that gunmen had to approach the enemy, shoot, and run back out of bow or spear shot, to reload (Fisher & Rowland 1971:220, & Kea 1971:207-13). Kea shows that, on occasions, having shot, gunmen found themselves with neither offensive nor defensive power and were cut to pieces by their enemy. Grassfields people seem to have solved the problem by combining spearmen and gunmen in attack: a small group of gunmen (five to ten) would crawl towards the enemy, followed by a group of spearmen. The gunmen would shoot and the spearmen would then rush forward to protect the gunmen and take advantage of the shock created by the noise, and perhaps the injuries, to attack in earnest[5]. The spear remained the main weapon. Thus, the offensive use of guns cannot be ruled out for the Grassfields. It is well documented in particular instances such as when Balikumbat, Bagam, and people of the Bafoussam area were called for by the Bamoum king to help him reduce some dissidents (Tardits 1980: 208). The Bamoum themselves used guns as offensive weapons in combination with spears (Tardits 1980: 810). However, most accounts that we have emphasize rather its defensive value.

The Bamoum kingdom, for example, expanded throughout the 19th century, but failed to progress when it met with the resistance of Bamileke chiefdoms using guns as defensive weapons (Tardits 1980: 139, 191, 215, 217). In January 1891, the German explorer Zintgraff attacked the chiefdom of Mankon with the help of a couple of thousand local warriors, and was repulsed though some of his men were equipped with modern breechloader rifles. In 1901, the German officer Pavel led a punitive expedition against the Bangwa (near Fontem) and came across several defensive walls guarded by warriors armed with muskets. It appears from Pavel's account that these avoided attacking, always preferring defensive tactics involving sizeable groups of gunmen (Pavel 1902). By that time the Germans had equipped the 'Schutztruppe' with machine-guns and breechloader rifles in front of which any resistance was vain.

Until the European conquest the spear remained the standard offensive weapon, for it was more versatile than the gun, and could be used in individual skirmishes as well as group fighting, besides being comparatively cheap and fully reliable. This appears in the war dances still performed by Grassfielders during public celebrations. The choreography of most of these is characteristic of a fight with spears, even when they are performed with guns. The movements of a gunman on the attack are usually forwards and sideways, ducking from one shelter to the next, holding his gun with both hands, pointed toward the enemy. By contrast, a spear-holder stands erect behind his shield, in full view of the enemy, leaping backward and forward at the limit of his opponent's striking range, holding his spear above his head ready to throw it. Both types of dances are performed by Grassfield's men. But the spear-dance is by far the most frequently performed, and, whereas it is often danced while holding guns, a gun-dance is never performed while holding spears.

Altogether, the introduction of the flintlock gun may not have had a very significant impact on patterns of warfare in the 19th century. This conclusion is fully consonant with those of the African History seminars on firearms held at the University of London from 1967 to 1970 (White 1971: 173), except that the differential impact of the defensive and offensive use of the gun did not appear in the conclusions of the seminars. In my opinion, the gun gave a slight but definite advantage to the defenders over the assailants in the Grassfields. It may have helped small chiefdoms to withstand the pressure of the larger polities that expanded in the 19th century, provided they had access to the long distance trade to Calabar and Douala.[6]

True, gun owners face serious maintenance problems. However being hand-made, these guns could easily be hand-repaired. The guns that can be seen nowadays in the Grassfields bear witness to the ingenuity of precolonial blacksmiths. The parts could be removed with the simplest of tools. The lock was a sturdy affair that could be repaired easily, and transferred from one gun to the next. Stocks decayed, but were always replaced with locally made ones, turned out from hard redwood resistant to termites and rot. Provided it was of fair enough quality, the trade gun was certainly very well adapted to the African hinterland and could be kept in working condition far away from the sources of spare parts and supplies.

How many men had guns? This, of course, varied from chiefdom to chiefdom. Those located closer to the main trade routes had more guns. Those of the northern and northeastern Grassfields had few. Zintgraff's accounts and photographs (1895) show that the chiefdom of Bali-Nyonga, at the end of the major route leading from the coast to the western Grassfields, had many guns. Perhaps up to half of the warriors were equipped with serviceable flintlocks. In the neighboring confederation of Mankon, according to oral tradition, one out of three or four men had a gun. The total male population was about 1500 in 1890, with perhaps 350 to 500 guns. In 1978, a total of 1561 dane guns were registered at the Sub-divisional Office for the Mankon Area Council. But a survey of some one hundred guns in the compound of their owners showed that more than half of the guns, owned by Mankon people were not registered, so that a number of 3000 guns for the

Mankon Area Council is a minimum (this total includes all the guns, even those that were out of order). The sample of guns consisted of 27% tafanga, 6% afurukwang and 67% of more recently made flintlock and percussion guns. Thus the 3000 guns may include some 800 tafanga and 180 afurukwang for an Area Council including five chiefdom (Mankon, Chomba, Nsongwa, Mbatu and Ndja) – Mankon being by far the largest. The figures obtained from oral tradition and from the count in contemporary Mankon coincide fairly well: granting that Mankon people did not get rid of their old imported barrels over the last fifty years, they must have had around 500 guns in 1890, for a total population of ca. 5000 within the confederacy of Mankon. However, these figures should not be taken as the last word on the matter: many guns may have been lost or put out of order during the colonial wars. Mankon men also tend to sell their tafanga guns because they consume too much gunpowder (about twice as much as any other gun), and to acquire recently made percussion guns instead. Some areas of the Grassfields were combed by dealers who collected flintlocks for the tourist market. All in all, however, the figures given above are certainly on the conservative side.

According to many informants, guns were seldom used in hunting. Instead, traps, nets and spears were used. The only exception may have been that of the leopard - the noblest and most valued game. Many oral accounts report leopard-hunting with guns. However, the actual tactics used in such hunts is not clear. It might be that the leopard, once sighted, was lured into attacking a group of gunmen. But even this way of hunting would have been highly dangerous because of the risk of misfiring, though the discharge of an 11 or 12 gauge smoothbore at close range must have been quite effective in stopping a leopard in full charge. It may be that hunters were willing to run high risks to win the rewards associated with the killing of a leopard. Often, it was the gift of a wife by the chief – an invaluable reward in a society where titled men monopolized the women and forced many junior men to remain bachelors for life.[7]

I was never told that guns were used for the protection of crops as suggested by White (1971: 178-79). It seems unlikely to me that the introduction of maize was linked, in the Grassfields, to the introduction of guns that made it possible to protect the crop from monkeys and other pests. For one thing, gunpowder was very expensive in the Grassfields, because of the great distance from coastal markets. The gain made by protecting the crops with guns would have been offset by the cost of gunpowder.

Guns and 'Prestige'

The popularity of guns in the nineteenth and 20th-century Grassfields may not be entirely explained by the comparative advantage they gave in warfare. Nowadays, as in the 19th century, they are displayed at death celebrations and annual dry season festivals. On such occasions, men parade with their guns, individually or more often in groups of kinsmen or friends. The parade is usually directed towards the bereaved family, to express respect and sympathy, as well as to honor the dead, or, during the annual festival, to honor the chief. Sometimes, an individual or group who want to honor a person or another group parade in front of them. The parade is a public display, and while leaping backwards and forwards, brandishing his gun, threatening and mock-fighting, the gunman tries to attract the attention of the crowd by his antics. The more grotesque the parade, the more fascinating it is. Well performed, the sight attracts the attention in an irresistible manner. At the end of the parade, the men come close to the persons they want to salute, brandish their guns, run to the periphery of the dancing field, and discharge a volley. The report is tremendous – much louder than that of a rifle or a modern shotgun. It livens up the proceedings. It adds to the atmosphere. Everyone obviously takes immense pleasure in these crakers, under the watch of a couple of weary government gendarmes waiting for the accident or the fight that occurs from time to time.

The noise has important connotations. Dillon (1973: 161) reports that in Meta', one of the peoples of Bamenda area, gun firing in anger is a kind of ritual statement that brings a sustained wrong to the attention of God and the village.

The gun, on such occasion, is something to be displayed. It is a symbol of wealth and manhood. At Mankon, a man without a gun is laughed at and called a woman. Before the European conquest, being given a gun by one's father or the chief was almost a rite of passage. A man was established when he had been given land, a wife and a gun.

In the 19th century, celebrations accompanied with gun-shooting were occasions of musketry practice. Other occasions were the periodical meetings of war clubs. During the meetings, there was no systematic training, but drinking, singing, dancing and gun-shooting. At least these meetings and other celebrations must have helped keep the guns in working order.

Before the European conquest, guns were traded from the coastal area together with gunpowder, cloth, salt, beads and brass rods, in exchange mostly for slaves. All these goods were exchangeable against each other and were convertible into brass rods. The conversion between slaves and imported goods could be made anywhere between the Grassfields and the coast. Around 1900 a gun was worth 30 to 60 brass rods in the Bamenda area, depending on its quality and condition. This is to be compared with the 150 to 200 brass rods or their equivalent in imported goods (including guns) that had to be paid for a slave at the same time in the same area. The goods of the long distance trade formed a network of exchange that was quite distinct from the regional trade in subsistence goods. It was controlled by wealthy and titled men, who by the same token controlled the distribution of such items as guns – the ownership and display of which brought 'prestige' – but, more importantly, which could be converted into household expansion through the purchase of slaves and payment of bride wealth. Nothing would be further from the truth than to see the acquisition and display of guns as a kind of conspicuous consumption similar to that which according to Fisher (1972/73), obtained with the horse in the central Sudan. One would rather apply to the guns of the Grassfields what Law (1975:2) wrote of the horse in reply to Fisher: "the importance of horses in 'conspicuous consumption' is only comprehensible as a secondary phenomenon deriving ultimately from their role in warfare".

Endnotes

1. First published in *Paideuma*, 26, 1980, pp.79-92. I wish to express my gratitude to Mr. H.L. Blackmore, curator of the small firearms collection at the Tower of London, who answered my queries and kindly guided my first steps in a domain quite unknown to me, and to Brian Cooksey for editing this article. My thanks also go to Pierre de Maret to whom Photographs 3, 4 and 5 are due. The other photographs were taken by the author.

2. After 1750 the Danish musket (Dane gun or long Dane) became the principal firearm export to West Africa, writes Kea (1971:199). Subsequently, the English took over most of the trade, but the term 'dane gun' is still in use for any trade gun in many parts of West Africa.

3. Efforts made to ban the trade, manufacture or repair of guns in that part of the world have always met with immense difficulties since it started (Rudin 1938:310-15). The import of firearms was banned in Calabar in 1885 (Latham 1973:132); the sale of firearms was banned all over Cameroon in 1909 (Rudin 1938:315); the import and sale of gunpowder is illegal in Cameroon nowadays. All this has been to little avail. Though the control on modern weapons is well established in Cameroon, the trade in 'dane' guns and gunpowder is much more difficult to eradicate, and in practice is tolerated.

4. Guns are manufactured by gunmakers and submitted to a proof house that assesses the quality of the gun before it can be put on the market. The proof house conducts two kinds of tests: one by visually examining the gun, the other one by firing one shot. Once these tests have been made, a 'view' and a 'proof' mark are engraved on the barrel of the gun.

5. Noise is an important psychological element in attack, stressed by all informants. Even in modern warfare it retains all its importance: Stuka bombers, during World War II, were equipped with a siren that was turned on during attack. Offensive hand grenades are usually devised to make great noise upon explosion.

6. It has often been said that guns were purchased by coastal slave traders to arm slave raiders asking for more offensive weapons to catch more slaves. If, as I think, the flintlock was effective mostly as a defensive weapon, the cycle of exchange between guns and slaves must have been more complicated

that it seems at face value: the insecurity caused by slave-raiding may have created a need for better protection, and hence a demand for guns. The fact that guns were exchanged for slaves put the onus of procuring slaves on the people who wanted protection against slave-raiding, induced them to catch slaves in order to obtain guns, and turned everyone into slave suppliers.

7. Percussion guns were introduced between the two World Wars and hunters started making use of these. The percussion gun is much more reliable than the flintlock and its hang fire is greatly reduced. Many owners of flintlocks have had them turned into percussion guns by the local blacksmith – a very simple and cheap transformation that makes a gun a better hunting weapon. Besides, all the guns traded or made since the beginning of the century are small bore, which are more adapted to hunting than the big tafanga.

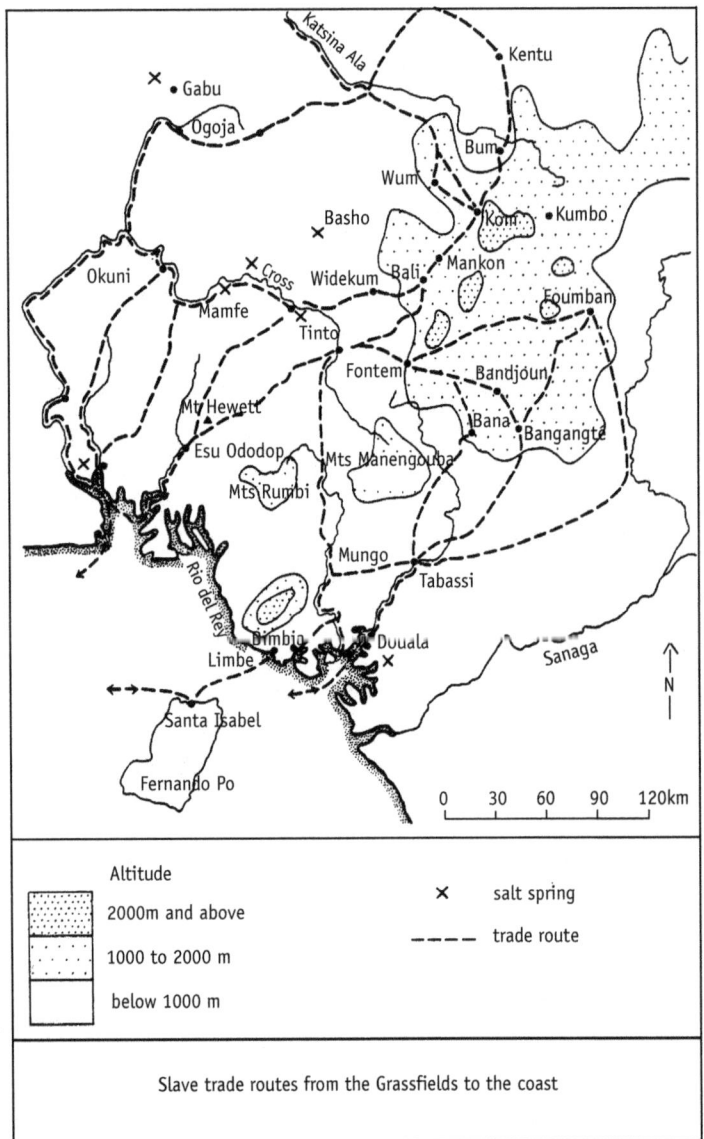

Slave trade routes from the Grassfields to the coast

Slave trading without slave raiding[1]

Until the slow demise of the inland slave trade in the course of the 19th century, the densely peopled high plateaux of West Cameroon – otherwise the Grassfields – were an important source of slaves. They fed the trade of the Bay of Biafra for three centuries. However, in contrast to what is observable elsewhere, the off-take of slaves was not effected, as a rule, by armed raids. It did not empty the regions supplying slaves, as was the case in the borderlands of the slaving states, such as Dahomey or the emirates that arose in the wake of the jihad of Othman Dan Fodio. The Grassfields case allows us to explore the controversial relations between the slave trade, slavery, long-distance trade, kinship and population. This paper aims at establishing that the slave trade of the Grassfields was long-lasting and on a large scale, that it was at the heart of social reproduction and that, notwithstanding it, the Grassfields have remained thickly populated up to the present day.

An old and substantial trade

The accounts of Koelle (1854/1963), Goldie (1964), Johnston[2] and the works of the historians of the Atlantic slave trade (Curtin & Vansina 1964, Curtin 1969: 188, 255, 295, Lovejoy 1983, Richardson 1989) of Calabar (Northrup 1978, Nair 1972) and of the Cameroon coast (Ardener 1968, Bouchaud 1952) inform us about the origins of slaves bought in the coastal ports of Duala, Bimbia, Rio del Rey and Calabar in the 19th century: a substantial proportion of these slaves came from the Grassfields (see map on page 68).

The sources show, likewise, that Grassfields slaves were numerous in the coastal areas and well-liked. Among other witnesses here is the Reverend W. Anderson, a missionary in Calabar in the middle of the 19th century in a letter addressed to T.J. Hutchinson, the British Consul for the Bay of Biafra:

"I have long wished to ascertain the position and distance from Old Kalabar of a country called here Mbrikum [the Grassfields]... Many of them are brought here as slaves. They are more liked in Old Kalabar than many brought from other countries. They are peaceable, honest, and energetic." (Hutchinson 1967: 322)

The strong demand for slaves in Calabar can be understood by reference to this port's history. From the middle of the 18th century onwards it was visited by an increasing number of European ships: the switch to so-called 'legitimate' trade at the beginning of the 19th century brought it more profit than it did to Duala, principally in the palm-oil trade. In 1855 Hutchinson (1970: 252) reported that Calabar exported twice as much palm-oil as Duala (4,090 tons as against 2,110). Subsequently, according to Latham (1973: 151) the traffic at Calabar rose to 7,365 tons in 1883 while it was stagnant at Duala. The development of palm-oil exports to Europe had two obvious consequences in Calabar, and to a lesser extent in Duala: the demand for slaves, despite the decline of the transatlantic trade, was maintained on the coast throughout the 19th century – it might even have increased; the hinter-land was implicated in the palm-oil trade and the distant interior was ever more drawn into it. The bulk of the trade profits made by the notables and kings of the coastal ports were not invested in fixed productive capital but in conspicuous consumption and in slaves. The latter were used to handle goods in the palm-oil trade on the inland waterways and as paddlers in the hundreds of dugout canoes owned by traders – these were used both as war-canoes and as a means of transport. Our sources strongly stress the political importance of these slaves that enabled each notable to swell his household "to make him strong", as 'King' William of Bimbia told Allen and Thompson (1848, II:231). Northrup (1978) has shown that this function had consequences unintended by the 'kings' who sometimes found themselves encroached upon by their clientages whose power had come to exceed theirs.[3]

This was the situation in the course of the 19th century, but one might well ask whether it was not much the same during the two preceding centuries. The following data establish a virtual certainty in this respect. First of all, we have the history of the trade in the four ports we have already mentioned. The accounts of Pacheco Pereira (1956) indicate that, from 1500, Portuguese vessels calling at Fernando Po occasionally picked up slaves on the mainland. Until 1600 European techniques of naval construction and navigation did not allow of anchorage at the Cameroon coast. But from 1600 onward this became possible and, on the basis of the works of Samuel Brun (1913), Gaspar da Rosa[4], Leo Africanus (1665), and Dapper (1668), Ardener (1968) concludes that contacts between European and African traders at Duala were already regular in 1614 and solidly established in 1650. With the first contacts slaves destined for the New World plantations figured in transactions, albeit in small numbers. Towards the end of the 17th century the slave trade expanded in Duala, some sixty to eighty year ahead of Calabar. The late date – the mid-18th century – assigned by Austen (1977:316-317) to the intensification of the Duala slave-trade seems to me to be wrong. Austen has revised it in view of the fact that it does not agree with the chronology of the trade established by Curtin (1969:150) and Ardener (1968), and proceeds from questionable interpretation of accounts collected from victims of Chamba raids by Koelle (1963/1854:11-13) which I have discussed elsewhere (Warnier 1985:128, 151-152). Finally, it must also be revised in the light of David Richardson's research (1989:13-19), one of whose most original contributions concerning the chronology and volume of the trade is to demonstrate, on the basis of unpublished primary sources, that the dates proposed by Curtin and Lovejoy for the development of the slave trade in the Bight of Biafra are too late and their estimates of the number of slaves exported too low, especially in its early stages. He writes: "Exports of slaves from the Bight of Biafra were, according to my figures, over seven times greater in 1710-1729 than Lovejoy assumed" (ibid.:19). There are other data that underpin the supposition that the trade between the Grassfields and the coast was substantial and that its beginnings go back several centuries. First there is the antiquity, continuity and density of the high plateau population which, as I have been able to demonstrate in an earlier paper (Warnier 1984, see chapter 2 in the present volume), can be deduced from the findings of archaeology, linguistics and anthropology as well as from the study of agro systems and landscapes. Archaeological research dates the advent of a Neolithic culture to the start of the fourth millennium BC, and the beginnings of the Iron Age to about five centuries before our era. Grassfields agriculture was based on the yam-oil palm association in which Thurstan Shaw (1976:13) detects one of the possible causes of the dense and ancient settlement of Igbo country. His argument applies just as cogently to the Grassfields. The diversity of Grassfields languages, which are genetically related to one another within the Benue-Congo family, likewise indicates a continuous, stable and anciently settled population.

Population densities of the order of 10 to 80 per km^2 according to region are attested in the 19th century by all sources, in particular in the evidence published by the first Germans to establish contact, such as Zintgraff (1895) and Hutter (1902), as well as by Moisel's map (Moisel 1913). The demographic history of Africa is still too halting to offer any clear account of the preceding centuries. But the humanization of the landscape, the long-standing evidence in both environment and society of regional economic specialization and commercial exchanges – all requiring a considerable population density – indicate a substantial and ancient population.

Between the Grassfields and the coast there intervene forest zones that are sparsely populated except in a few patches, such as the Mamfe and Cross River basins; these were not, in any event, capable of supplying the large contingents of slaves referred to in historical sources.

Grassfields societies, then, were in exchange relations with those of the coast for several centuries, perhaps even for one to two millennia. I have shown elsewhere (1985:173-177) that the mild steel items possessed by the coastal peoples were likely enough to have originated in the Grassfields, at least from the 16th century onwards. The biographies of Koelle's informants (Koelle 1963/1884:11-13) show that the slave trade between the Grassfields and the coast was well-established before their capture, that is, before the start of the 19th century.

To sum up, one can assume that the slave trade between the Grassfields and the coast certainly started before 1650, that it was intensified first with Duala and then with Calabar, to the same rhythm as for the Bay of Biafra, and that it was not extinguished until the beginning of the 20th century.

It remains to estimate the volume of the trade. The sources of information for the Atlantic trade seldom refer to the first origin of slaves. The attempts made in this direction by Curtin and Vansina (1964), Curtin (1969: 188, 255, 295), and Richardson (1989) need to be completed by inquiries in the field, problematic as these are. Consequently I have made some estimates for the 19th century in a limited area – that of the Bamenda plateau – based on the number of trade guns and the mass of brass currency imported against slave sales. These two consumer durables are, in fact, quantifiable by local inquiry and archival research. In 1985 I estimated that the average annual off-take of persons from the population to supply the slave trade was about 1.7 per thousand of the Bamenda plateau population. This figure, however, takes no account of slave sales against non-durable consumption goods – necessarily impossible to quantify a hundred or a hundred and fifty years after the event, namely cloth, gunpowder, salt, beads, chinaware, etc. Nor does it take into account the export of slaves to the middle Benue and Adamawa nor of the inroads of the 19th-century raids by the Chamba and Fulani.

So this figure, which I put forward in 1985, now seems to me a considerable underestimate. I am now inclined to think that some 0.5 percent of the population left the Grassfields annually in slave caravans. So, for a total Grassfields population of 300,000, this would imply an annual loss of 15,000 individuals. This would seem to be a large loss in terms of a Malthusian demographic situation, but it was incontrovertibly one that did not arrest population growth in the longer term – we shall see why. This estimate is compatible with oral sources from the Bamenda plateau, the Bamileke region and the Western Bangwa at the exit point of the main slave routes, as evidenced by Brain's study (1972).

To understand the import of these estimates, the reader must realize that the chiefdoms and kingdoms of the Grassfields did not draw these slaves from peoples external to the high plateaux, but from their own stock.

Slavery in Grassfields societies

At the end of the 19th century the Grassfields societies were organized into chiefdoms more or less independent of one another. The smallest had a few hundred citizens, the largest – the Bamum kingdom studied by Tardits (1980) – about 60,000, a large proportion of whom were of servile condition. Each chiefdom federated unrelated descent groups.

The region was criss-crossed by exchanges of subsistence goods and goods of high value of varied and distant origin. Superimposed upon these mercantile transactions were gift-exchanges between rulers and notables, networks of matrimonial alliances and all sorts of other social interactions. Some chiefdoms, those I shall label 'central', took an active part in exchanges, and possessed a hierarchy of notables able to impose its authority on the population, put it to work and intensify production and exchange for its own benefit. Other local communities, to which the term chiefdom cannot be accurately applied, and which one can term 'peripheral', only participated in exchanges at the tail-end of trade circuits which were mediated by the central chiefdoms. They had no hierarchy of notables – or barely so – and were not remarkable for any special keenness for productive labour.

These societies recognized a servile status denominated by *buk* in the Mbam-Nkam and Momo language groups (the latter south and west of the high plateaux) a root which the Grassfields Bantu Working Group relates to the proto-Bantu root *pika* reconstituted by Guthrie (1967-1971)[5]. Another root *kot*, reconstituted by L. Hyman (1979), was used in the central and northern region of the Ring group of Grassfields languages. The semantic field covered by these nominal roots that, in a first approximation, one could translate by 'slave', is great.

The inhabitants of the central chiefdoms considered those of the peripheral palm-oil producing regions as 'slaves'. But there was no relation of dominance of one over the other. At most there was an invisible transfer of surplus value to the central chiefdoms within the framework of regional exchanges; this contributed to the prosperity of the centre and to the increase of its rank in the regional hierarchy. To the extent one can recover the evidence after some hundred years of colonial suppression, domestic slaves were rare. Production in the

Bamenda Grassfields did not rest on the exploitation of servile labour, but on the putting to work of juniors and women – we shall return to this later. However, one still comes across aged slaves or their descendants whose genealogy makes it clear that they have been fitted out with borrowed kin, while retaining the stigmata of their origins.

The third and last category of slave consisted of individuals who were sold outside the Grassfields in the context of long-distance trade and who were designated as such. Only the slaves in the last two categories were bought and sold.

The field covered by the nominal roots *buk and *kot is thus huge. In outlining servile institutions my design was not to engage in a search for semantic precision, which is full of pitfalls as the debates between Meillassoux, Lovejoy, Miers, Kopytoff, Inikori and others exemplify. I was concerned, in the first place, to outline the socio-political framework (chiefdoms, regional hierarchies, local hierarchies, varied servile institutions, exchange networks) within which the process of the withdrawal of slaves occurred. And secondly to suggest that domestic slavery was almost nonexistent and anyway of a nature which could not have supplied the external slave trade. How was it then supplied?

The provision of captives

I shall discuss, in turn, war, fraudulent sale by agnatic kin and affines, and brigandage in order to demonstrate that armed violence had a minimal role in the acquisition of persons for sale and that the Grassfields were, in this respect, an exception, at least in so far as our present knowledge goes. The latter, in fact, is principally based on the study of the great slave states of West Africa and in particular on the Dahomeyan archetype. R. Law (1986: 237-267) has demonstrated the important part played by Dahomey in European representations of slavery from the first contact period up to the present. My aim will be achieved if I can establish that other models of slave supply do exist, despite the fact that they are rarely recorded.

War first of all. Grassfields societies distinguished between a 'fight' and 'war' (*filam* and *ntso* in Mankon). A fight between kinsfolk, affines or fellow-citizens was undertaken with wooden weapons. The use of iron was forbidden in such cases and reserved to proper war such as might take place between descent groups or communities which were strangers to one another. It is useful to distinguish between three types of wars which I shall call wars of honour, wars of capture and predatory wars. In contrast to the categories of 'fight' and 'war' – distinguished in Grassfields societies by practices, representations and vocabulary – these three sub-categories are not differentiated by the societies themselves: these are terms I have invented.

What, for lack of anything better, I have called 'wars of honour' were undertaken by the societies of the high plateau in the context of competition between local communities – for the symbols of the rank occupied by local communities. To be sure this ranking was not lacking in important economic stakes – ownership of land, the protection of one's subjects, especially traders, the rendering of tribute, and so on. As a rule such conflicts were initiated by a chief (*fon* or *mfe*) whose ambassadors presented two containers to another fon, one filled with ashes, the other with camwood powder. The fon had to choose either the camwood, implying his subordination and the, at least, partial abandonment of his claims against his opposite number, or ashes, which signified that he accepted battle, the date and place of which was agreed between those present. These preliminaries immediately placed the war of honour in a ritualized and symbolic context. Each belligerent considered his war aims had been achieved if he had made a demonstration of force, killed a few of his opponents, set fire to a few dwellings, and proved that he would not give way to intimidation. Few prisoners were made. These were ransomed, exchanged, sometimes extradited, but very seldom sold. The peace which followed the exchange of prisoners was ritualized. In no way could the slave-trade have been a by-product of such wars of honour.

It was not at all the same in wars of capture, the object of which was to acquire slaves. An example of this type is provided by the Kingdom of Bamum described by Tardits (1980: 806-816). The annual campaigns were there considered as 'the work of kings'. Their aim was to take captives from neighbouring chiefdoms in order to furnish the royal domains and those of the nobility with servile manpower. Tardits (ibid: 165-167, 363-364) has shown that these wars of capture did not furnish slaves for the external trade, except on a very minor scale. The Kingdom had such need of servile manpower that it kept almost all its captives. They were put to work within an autarchic domanial economic system that contrasted sharply with the household economy geared to the regional market so characteristic of neighbouring societies. I have suggested elsewhere (Warnier 1985:238-259) that this system resulted from the implosion of a regional system of exchange in which the centre absorbed the periphery and substituted a closed circuit economy for the regional specialization and mercantile exchanges found elsewhere in the Grassfields. Other highland kingdoms practised these wars of capture; it was the case in Bafut, and in Kom and Nso' perhaps in the second half of the 19ᵗʰ century.

From the onset of the 19ᵗʰ century onwards the Grassfields were subjected to a third type of war – predatory war – practiced by Chamba and Fulani bands. Fardon (1988) has provided a detailed analysis of the processes at work in these enterprises. By contrast with wars of capture which were not intended to supply an external or internal market but, rather, a redistributive economy dominated by the ruler, predatory wars were aimed at supplying the long-distance slave-trade within the framework of what Meillassoux (1986) calls 'esclavagisme' – comprising both slaving and chattel slavery.

To summarize: wars of honour did not produce slaves; wars of capture produced them but not for the trade; predatory wars produced them for the trade. Wars of the two first kinds were practiced by the autochthones of the Grassfields. The third type of war was undertaken in the Grassfields by allochthones: these sent their captures to Adamawa or the emirates formed by the jihad. Yet the 'Mbrikum' slaves sold to the coast were certainly highlanders. And they were numerous. If they were not produced by war, how were they?

Sales of blood-kin, sales of affines, and brigandage

Let us start with a partly fictional case. We are in 1875. Awa' is 34. A junior bachelor, he lives with about ten half-brothers in the same condition as himself in the household of his father Furu, a notable of the Mankon chiefdom. Furu has seventeen wives. He has obtained wives for six of his sons. Of these, three, not having acquired a second wife who would enable them to establish a separate domestic unit, either by their own or their mothers' efforts, are still living with Furu. Awa' takes part, under his father's direction, in regional trade activities: the carriage of palm-oil, small livestock, iron-wares, cereals and pulses, and tobacco between trading households and the marketplaces, the representation of his father at rotating credit clubs and mourning celebrations and in debt recovery. He undertakes work for the household: the clearance of farmlands, the herding of small stock, the maintenance of banana groves, tapping raffia palm wine, the construction and repair of buildings.

Awa', like others of his kind, is sure that his father will get him a wife at an appropriate time. Don't fathers have the duty to obtain a first wife for each of their sons? He is no more conscious than others that this can only be a futile expectation, given the large-scale polygyny of notables. He shares the general illusion that women are more numerous than men. He works to the best of his ability, realizing that only his personal merits will win him the reward of matrimony and the exercise of genital sexuality denied him in this repressive society. Up to now the years have passed without any such reward being firmly promised. His fits of ill-temper are taken for proof of his waywardness. One of his younger brothers, whom he loathes, has been preferred before him and given a wife. She has come to live in Furu's household bringing with her a *ndimon* ('elder of the new-born') – the child (girl or boy) who accompanies all brides to help with young children and do household chores – a sort of baby-sitter. In this case it is a twelve-years-old boy – Ade, the bride's half-brother, and affine to Furu and Awa'.

Furu suddenly dies in 1876. The corporate estate he catered for – name, title, symbolic capital, wives, children, land, raffia stands – is inherited in its entirety by one of his married sons, Tche, in accordance with a positional succession which is the rule for all notables. Awa', formerly his half-brother, now becomes his 'son'. His hopes of getting a wife diminish. To be sure, Tche has inherited Furu's rights (from now on he is not only called Furu, he is Furu). He has also inherited his duties as a father. But when will he have the inclination to honour them?

During the eight days of mourning Furu's homestead is never empty. Kinsfolk, affines, visitors, men's and women's societies succeed one another, day and night. Awa' decides to take advantage of the confusion and the crowds of people. He goes to see Zama, chiefdom notable and trader in high value goods and holder of a 'slave rope' (*nki bu'* – a license to trade in slaves, to which we shall return): would he like to acquire Ade? The risks are weighed. Like the woman he came with, Ade comes from a small neighbouring chiefdom. No worries need be expected from that quarter. In the course of a wake, who is in a position to supervise the comings and goings? The bargain is struck.

Back home in Furu's homestead, Awa' keeps a watchful eye on Ade. He waits for a moment when he can speak alone to him. He asks him to come at once to help fetch a goat, a mourning gift, from Zama. Ade obeys. Nobody sees them leave. They arrive in Zama's compound at nightfall. Ade is fed and pampered. He is flattered to be allowed to take part in the affairs of grown-ups. His watchfulness is lulled by the consideration shown to him. Next day, they tell him that Awa' has had to return to the site of the mourning, that he will explain Ade's temporary absence, that no goat is handy but that very evening one of Zama's sons will go with Ade to a neighbouring village to get hold of another. Ade, in his innocence, enjoys all the pleasures highly prized by the high plateau people: travelling about, breaking the daily routine by visits and discussions. Five days later, at the end of more and more unbelievable episodes, he finds himself some 70 kilometres from his starting point. He does not know the way back. The people speak an unknown language. His successive travel companions have vanished. He is now treated with severity. Nothing is spelt out but he gathers that slaves are being talked about and so is he. His voyage to the coast has begun. Several informants have mentioned that herbal drugs were used to allay the suspicion of the sold person.

Awa' is credited by Zama with 80 brass rods, three-fifths of a minimum bride-wealth which only conveys rights in uxorem. What remains to be done is to do some money laundering, according to an expression today in use, to complement the sum and persuade Furu junior to undertake the marriage negotiations. Awa' manages all this in a couple of years with the discreet complicity of his maternal uncle, while Ade's disappearance (which gave rise to a fight between his relatives and their Furu in-laws) has become blurred in people's memories. Some suspicion hangs over Awa', but in fact nobody knows exactly who brought off the coup. Some wags even put it about that it was Ade's own relations who came to look for him. Awa' took a wife at over 36 years of age. On that day he became a man. Aren't all men married? Doesn't it go to prove that women are much more numerous than men?

This case allows one to understand the mechanism of the supply of captives. Some of the important notables of the central chiefdoms of the plateau had permission to trade in slaves. This took material form in a rope (in Mankon *nki bu*; 'rope-slave') made of vegetable fibres entwined with human hair. It was granted to them by certain fons or clan heads that had rights to give them out. The father and mother of the trader concerned had to pronounce a blessing on the rope when it was transferred. His kinsfolk and the notables forbade him to sell members of his own clan; however this did not limit the trade since a chiefdom like Mankon was composed of nine exogamous clans, seven of which possessed the slave rope, so that a man unable to engage a trader of his own clan could always find another notable willing to oblige him. These traders were in touch with one another in a system of relay trade that enabled them to supply the big markets largely in the direction of the coast. It was thanks to complicity between a relative, agnatic or affinal (the 'Judas') and a non-relative (the trader) that a person could be sold.

The business was, for the most part, stocked up by private persons. The semi-fictional case given above illustrates the processes that eventuated in the fraudulent sale by individuals of agnatic or affinal kinsfolk, often in periods of crisis (succession or conflict). Most often children or young adults were the victims. I stress the point that they were in no way marginal to society. They had the following characteristics: they were members of a descent group, of good tradeable value, and likely to be deceived by the seller. I also stress the point that the primary agents of the sale – the Judas to put it briefly – entertained close relations of kinship or affinity with the victim in most cases. It was the familiarity between seller and sold which made the operation feasible. For a sale to take place, moreover, there would have to be no conflict of interest between the seller and the sold, but rather between the seller and another person with rights in the sold person. Such conflicts were rooted in the nature of marriage and kinship. They opposed persons with close ties: cadets were opposed to their father, half-brothers aspiring to marriage were opposed to each other, wives-givers and wives-takers were opposed. We have, on this topic, statements which are both numerous and unequivocal.

A detailed analysis of kinship would enable one to list the various types of situation in which sales occurred. It is not possible to set it out here. By way of illustration, however, here is a schematic presentation of the types of marriage prevalent in the Grassfields in the 19th century and the types of conflict they engendered.

The societies here considered practiced, with differences in form, marriage by deferred exchange. In such cases, a man of lowly status received a woman in marriage without bride-wealth payment but ipso facto lost his rights to dispose of the female issue of the marriage, which returned to the wife-giver (often called *ta ngkap* or 'father of money'). The boys born of such a marriage also owed renders to the wife-giver. Grassfielders credited (and still credit) the ta ngkap or the maternal grandfather (or his successor) with occult powers over the issue of the woman he has given in marriage. Notwithstanding these powers he was not always in a position to ensure that his rights over his daughters' issue were respected; they might be living at a distance and were liable to be numerous and dispersed if he was an important man who controlled a number of women. Such marriages gave rise to litigation. Did the ta ngkap have rights over one daughter or several? When the woman bestowed was prolific had not her husband acquired rights in genetricem by returning two women of the children's generation to replace the one of their parents' generation?

A structural analysis of this type of marriage, centred on the norm, does not allow one to grasp what it concealed in terms of potential violence and abuses as Brain attests (1972: 179-180). The same can be said of sisters-exchange marriage, forbidden by the British colonial administration among the Tiv for the same reasons. Is not marriage by deferred exchange equivalent to sisters-exchange marriage staged over two generations, were it not for the fact that matrilineal rights are disjoined from descent and that it develops in a context of inequality?

Among equals most Grassfields societies practiced marriage by bride-wealth payments that transferred entire rights in uxorem and in genetricem to the bride-taker: this type was unlikely to provoke litigation. But the same societies also practiced a form of marriage intermediate between deferred exchange marriage and marriage by full payment. What is involved is marriage with small or incomplete payments which only transfer rights in uxorem and allow the ethnologist to distinguish between a 'child-price' (not paid by the bride-taker) and a 'bride-price' (which he paid). As in marriage by deferred exchange, this type of marriage offered possibilities of conflict over issue, all the greater since it coincided with unequal power relations between affines, the bride-givers having the upper hand. The type of marriage practiced in each particular case depended on the affines' respective ranks in the social hierarchy and their matrimonial strategies. Thus, at a second level, it depended on the existence of hierarchies and their spatial distribution. Conflicts were stirred up by social inequality and large-scale polygyny. Genealogies collected in the central chiefdoms of the Bamenda plateau demonstrated that the notables of lineages, clans and chiefdoms all had more than ten wives and that a chief or fon had from fifty to a hundred and fifty in the 19th century (at the end of the 20th around forty is not unusual). The fon alone could mobilize 5 to 10 percent of the women of the chiefdom. Younger sons married late or not at all, and often died as bachelors. It is also important to realize that, in contrast to the forest societies described by Laburthe-Tolra (1981: 234-239), the central societies of the Grassfields were notably repressive in matters of sexuality[6]. Girls were supposed to be virgins before marriage. Wives owed fidelity to their husbands and everything suggests that the bans, and the fears that went with them, were (and still are, at least in respect of the conjugal fidelity of women and post-natal abstinence) sufficiently great to ensure the general acceptance of social norms. Adultery with a fon's wife was punished by the ignominious death of the lovers.

These societies denied to a considerable part of the male population – the majority of men up to the ages of 25-30 and a considerable if declining number thereafter – not only access to marriage, but the exercise of genital sexuality. To assert that this repression was deliberately organized to extract labour from junior men and their mothers (in whose interest it was that their sons should marry) would be going too far. On the other hand it is undeniable that the control of marriage circuits and the repression of sexuality had the effect, whether or not consciously sought, of putting women and male juniors to work, given that marriage was a consequence of recognized merit or of the money gained by working.

In cases of conflict over rights to persons, a man might take the matter into his own hands. The simplest method was either to sell the person claimed, or else a substitute, in order to acquire the equivalent capital sum.

One has seen how these disputes could degenerate into fights and wars, but these outbursts of violence remained controlled – there was no bloodshed in fights and very little in wars. The notables were the only beneficiaries of the intensive labour of younger men and wives, of large-scale polygyny, of regional exchanges and the slave trade. It was not in the least in their interest to allow conflicts to reach the point of challenging the system. One can say that – for reasons nobody agrees about – they lost control of the situation in the Bamum kingdom and in Bafut with, in consequence, the development of wars of capture, the hypertrophy of royal power, and the obliteration of a notability independent of the palace.

Cases of implosion, of the Bamum and Bafut type, were exceptions. They were due, it seems, to structural imbalances in regional exchanges. Elsewhere the exploitation of juniors and women and the fraudulent sale of agnates and affines were carried on under the control of, and partly to the benefit of the polygamous notables. These mechanisms were at the heart of social reproduction. The sales, even though considered as instances of individual fraud, were institutionalized by the artifice of the slave-rope and were never repressed, save by fights, which offered a convenient safety-valve for the feelings of the protagonists. In this sense, they turned out to be functional. The ideology of inequality legitimized the domination of notables, large-scale polygyny and the celibacy of juniors. It was not questioned by anybody, not even, it seems, by the bachelors who, despite the evidence available to anyone with a glimmer of demographic understanding, went on believing that the marriage was possible. One remains amazed at the potency of the ideological discourses which maintained that women were much more numerous than men (true up to a point given the difference in the age of marriage by gender, but not in the proportion of 5 or 10 to 1, as the notables aver). One is equally perplexed by the semantic conjuring tricks that allowed people to claim, in complete good faith, that not a single 'man' (*ngwo* – person) was unmarried precisely because a bachelor, whatever his age, was not regarded as a 'man', but as a 'child' (*mu*).

To return to the sale of kin and affines. It could happen in broad daylight. My inquiries on the Bamenda plateau had indicated that Kom, a large matrilineal chiefdom north of the Bamenda plateau, used to sell numbers of children for subsistence goods, so I turned to E. Shanklin who was working there. She informed me that in periods of food shortage a father sold one of his children – a member of his wife's lineage – in exchange for food. The next child to be born was surnamed 'maize grain' since the cereals obtained by the sale of his elder sibling had probably saved his life. These sales for food, not unfrequent in Kom for reasons unknown to us, do not seem to have obtained elsewhere.

On the Bamenda plateau, where patrilineal descent was prevalent, men sold their half brothers to assemble marriage-payments. Those with rights over them, when they happened to hear of the event, protested but nevertheless did not refuse part of the profits. In such circumstances it is not surprising that an institutionalized brigandage flourished; this also was under the control of notables. At the end of the 19th century the fons of the Bamenda plateau maintained retainers half spies, half strong arm men, called *bigwe* (sing. *gwe* = a term of Bali-Nyonga origin it would seem). The notables of the chiefdom's constituent clans, as well as licensed slave-traders, lent a hand to their enterprises in which abductions occasionally degenerated into forceful kidnapping or small-scale fights. But the favourite mode of action of these sbirri was not in commando style but by use of seduction and ruse, both more effective and more highly regarded by themselves.

Tamwa Hamkong (1983: 100) provides evidence for similar practices in Bamileke country. The account given by of one of his informants (Tokpa Senga Metoua) is worth quoting in extenso:

"The slaves sold by the Baham a little before 'the years of the Whites' came from all parts. The troublemakers called *sam'su* in the Baham language were maintained by, and were in collusion with, the chief. These troublemakers met with children or ignorant people, flattered them, and lured them, alone, away from their native village. In a distant village, some two days' walk away, they abandoned the poor child in a corner and told him to wait. The slaver went to find a client or a taker and pointed out the unfortunate creature. When the sale price was agreed, the troublemakers went home. The buyer observed the child, who had thus become a slave, closely, flattered him and gave him food repeatedly. It was only in time of war that force was used. Nevertheless some outlaws stole children by force or fraud. Such cases were rare, because the professional success of a sam'su depended on his discretion. All the slave-traders were in the chiefs' service or that of some very powerful notables. They were credited with magical powers. Bangwa had a corner for slaves in the market.

The slave-traders were distinguished from others by carrying a rope. Even today, to show respect to the wife of a powerful man, one addresses her as *Ngo magwa* (descendant of a rope owner)."

Having appreciated the arts of seduction, the inventiveness and craftiness of Bamileke merchants for myself I have no difficulty in presuming that the taking of slaves, in these regions, derived from a trading rather than a warrior habitus. After all, why fight and risk one's life when one could obtain slaves much more advantageously? This reasoning is indubitably that of trading societies, save in the Barnum case.

Brain (1972), who did his research on the western slopes of the Bamileke plateau, presents a similar picture, mutatis mutandis, to that of Bamenda. Let us consider: "The backbone of the 19th century economy of the Bangwa was the slave trade" (ibid.: 15) or this longer, eloquent quotation:

"Human beings were a traditional item of privately owned property. Most slaves came from the east, although many Bangwa were also sold abroad as a punishment for witchcraft, adultery, or treason. Women slaves were kept in the country: the Bangwa division of labour meant that women had a local value as wives and farmers and large polygynous compounds were part and parcel of the trade. Boys had some value as servants and male slaves worked the royal oil-palm plantations. But on the whole men were sold away from Bangwa: retainers were available among the free population or from the children of slave women. This was the situation in which the Bangwa tangkap system evolved: women were kept in the compounds of traders and chiefs for distribution to loyal subjects, impecunious retainers and sons and successful warriors. Women were used as gifts to chiefs, payment of society fees and death dues. When a female slave was given out in marriage tabs were kept on her children, and even today the patrigroup of the original slave-owner possesses bridewealth and wardship rights on the matrilineal descendants of these slaves. This is what the Bangwa who are fighting the institution mean when they call marriage lords 'slave owners'." (ibid: 98-99).

One will note, here, the absence of any reference to armed raiding, the intertwining of kinship and slavery, and the importance of the trade in women from Bamum, vetted by the Bangwa.

Let us return now to the Grassfields of the northwest. The earthworks which surrounded the chiefdoms of the Bamenda plateau and the Ndop Plain (see map) in particular Mankon, Nkwen, and Bafanji, are characteristic in one respect: they are designed in the main to control exits rather than entrances. These densely inhabited chiefdoms were surrounded by a trench about 3 to 5 meters wide and deep. Large entrances guarded by sentinels permitted passage. When a suspect disappearance – which usually occurred at wakes or on market days – was reported the notables had the call-drum beaten and the sentinels block the passageways to prevent departures. Then the town was gone over with a fine toothcomb. At Bafanji, circular pits hidden by a raffia lattice covered with grass were made to trap escapers. These traps, still visible, were placed inside and not outside the trench. This clearly shows that they were designed to catch people leaving the town, not attackers. The instructed reader can now understand why and how the Grassfields could supply a substantial trade in slaves by means other than armed and bloody raids.

According to oral evidence the internal trade of the Grassfields showed a preferential demand for women. The sex ratio of the external trade is unknown. But the price of slaves was reversed in favour of men at the southwest limit of the Grassfields, in the direction of Calabar, indicating that the demand for men there was not completely satisfied. The sex ratio of slaves exported from the Bight of Biafra, as reconstructed by Northrup (1978) and Geggus (1989), was the closest to the normal for the whole African coast. These data suggest that the Grassfields doubtless exported more men than women, but not all that much more.

We can thus feel surprise that the slave trade, despite an annual off-take of persons that I estimated at 0.5 percent, did not have a more obvious impact on population. At most one notices a lesser density of population in the centre of the Bamenda plateau – a big exporting area – than on its western periphery whose inhabitants, though qualified as 'slaves' by their neighbours, provided negligible contingents to the trade. Finally – one thing explains another – these peoples were organized in weakly hierarchised polities, lacked notables and were barely engaged in the long-distance trade.

Geggus (1989:38), following Fage, Manning and Northrup remarks on the strong correlation between a more even sex-ratio in the exported slave contingents on the one hand and dense populations in their areas of origin on the other, especially in the hinterland of the Gulf of Benin and Biafra Bay. He adds (ibid.): "This might suggest that not only was a high volume of slave exports linked to population pressure, but so, too, was an indigenous willingness to part with females." A bride-giving group was obliged to replace a wife if she proved sterile. Such replacements often led to conflicts. It is possible that barren women were sold more regularly than others. If such a woman was not replaced, her sale was the sole means of acquiring the money for bride-wealth.

In 1884, when Duala was occupied by the Germans, its hinterland, the Grassfields, though unexplored by Europeans, already had the reputation of being a densely-populated labour reservoir. It was in order to establish trade links and recruit labour that Zintgraff undertook his first expedition in the dry season of 1888-9. In the subsequent years the Imperial Government attempted to recruit male labour there on a large scale for the coastal plantations and its public works through local intermediaries, especially Bali, Bana and Bamum. Rudin (1938) and Chilver (1967) have shown that these removals were far beyond the capacities of these societies. They had even more devastating effects on the local economies than the mortality in the plantations and on road works that, though not accurately known, could reach levels of 50 percent or more, as Rudin has shown (1938:327-328).

After the Franco-British conquest of 1916 and the mandates granted to the French and British by the League of Nations, this unbridled recruitment gradually abated, but labour migration offered an escape-route to young unmarried men and became established in the wake of the slave-trade and German recruitment as a fundamental feature of the economy of the high plateaux. Following the urbanization of Cameroon, migration to the towns and the constitution of a Bamileke and Bamenda industrial and plantation proletariat prolonged this schema, which can be followed in the works of Dongmo (1981, I:187-221 and II) and Champaud (1983: 126-210).

Slavery systems, war, population, kinship

In his analysis of slavery systems Meillassoux (1986) has shown that such were characterized by the absence of reproductive replacement among slaves, and by the reproduction of the system itself by means of wars of predation and by trade. Such systems are essentially unstable since they empty their borderlands and have to seek slaves from further and further afield. Having reached their limits they must either disappear or radically transform themselves. On the other hand, the Grassfields case suggests the existence of a longer-term slave system – not that the Grassfields themselves offer examples which fit the above definition, as has been shown[7]. But as permanent slave providers the Igbo and Ibibio societies described by Northrup (1981) and those of the Grassfields enabled the New World slavery system to maintain itself over a long period without using up all its sources of supply. One might deduce that the same situation obtained among the southern Igbo and the Ibibio (including the Efik of Calabar) described by Northrup. But one must underline a major difference: Northup's analyses show that a slavery system of the type Meillassoux describes was not present and that, in the course of the 19th century the conditions of biological reproduction among slaves together with social mobility in southern Igboland would have prevented its maintenance as such. This would only have been possible in the northern part of the country that specialized in the production of yams for export. Without abolition and the European conquest it is theoretically conceivable that, instead of vanishing for lack of slaves, these varied systems would have persisted well into the 20th century provided that oil-palm cultivation had been succeeded by that of rubber trees, cocoa and the banana.

I shall not be arguing the case of the Grassfields against the controversial thesis advanced by Inikori (1982:19-38) for whom the Atlantic slave trade is the prime cause of African under-population and under-development. Who will deny that the external and internal slave trade, with its train of predatory wars and ruin has durably depressed whole regions? What I am trying to show is that the processes of slave supply in the Grassfields allow us to put forward possible reasons for that absence of correlation between the volume of exports and the density of population in the corresponding hinterland, to which the regional statistics of the slave-trade bear witness. The 'Grassfields mode of slave-taking' also allows one to see why the cycle of slaves-guns-predatory wars – so clearly evident in Senegambia, for example – is no more present in the Grassfields than in Akan country, as Metcalf (1987) has pointed out already. In the Grassfields the sale of slaves certainly enabled guns to be purchased. Guns were used in wars of honour, at mortuary ceremonies and chiefdom festivities; since wars of capture and predation were not practised guns were not used for making captives[8]. In terms of the production of slaves they were useless. But, like slaves, they were part of the capital of symbolic goods and high-value merchandise the circulation of which was regulated by the notables. In the Bamum kingdom wars of capture certainly took place with the object of taking slaves, but they were carried out with edged weapons, since the kingdom, not an important exporter of slaves, was short of the means of procuring guns. The slaves-guns cycle was nowhere evident in the Grassfields.

What I am stressing here is that the connexions between war, weaponry, slavery, the slave trade, population, and kinship systems, differ so much from region to region that a macro-sociology of African slavery, despite or perhaps because of the numerous studies published in the last fifteen years, should now be based on regional, micro-sociological studies aiming at a thorough analysis of the different cases presenting themselves.

Slavery and kinship

In his construction of the concept of the slave economy, Meillassoux (1986: 23-40), in the wake of all the analysts of slavery including Lovejoy (1983), and Miers and Kopytoff (eds. 1977), posits the slave as 'anti-kinsman'. This conception figures in the case of a slave based economy which is constantly renewing its stock of slaves by imports rather than by natural reproduction. On this particular point the Grassfields case does not enter into any argument in contradiction to Meillassoux's concept of a slave-based economy. At best it allows of some extension to what Meillassoux writes about the production of slaves, so that the fraudulent sale of agnatic and affinal kinsfolk can be given a better place – if one can so put it – alongside of war ('the belly of iron') and trade ('the belly of money') in the 'process of production' of slaves.

On the other hand, Meillassoux (ibid.: 27-28) thinks that an "exploitation of the work done as a consequence of the celibacy of juniors could only be of limited economic significance as well as putting into question the basis of the physical, structural and ideological reproduction of the domestic community". And further on: "Such a denial [the forced celibacy of juniors] could, if necessary, only be exercised in respect of juniors whose kinship links were weak or non-existent." A rapid and superficial reading of these texts might lead one to think they are contradicted by the Grassfields case. This is not certain, to the extent that Meillassoux is here explicitly concerned with the domestic mode of production (thus excluding the Grassfields case) and imputes to trade, long-distance trade in particular, the causal antecedents of both the slave-based economy and the corruption of kinship relations by money.

We have seen that the Grassfields societies were merchant societies and had indeed been so for several centuries. One can, in their case, reverse Meillassoux's statement, and say that the exploitation of the labour of young bachelors had significant economic consequences without its putting the foundations of the physical, structural and ideological reproduction of the household at risk. But more: the intensification of the work of women and junior males by celibacy and the control of sexuality was here one of the conditions, necessary but not sufficient, of this physical, structural and ideological reproduction of the polygynous household and the social hierarchy. One could equally say that junior males, whether sold or themselves purveyors of slaves, were on the way to marginalization but that they were in no sense non-kin or anti-kin. On the contrary, it was what remained of their agnatic or affinal links which enabled some of them to be reintegrated into society as agents of the trade, at the expense of those they sold and their exclusion from it. Juniors, bachelors or otherwise, potentially sellers or sold, formed a social category. It seems to me that this category was so completely dominated that the individuals composing it had contradictory interests that could be played upon by the dominant group. This system could not be perpetuated without being reproduced. So as regards the relations between slavery and kinship, there are at least three possible variations of them according to whether one is dealing with the domestic unit (or 'domestic mode of production'), with a trading economy not based on slavery (the Grassfields case), or with a slave-based economy as defined by Meillassoux.

Now, can one say that the intermediate case is operatively transitional and gives grounds for detecting the origins of master-and-slave relations in those of kinship? I would agree with Meillassoux (1986:28 sq.) when he says that "the probability that slavery, sui generis and systematic, arose out of the functioning of domestic society left to its own laws (in particular those of kinship) seems to me to be a hypothesis with little foundation".

On the other hand, if there is indeed an antinomy between kinship and slavery in the context of a slave-based economy (what Miers and Kopytoff call 'chattel slavery') one cannot infer from that that there was an incompatibility between kinship and the off-take of slaves. But, it might be objected, in the Grassfields case, should one not assign the origin or cause of slave production to the commercial economy rather than to the kinship system? Put in this way, the question has every likelihood of remaining unanswered because, besides the general problems of the search for causes in the field of history, the detailed documentation that would be necessary is lacking.

It is for this reason that the analyses presented by Kopytoff and Miers (1977: 3-81) seem to me to be of great interest, notwithstanding the criticisms advanced by Meillassoux (1986: 12-15) because they revolve around a whole set of institutions which include both slavery and kinship.

No doubt an explanation is called for. Meillassoux's criticisms concern the causal connexions between kinship and slavery. To take him at his word, the two American authors supposedly think that the 'effect' of the transformation of kinship relations into slavery is to be imputed to kinship (ibid.: 13, 28), and that the 'genesis' of slavery is to be sought in African kinship systems (ibid: 235). After a careful reading of the text I cannot detect anything of the kind in Miers and Kopytoff (1977: 66-69) who categorically refuse to pose the question of origins, which they judge to be 'unanswerable and meaningless', or that of causality. The vocabulary they use to qualify the relations between kinship and slavery avoid every connotation of causal links in either direction. Here are examples to judge by: "transformation, merging, overlap, intertwined, integrated, intermingling, continuum, involved, reflected, redefinition, coordination, ambiguity, manipulation, response". There is nothing else there, it seems to me, than what Meillassoux recognizes in this passage: "What is true in Miers' and Kopytoff's theory is that kinship relations are constantly manipulated." Indeed, I would have expected, rather, that these authors would have been reproached for their timidity on the issue of causes and that they might even have been accused of empiricism.

Let us close this exegetical excursus. What can we retain of the approach adopted by Miers and Kopytoff? The 'givens' are the existence of slave-based economies in the New World and in the emirates issued from the jihad; the demand for slaves on the African coast; the commercial links between the Grassfields and the systems in question; the inegalitarian politico-social organization of Grassfields chiefdoms; given all these, the relations of marriage and descent, the configurations of the notability and descent groups and the privileges represented materially by the slave-rope and regulated by clans offered to some agents access to persons and to information which enabled them to engage in selling them without recourse to armed action. Kinship was manipulated by these agents within a setting of individual and collective strategies with varied ends in view. Among them were the settlement of conflicts, the acquisition of wives, titles and privileges, obtaining means of subsistence, increasing symbolic capital, entering into the nobiliar game of gift-exchange, the advancement of one's own lineage.

One would only have been surprised to observe slavery flourishing in the terrain of kinship relations if one had been unaware of the potential for violence these relations conceal. Kinship is no more incompatible with conflicts and domination than it is with the exercise of power. One could conceive with Godelier (1989) that the latter proceeds from it. Kinship constitutes a field of action in which abuses are potentially numerous and express themselves either openly or, in African agricultural societies including the so-called subsistence-based ones – in the discourse of witchcraft. In so writing, I am not prejudging the causal link between kinship organization and the slave-trade nor the whole question of origins: the possible pre-conditions for the configuration described in this paper are so numerous that they obscure causality – a social hierarchy, the intensification of labour and trade, the concentration of power, the density of population, etc. However, one is left with the strong impression that one has to do with a complex causality and one which, to some degree, makes up a system. The kinship system is no more a cause of slavery than the humus of the underwoods is the cause of the sprouting of mushrooms and toadstools. But it seems to me undeniable that it offers a favourable field for parasitic invasion: the role of Judas, after all, has to be played by someone on the inside.

I return now to the articulation between the slave-trade, witchcraft and kinship, and if I mention its existence it is because I can turn for support to the transposition into the realms of imagination which the slave trade has undergone among present day Cameroonians, witness the Duala belief in Kong and the Bamileke belief in *famla*. According to these beliefs a man can join a club copied from the model offered by the rotating credit association. The contributions take the form of persons of the kin groups of the members. Each member in turn offers the name of an agnate or affine, who dies, while the member of the association is enriched (just like Judas). The person who has died (was sold) is reckoned to have departed for the south to secret plantations sited by popular imagination in the mountainous massif of Manenguba. His wages are believed to be paid directly into the association member's bank account. The beliefs in famla' and Kong are based on and developed by the disappearances due to the slave trade, the wealth of the slave-traders and their agents during the period of the slave trade, on the mortality in the plantations and the wealth of recruiting agents and chiefs during the colonial period, on the inequalities experienced in illness and death, and the ostentatious fortunes of the big men in the public service and in business in the independent state.

Are the Grassfields an exception?

To conclude, in the Grassfields, and given the exceptions presented by Bamum, the Chamba and Fulani, slaves were not furnished by armed raids. They were mainly supplied by the fraudulent sales of neighbours, members of one's own lineage and affinal relatives, and by the institutionalized practice of brigandage employing cunning and seduction rather than arms, which were rarely used.

This process of obtaining slaves emanated from an inegalitarian social and political organization, the existence of a hierarchy of polygamous notables actively participating in long-distance trade, from the exploitation of juniors and women through the bias of the matrimonial systems and the repression of sexuality, from the development of regional exchanges and the merchant economy. Wars, which were undertaken, had aims other than the taking of captives. Those I have called 'wars of honour' were not very lethal. The Bamum, Chamba and Fulani raids were circumscribed in time and space. Consequently the Grassfields population was able to supply significant numbers of slaves to the coastal societies and to the slave economies of the New World without suffering any glaring loss. For the rest, the slave trade might even have had positive local demographic effects to the extent that it favoured the growth of the reproductive potential of those societies who were economically well-placed. Hence the high densities of population, reported in the course of the last two centuries save, as might be expected, in the regions exposed to predatory raids (the Bamum Kingdom, and the north and north-west of the Grassfields).

During the last thirty years anthropologists and historians of Africa have taken note of the fact that African history is not reducible to the history of African states. Interest has been aroused in societies in which power is decentralized and diffuse. I am by no means persuaded that this movement has come to an end. The great slave states were plural states. During the last three centuries they permitted the survival, internally and interstitially, of dominated societies that composed the bulk of the continent's population. In the tragedy of the slave trade, were such societies merely the pitiable victims of predatory raids? The Grassfields case, which may appear as an exception, suggests that we can take account of the possibility of large-scale participation in the trade by the societies of origin of the slaves themselves. It was always known. But one thought in terms of marginal, penal slaves, captives taken for blood-debts. In the Grassfields we meet a different situation, one that, to the best of my knowledge, is partly unpublished. Is it really an exception? Fage (1978: 267) estimated that a little less than half of the slaves shipped across the Atlantic had been members of the society that enslaved them. The researches of Northrup (1981) and Metcalf (1987) go in the same direction for the trade of the Bay of Biafra and the Akan country respectively.

Consequently it seems to be necessary to distinguish between the mode of acquisition and the mode of exploitation of slaves and to say that there is no necessary correlation between a particular mode of exploitation and a particular mode of production. Thus, if I agree with Meillassoux's description of the slave-based economy, I part company with him when he gives pride of place to war and trade as the process of production most closely related to it. Upriver from trade is there nothing but war? On this point I agree with the only reservation voiced by Miers and Kopytoff (1977: 67) concerning it. In fact, if one could follow the individual trajectory of a person sold in the Grassfields one would observe that it could end in many ways in complete adoption into a descent group in a neighbouring chiefdom or into a coastal house; in the position of a celibate bachelor or spouse of servile condition in the Grassfields, or as a slave within the slave economy of the southern Igbo or of the New World. In the last case the slave would find himself a member of a servile category recruited at the end of very different processes: armed raids, sale by relatives, payment as war indemnity or in compensation for a blood-feud, etc. The slave trade, near or far, ensured the sealing-off of the manner in which slaves were first obtained from the subsequent process of integration or exploitation.

Finally, I would emphasize that in contemporary Cameroon, labour migrations, and the transposition of the enrichment of a minority, of social inequalities and misfortunes into an imaginary slave trade are both present to bear witness to the fact that history is prone to quote itself; in its travesty of the facts popular memory is, in its own way, as faithful to the past as the anamnesis the historian strives for.

Endnotes

1. The idea for this study was given to me by Bongfen Chem-Langhëë who, in 1981, originated and encouraged a collective study of slavery in Cameroon among members of the teaching staff at the University of Yaoundé. The numerous works concerning slavery and the slave trade published since 1981 – in particular that by C. Meillassoux (1986) – led me to undertake a thorough revision of the text I had in hand. I thank C. Meillassoux for having given a very careful reading to the recast version. His criticisms enabled me to qualify and refine some analyses: they diverge from his here and there and I remain wholly responsible for them.

This paper was first published in *Cahiers d'Études Africaines* 113, XXX, 1 (1989) and it has been translated for me from its original French version by Mrs. E.M. Chilver to whom I am very grateful. It was then published in English in *Paideuma*, 41, 1995: 251-272. It is reproduced by kind permission of the editor whose copyright it remains.

2. Johnston, *Report on the British Protectorate of the Oil River*, 1888, Public Record Office, London, F.O. 84/1882: 106-234.

3. The reader can refer to an earlier publication (Warnier 1985: 173-177) in which, for the 19th century, I appraise the various sources that enable us to establish the origins of these slaves and the routes they followed from their regions of origin.

4. "Lembranças de Gaspar da Rosa (1618?)" in Brásio, 1955: 346-350.

5. Unless otherwise stated, words are given in the singular.

6. There are long-established stereotypes about African dancing and sexuality: but who can ever describe the inexpressible boredom of the mixed dances of the Grassfields? In almost 20 years of intermittent residence I have never observed the slightest touch of eroticism. I am not speaking here of the men's masked dances – they are spectacular and entertaining, and not entirely free of erotic associations – but of domestic ones in which men, women and children all take part. How far one is from the dances of the forest, whose sensual exuberance and liberty of expression have led foreign observers and modern ethnologists (cf. Laburthe-Tolra, 1986) to consider them as archetypical of the *Naturvölker* of Africa!

7. I am not convinced that the Bamum kingdom fits Meillassoux's definition to the extent that Tardits (1980: 467) states unambiguously that the slaves were integrated into a family organization and reproduced themselves on the spot.

8. As indicated in chapter 6 in this volume, they were very ineffective weapons anyway.

8

The transfer of young people's working ethos
from the Grassfields to the Atlantic Coast[1]

This chapter highlights the fact that the Grassfields chiefdoms of the northwest and western provinces of Cameroon evolved a working ethos that was unique in the wider region in the pre-colonial era, and that this ethos was most strongly embodied by the young men and women of these chiefdoms. The argument is then made that the numerous young people who were exported from the Grassfields as slaves in the 19th century carried this ethos with them to the Atlantic coast.

The Grassfields working ethos

In the period immediately preceding the colonial occupation by the Germans, there were about 150 chiefdoms in the Grassfields. They were then engaged in a permanent process of splitting and aggregation. The hierarchy of each chiefdom consisted of a king, who was at the same time the head of the royal descent group, and of a number of notables and heads of larger or smaller descent groups. The king and notables accumulated in their respective bodies the ancestral life and reproductive substances. They were understood to receive these substances from the dead elders and to give them out in the material form of breath, speech, spittle, raffia wine, semen and the palm oil and camwood rubbed on persons and things. Since the kings and notables were believed to be the only males filled with reproductive substances, they exercised a monopoly over the women, and practiced high levels of polygamy. Most kings had 150 wives and above. As a result, one out of two adult males remained a bachelor for his lifetime, and, in most kingdoms, was effectively barred from access to genital sex, reproduction and wealth accumulation. The other men were co-opted into the hierarchy by being given a wife by the descent group head, and by succeeding to a vacant title.

It is fairly easy to reconstruct the Grassfields economy from 1800 onwards. In the 19th century, this region – roughly the size of Belgium – was densely populated (with about 30 people per square kilometre on average). The agrosystems were based on a combination of forest and savannah crops and small livestock rearing (poultry, goats, Djallonke sheep, pigs). Social inequality and competitive conditions among bachelors and women (who tended the fields) intensified agricultural labour. Local economic specializations and regional trade had a multiplying effect. Altogether, it was a developed 'traditional' economy, with efficient centres of craft production (ironware, raffia and cotton textiles, carving, and pottery) and agricultural production (cf. Warnier 1985).

Market exchange was equally developed over vast regional networks, with various currencies (including cowries, iron, brass rods and salt in bags), local and regional marketplaces, rotating credit associations and formal alliances between traders, as analyzed by Rowlands (1979) and Warnier (1985).

In the organization of production and trade networks, women and male bachelors constituted the labour force. Men engaged in intensive labour in the hope of being rewarded and given a wife and, in the end, succeeding to a title. There is much evidence that hard work was internalized as a habitus by men and women alike.

The potential conflict between the bachelors and the notables was diverted and turned into a sometimes violent competition among the youth. Married women were drawn into the competition through their sons, by working to accumulate bride wealth or by plotting with the head of the descent group or household to secure a wife, succession, or a title for their son.

The working habitus was associated with moral values of subservience to the young women's and bachelors' 'fathers' – dead or alive – willingness to work, and the avoidance of jealousy or of witchcraft activities. Thus the working habitus assumed the shape of an ethos. It is striking to see the high degree of genuine consent and subservience to such an ethos that obtained among the youth until the 1970s, and, to some extent, down to this day. This raises the Gramscian question of explaining such a degree of consent, or of assent, by the exploited to the basic tenets of the social and economic organization. This is a key issue in the present debate, as it is a prerequisite for the transference of the working ethos to other societies by the slaves who were sold out by the kingdoms.

The kings and notables of the Grassfields engaged in long-distance trade, especially southwards towards the Atlantic coast some 200 km away as the crow flies, and also towards the Muslim north. To the south, slaves were the primary commodities exchanged for European imports (including guns, cloth, Toby jugs, etc.). In contrast to the prevalent assumptions about the slave trade, most Grassfields slaves were procured not through warfare, but by purchase from their own kin (Warnier 1995, chapter 7 in the present volume). Young people and children were sold and smuggled out in secret.

This point may seem shocking and perhaps dubious to the twenty-first century reader, and needs some elaboration. As I have said, unmarried men competed among themselves to be given bride-wealth, a title of nobility or a wife by their father. However, there were alternative ways of getting a wife. A bachelor could seek the help of a notable within his descent group, or of his maternal grandfather, to approach a slave dealer. On particular occasions such as market days, funeral celebrations or commercial ventures to neighbouring kingdoms, the bachelor had the opportunity to lure or trick a member of his kindred whom he knew well (often a closely related child) into going astray. Food, flattery and drugs were part of the trick. The person who had been targeted fell victim to the plot, unnoticed for long enough to be smuggled out of the kingdom beyond recovery. All the parties involved got secretly a share in the bargain: the king, the slave dealer, the go-between and the bachelor. The latter obtained enough to complete bride-wealth payments and secure a wife, often with the help of his mother's savings. This was by no means the only scenario of enslavement, but it is emblematic of the means of 'peaceful' slave procurement.

Slave dealing was more than tolerated at the level of the kingdoms. In the kingdom of Mankon, for example, the king and half a dozen notables had a slave-trading license in the form of a 'slave rope' made of human hair and vegetable fibres plaited together and wound around their walking stick. The dealers gave a commission to the king for each slave they sold. Thus the kings and notables had a vested interest in slave dealing while keeping it within reasonable demographic and political limits. The number of unmarried men actually present in the chiefdom was thereby reduced from about 50 per cent down to 30 per cent of the total male population, thanks to the practice of exporting a proportion of the bachelors.

The authority of descent group heads, the pressure and violence exercised by forced bachelorhood and the threat of being sold out by slave dealers and by the king were enormous. This explains to a certain extent the obedience and compliance of the cadets. However, it would be a mistake to think that it was enough to explain both the compliance of the cadets and their working ethos. The violence was successfully hidden under an ideology of benevolent protection by the notables and the king that turned the pressure they exercised into a horizontal competition between cadets and between their mothers.

From what information can be collected from Brain (1972), Latham (1973) and Northrup (1978), as well as from genealogical and oral sources, slaves were exported from the Grassfields at a ratio of two males for each female. They were delocalized and left the Grassfields in caravans through the Western Bangwa, south of the Kwa mountains, and then to Calabar, or through the Moungo River towards Douala and Bimbia. It is not possible now to conduct a census, but my educated guess is that throughout the 19th century, the slaves exported annually could be counted in five digit figures, perhaps 20,000 to 40,000 for the Grassfields as a whole (Warnier 1985). Thus, the kings and notables not only profited economically from the trade, but ideologically as well. The slave trade had the advantage that it hid from the population the true extent of bachelorhood due to the wife-taking of the elite by exporting many bachelors and thus excluding them from an 'emic' calculation of the demographic situation.

If the number of lineages founded by successive kings is any indication of their wealth and of the number of their wives, the slave trade in the Grassfields seems to have gained momentum towards the end of the 17th century. It lasted until the beginning of the 20th century, to be replaced at the onset of colonization by labour recruitment, then by migrations to the coastal plantations and, after the Second World War, by rural-urban migrations. For the bachelors, the migration provided opportunities of access to wealth accumulation and marriage, although at a cost for them since their father was expected to obtain the lion's share of their earnings.

From the 1930s onwards, and much more so in the 1950s and subsequent decades, forced or voluntary migration gave access to entrepreneurship to growing numbers of Grassfielders, who nevertheless always remained a minority among their countrymen. Rotating credit associations, thrift, low levels of consumption and the exploitation of younger dependents became key factors to success in a history that owed much to its ancestry in the slave trade (Warnier, 1993).

The transfer to the coast of the working ethos of Grassfields youth

A number of sources indicate that slaves originating in the Grassfields were numerous and well known in the coastal polities of the Bight of Benin, including Calabar, Bimbia and Duala throughout the slave trade era. Koelle (1854: 11-13), who conducted enquiries with slave recaptives in Sierra Leone, refers to the speakers of seventeen Bantu languages of Cameroon including ten Grassfields 'Moko' languages. Before Koelle, the term 'Mbudikum' was more loosely used by Sandoval, Ogilby, Baikie and others for a vast geographical (as against linguistic) area in the coastal hinterland of Calabar, including Ibibio country.

From around the 1850s, 'ethnic' or linguistic categories became more refined on the coast, and slaves from the Grassfields became clearly named as Mbrukim, Burukem (Baikie 1856: 351, 439), Mburikum, Mbrikum, Mbudikum (Hutchinson 1861: 322) or Mbudikom (Goldie 1862) – obvious variations of a single name. 'Mukom', the Duala version of the word, is synonymous with 'slave' (Austen 1977: 308). From the descriptions that the slaves themselves gave of their country of origin, the main physical characteristics of the Grassfields environment came to be well-known on the coast: well watered mountains and savannah, kingdoms of various sizes (the largest ones like Nso' and Barnum being the most famous on the coast), proximity with the Muslim world and the presence of mounted raiders were all mentioned by traders and missionaries who collected this information from slaves living on the coast.

At face value, one would expect the slaves to have dropped their working ethos somewhere along the road from their homeland to the coast and to have slackened the efforts they put into their work, except under duress. What actually took place was rather different: all known sources agree on the facts that, on the coast, the Mbrikum were exceptional in their willingness to work and comply with their masters.

Hutchinson (1861: 322), the British consul for the Bight of Biafra, quotes a letter addressed to him by the Rev. W. Anderson, a missionary in Old Kalabar, stating inter alia of the Mbrikum that "they are peaceable, honest, and energetic". According to Goldie's Efik Dictionary (1862: 320), "the slaves from this region are much esteemed". Summarizing Douala sources, Austen (1977: 319) writes that the Grassfields was "probably the most important source for slaves" and that the latter had acquired a reputation for loyalty and docility among the Duala.

There is obviously no simple explanation for this state of affairs. For one thing Austen (1977: 311) points out that Duala masters were responsible for providing their slaves, as they did their sons, with wives. Thus, slaves had a better prospect for marriage in slavery on the coast than at home. Besides, they could accumulate wealth of their own, which was impossible for young bachelors in the Grassfields. This contributes to explaining the failure of the attempt made in 1892 by the German explorer Eugene Zintgraff to induce Grassfields slaves from the kingdom of Bali-Nyonga to leave their Duala masters and return to Bali (Austen 1977: 311). They were better off in Douala than in their home kingdom. However, one may also take into consideration the threat of being sold again if they were to go back home. Whatever the case, it is clear that, compared with slaves of other origins, those from the Grassfields retained their habitus of compliance and work (which is precisely what an habitus is all about – a second nature).

Historical research conducted on the coast of Cameroon and Nigeria by Latham (1973), Northrup (1978), Austen (1977), Austen and Derrick (1999), Wirz (1972) and others makes it clear that until 1859 (the date of the last legal shipments going to Brazil) slaves were either sold out in the Atlantic trade, kept in the coastal polities and established in slave villages, or integrated into the households or estates of coastal big men or 'kings'. Slave women were married to men of servile status, taken as concubines by free men or trans-shipped across the Atlantic. The male slaves were employed in various capacities (though not much in palm plantations it seems), mostly as 'pullaboys' manning the large dugout canoes that went up the Mungo, the Calabar and other coastal rivers to fetch the palm oil that fed the legitimate trade. A minority were employed as domestic labour. All of them contributed to agricultural work to some extent. A tiny minority was adopted in local lineages, and had offspring of their own within a lineage. Some Douala genealogies bear witness to such adoptions. All of them contributed to the status of their master and 'made him big'. The picture would be incomplete if human sacrifices of slaves at the death of big men were not mentioned.

Thus, Grassfields slaves represented a different civilization from the local one in coastal polities. Self-perceptions of the slaves' difference had a direct impact on their behaviour and on their relationship with the local community. In their studies of Duala history and socio-political organization, Austen (1977) and Austen and Derrick (1999) show that the servile population was part and parcel of the Duala polities and an essential component in their multiethnic and stratified society. It had a place of its own in accordance with the dominant ethos of the Mbrikum despite their condition as an 'economic and political chattel'. From the mid-19th century onwards at least, the Duala could not make do without them. It would be misleading to consider the delocalized slave some sort of culturally and politically neutral import that was dissolved into the local population with no clear and lasting identity of his or her own.[2]

This argument can be generalized for the entire area encompassing the Grassfields, the coastal areas and the forest societies in between: all of them were stratified, multiethnic and multicultural societies in a number of different ways. The Grassfields kingdoms were composite communities but did not maintain resident groups of slaves. The forest and coastal polities on the other hand established dedicated slave settlements in the vicinity of their villages, outside the settlement of the local free people. In all such cases, however, the slaves were not conceived of as a foreign body within the coastal polity. Rather, they were part and parcel of its definition. They were an essential component of the social and political fabric of the forest and coastal areas, with their languages, technologies, musical repertoires, associations, etc. However despised, they interacted a lot with the freeborn, with whom (rather than to whom) they belonged.

Conclusion: a specific Grassfields ethos or habitus?

Contemporary ethnography can still document the ways in which young people in the Grassfields incorporate working habits and values to such an extent that they retain them in quite different social and economic settings through urban and international migrations. It may become an asset in a diaspora setting in which they enjoy more autonomy and freedom than at home. Thus, whereas Grassfielders represent no more than 20 per cent of the total population of Cameroon, they provide 35 to 90 per cent of the country's urban entrepreneurs, depending on the branch of activity (Warnier 1993). The Weberian notion of ethos and the notion of habitus, developed by Aristotle and Thomas Aquinas, and picked up by N. Elias and P. Bourdieu may contribute to explaining how the subservience, honesty, energy and willingness to work of young people in the Grassfields could be internalized and incorporated to such an extent that they survived (and presumably helped to overcome) the trauma of sale and exile.

Moreover, although we write today as if slavery belonged to a distant past from which we have clearly emerged and in contradistinction to which we can posit a present of free social relations and labour contracts, the era of the slave trade is not temporally or socially distant. It is still present nearby and palpable, if disguised, in the memory of the coastal populations of contemporary Cameroon and southeastern Nigeria. It persists in attitudes of social prejudice that perpetuate past relations under new names. This may contribute to explaining why, to this day, the Grassfields working ethos is still identified in popular representations with the urban migrants of Grassfields origin. Douala, with more than two million inhabitants, is overwhelmingly a Beamlike/ Grassfields town and associated with an inferior condition. It has become instrumental in stigmatizing wealth accumulation – supposedly at the expense of non-Grassfields people but actually at the expense of the lower rungs of the Grassfields hierarchy – and in fostering ethnic prejudice and conflicts. Thus it has become part of the local social, economic and cultural setting, yet with the status of a trans-local reality.

Endnotes

1. First presented at a panel organized by Stephan Palmié and Ute Röschenthaler at the 2003 ASA conference in Boston. Then published, under a revised form, in *Social Anthropology* (2006), 14 (1): 93-98, and reproduced here with the kind permission of the editor whose copyright it remains. I am extremely grateful to Nicolas Argenti for editing this article and for contributing valuable comments. I also wish to thank Ute Röschenthaler and Stephan Palmié for having organized the panel and invited me to participate in it, and for their comments and discussions.

2. Yet we cannot assume that they were 'ethnicised' as we, and they, perceive them today after a century of colonial and post-colonial production of ethnicity.

An African sacred king

Back from his visit to the ancestors' graveyard, the king,
filled with their blessings,is the source of all life and wealth.
(Mankon, 2009, courtesy of Manuela Zips-Mairitsch.)

Part III

Grassfields sacred kingship

The third part of this book deals with the political organization of Grassfields kingdoms and, in particular, with four aspects of it. Chapter 9 considers any kingdom as a bounded unit. Why is there such a need for closure and control at the gates of Grassfields kingdoms? Following Robin Horton and Igor Kopytoff, one may consider that one of the basic problems in an African 'frontier' situation in which people and things are highly mobile, is to construct some kind of organization bringing together unrelated and mobile people, and to regulate their interactions. The means to achieve this end is to produce independent kingdoms as so many bounded, localized and unified entities in which people can be subjected to a unifying principle embodied by the sacred monarch and the ancestral life principles he receives from his ancestors.

Part III analyzes this type of organization under four headings. Chapter 9 focuses on the principle of territorialisation of people and things achieved by the kingdom. Chapter 10 underlines the functions of containment fulfilled by the king's body and his embodied material containers. The logic of containers and contents, surfaces, apertures and transit are key elements that help understanding the position of various categories of persons in the political hierarchy: the king as an arch-container of ancestral substance, the notables and descent group heads as receptacles brimming with reproductive substances for the benefit of their own groups, and the male cadets, empty of any reproductive substance, and whose bodily envelope has not been the object of ritual practices that would turn it into a leak-proof vessel capable of storing ancestral substances on its own rights. This is a key to understanding the historical position of male cadets, from the slave trade era in the 19th century to massive urban migrations in the 20th century and also as regards their possible involvement in various forms of violence meted on them or exercised by them, and rebellion from the colonial conquest onwards. Accordingly, chapter 11 is devoted to discussing the position of male cadets in the political hierarchy of the kingdom.

One of the implications of the politics of containers is that one may consider the sacred king as having (or being) three bodies: his own, full of ancestral substances, the palace where he lives at the heart of the city, and, third, the kingdom as a whole. One is allowed to consider those three entities – the king, the palace, the city – as the three bodies of the king on the grounds that they possess the same structure (an envelope and its apertures); that they have the same contents (the ancestral life substances, and everything they help producing and reproducing: the camwood, medicines, etc. stored in the palace, and the children, crops, livestock, wealth, good health, etc. they produce); and that they fulfil the same functions of containment, unification, control and transformation of the contents, things and people that go through the apertures of the three envelopes, either on their way into or on their way out of any of those containers. Accordingly, the last chapter of this third part (chapter 12) deals with the palace as the second body of the king, with its layout, functions and organization.

Matter for territorialization
An inroad into a contemporary African kingdom[1]

King Ngwa'fo of Mankon rules over a people of some 60 000 to 100 000 subjects. His kingdom is perched in the highlands of Western Cameroon, a space he shares with some 150 other kingdoms of various sizes. He succeeded his father in 1959. Before that, he had read agricultural engineering at the University of Ibadan in Nigeria. In addition to his royal headgear – one cannot say his crown – made of the tips of elephant tails, he wears several other caps. He is a prominent businessman with interests in agriculture, breweries and real estate. He is also a politician of national importance, for a long time the President of the Provincial (now Regional) section of the ruling party. He has also been a Member of Parliament. He is a modernizing king in economic, technical and social matters, yet sharing in the politically conservative hegemonic alliance established by the two successive Cameroonian Heads of State, Ahmadu Ahidjo and Paul Biya, for which he does not see any viable alternative. He entertains a drive towards a conservative modernization, frequent in Sub-Saharan Africa. His palace, provided with a museum and a superb catalogue since 2005 (see Notue & Triaca 2005), has a web page – [www.museumcam.org/mankon/kingdom.php] – on which one can see, amongst many other images of interest, a photograph of President Paul Biya having a conversation with him at the Presidential Palace showing how personally close he may be to the Head of State.

He also participates in the 'come back of the kings' in the forefront of national politics that has been taking place since the 1980s. Claude-Hélène Perrot & François-Xavier Fauvelle-Aymar (2003) have devoted an edited volume to this noteworthy political phenomenon. This come back makes sense if, following many analysts of African politics such as Jean-François Bayart (1979, 1989), one considers the post-independence States as rhizome-States connecting together the urban elites, the local and expatriate economic operators, the regional interest groups and the kingdoms of various origins benefitting from an important legitimacy and political backing, etc., in brief, many elements that, despite their heterogeneous nature, contribute to the formation of the State by a process of social divergence and hegemonic alliance.

In the present essay, I propose to show that the *body* of the king is a means of territorialisation and de-territorialization of subjects and things. When talking about the body of the king, I am not alluding to the social representations pertaining to the body of the monarch, but its very materiality – that of a body with flesh and bones – physically quite prominent, in accordance with the corpulence he cultivates and that befits a king-container of vast bodily capacity.

The king procures matter for territorialisation thanks to the bodily substances he contains: breath, speech, saliva, semen, that are considered as being loaded with life and reproductive essence given out to the king by his dead predecessors. I will have to give more information on those substances and on the bodily techniques that pertain to them before I am in a position to deal with the issue of territorialisation.

The 'burden of kingship': receiving, storing and giving out

I will start with the description of the gestures accomplished by the monarch towards the end of the annual festival that brings to a close the agricultural cycle and gives the start to a new one. It takes place late in the month of December of the Gregorian calendar. On that occasion, the king dances amidst his subjects. He holds his drinking horn in his right hand. A palace steward stands by him, holding a calabash full of raffia wine. The king proffers his drinking horn. The steward fills it up with raffia wine. The king brings it to his mouth, fills it up with the beverage, washes his mouth with it, and sprays it on his subjects who congregate around him, on their skin and garments (very much a second skin) on which the royal substance falls like a milky mist.

This gesture, called *fama* ('to spray') in the vernacular, exemplifies the calling of the king. The body of the monarch receives, accumulates, and stores the ancestral life essence that inhere his bodily substances. He gives them out to his subjects. He is the single origin, spring and principle of the life essence needed by the subjects to reproduce, bear children, produce successful crops and breed livestock. His power is an essentially monarchical one in the true sense of the term since he is the single origin of all life and wealth in his kingdom. However, since his bodily substances are in limited supply, they are as it were expanded upon and multiplied by such substances as raffia wine (mixed or not with his own saliva), palm oil, camwood powder taken from the wood of the *Pterocarpus soyanxii* tree, and medicines. These substances are medicated by the king when he spits on them and utters performative words upon them. They are stored in so many containers (raffia bags, calabashes, mixing bowls, drinking horns) incorporated in his bodily schema or his image of the body, as Paul Schilder (1935) would put it, and in his sensori-motor conducts. They are used to smear the skin of the subjects or the envelope of many things (houses, containers, musical instruments, weapons), or, as with raffia wine, to be sprayed upon people's skin.

Consequently, the task of the king consists in doing all the gestures and implementing all the sensory-motor conducts of receiving, storing, opening up the apertures, expelling, pouring, blowing, spraying, ejaculating, anointing, in order to strengthen the bodily envelopes of his subjects and to fill them up with life and reproductive substances, beginning with his own numerous wives. Such is the burden of kingship mentioned by Frazer: giving out again, again and again. And in order to give out, take in, contain, safe-keep, and accumulate. The king is a 'pot-king' to which I devoted a book (2007 for the English version and 2009b for the French one). In French, one may make a pun and call him a '*roi-peau*' – a skin-king – that sounds very much like the '*moi-peau*' – the 'skin-self' after the title of a book written by the French psychoanalyst Didier Anzieu (1985) who claims that the self is constituted by anaclisis on the lived experience of one's skin. Everything that he writes on coetaneous envelopes in their relationship to the self would apply to the king's skin and body. And, in French, in the expressions 'roi-peau' (skin-king) and 'roi-pot' (pot-king), peau and pot are pronounced exactly the same way[2].

Since the king is directly connected with the ancestral origin of all life and reproduction, there can be no doubt that he is perceived as the most fertile man in the kingdom. The polygamy practiced by the Grassfields kings procures a gage for the fertility and sexual achievements they are credited with. In 1959, when he succeeded to the throne, Ngwa'fo inherited 79 wives from his late father. In 1971, when I met him for the first time, there were still some fifty of them. One never alludes openly to the king's sexual life, although it stands out as a prominent technology of power. A monarch, in that respect, is put to the task and has to show results.

Calling at the fuel station of the ancestors

The king contains the ancestral substances. However, he does not contain them once and for all as from the day he succeeds his father. In order to be in a position to give out in plenty, he must, as it were, call time and again at the fuel station of the ancestral substances and fill up the tank. He calls there following a double cycle: a yearly one and a weekly one. Each year, at the end of the agricultural cycle, the king and his entourage call at the royal graveyard. The king purifies himself in the local stream before addressing the dead kings. Royal notables and the king then make offerings to the dead monarchs, read the signs allowing to see whether the offerings have been accepted, and utter performative words. In case the offerings have been accepted, the words convince the king and his entourage that he is now in a position to engage into a new yearly cycle. The discourse of the king and his entourage explicitly express the complaints of the kingdom and request newborns, good health and abundant crops and livestock for the kingdom. However, it is never said in so many words that such blessings will be channelled through the bodily substances of the king and their extensions. This is acted, performed, but never expressed in words. Once the king has visited the royal graveyard, he is considered as fit to give out the life substance to his subjects during the annual festival and throughout the following year. Those offerings are complemented, following a weekly cycle, by libations performed on the graves of the last two kings.

The bodily and material culture of receptacles and the production of subjectivities

The technologies of power implemented by the king and his entourage are, to a very great extent, embodied and materialized. The bodily cum material culture of containers, substances and bodies is an essential component of power. It cannot be separated from the techniques of the body and the bodily motions and emotions associated with it. One may distinguish between two sets of materialities and associated bodily conducts, that is, the containers, each provided with an envelope and an aperture on the one hand, and the contents of the receptacles that may transit through the apertures and be stored or made available on demand, on the other hand.

On the side of the containers, one finds the bodies of the king, the notables and the subjects, the bags, calabashes, drums, pots, bowls, drinking horns, caps, garments, houses, buildings, the palace of the king and the city as a whole that used to be enclosed by a broad and deep ditch and by medicines spread across the gateways. The apertures – whether they belong to human beings or to material containers – are universally named 'mouths' (ntsu, sg. in the vernacular).

The contents are bodily substances or their extensions such as raffia wine, palm oil, camwood powder and medicines, but also the children engendered by the male and female bodily substances together with ancestral life essence, and born by the women. The larger containers (houses, hamlets, enclosures, dancing field, marketplace, palace, courtyards, city) contain the subjects themselves, the livestock, the crops, the commodities of the regional and long-distance trade that may transit through their apertures.

As a rule, the containers are inalienable and sacred, whereas the contents are profane alienable commodities that circulate from inside to outside or vice-versa, or from one container to another. They are transformed in the process. The contents, being alienable, are more profane than the containers. However, a container may be stored as some kind of content in a larger one, just like a Russian doll. Such objects may therefore assume the two conditions of container and content.

Underlining those comments, there is a theory of bodily and material culture. Marie-Pierre Julien, Celine Rosselin, a few others and myself have developed it elsewhere[3]. There is no point summarizing it here with two exceptions: in the present case, material culture is not taken for its sign value in a system of connotation or communication, as exemplified by the work of Roland Barthes (1957), but for its praxic value in a system of agency that produces given subjectivities. The question that is being raised is not 'what does *material culture* and objects *mean?*' But 'what does bodily and material culture *achieve?* What is their practical impact on subjectivities and on power relationships?' The bodily and material cultures are embodied and put to use following a procedural knowledge that cannot be easily verbalized by the subjects. It is learned by apprenticeship in daily life since birth. It shapes the subjectivities of the monarch and his subjects to the effect that, in Foucauldian parlance, it produces a governmentality of a certain kind. It is a governmentality of containers, contents, transit and transformations.

Little wonder that the subjects implement techniques of the body in the terms of Marcel Mauss, and techniques of the self in Foucauldian parlance. At this point, I will not belabour the questions of definitions and terminology. All such techniques make use of the same kind of sensori-motor repertoires, whether they apply to the king or to his subjects illustrated by the daily and thorough massaging of the babies, or by smearing the body of adults with various substances. One can also see such techniques of the body/self in the identification of any subject to his palm oil bowl called *azo'* in the vernacular, the identification of the married subjects (whether male or female) to their individual house, in conducts of absorption and excretion, in innumerable motor algorithms in tune with crossing thresholds, walking along paths, passing through barriers and gates, etc.

As an example, I will mention the succession rituals. The kingdom is made of nine exogamous clans totalizing thirty-two named lineages. Each clan and lineage head, and some of the lesser descent group heads are said to be a notable (or lords – *kum*, sg. in the vernacular) who stores and gives out the ancestral substances that belong with his descent group. Consequently, he fulfils for the benefice of his own descent group the same kind of functions fulfilled by the king for the benefit of the whole kingdom: he calls on his dead elders, he stores in his own body the life and reproductive substances of his corporate group, and gives them out to the members of the latter; Accordingly, being perceived as a most fertile man in his descent group, he has many wives.

The succession ritual to such a title of lord or notable has to answer the following question: what can one do when the notable dies, when his body as a material receptacle of ancestral substances disintegrates, and the substances he contains are at a risk of being lost in the process? This question is never verbalized in so many words. It is a question raised by the anthropologist who has provided an analysis of the governmentality of containers. The answer is this: the senior members of the descent group get hold of a son of the deceased, usually, but not always, designated by the latter before his demise. They have him seized by a few strong men who drag him by force into the house of his late father. This is done as soon as possible after the death of the notable. They strip him of his clothes, anoint his body with a mixture of palm oil and camwood, address the dead elders, offer them ritual libations and food, and, there and then, dress the incumbent successor with the loin cloth and paraphernalia of his father, the most important of which is his drinking horn. Then they give him the very name of his late father. One may conclude that the succession is indeed achieved by the utterance of performative words, but also, in an essential way, by the implementation of the techniques of the body applied to the coetaneous envelope of the incumbent, and to the material extensions of his *Körperschema*, as Schilder (1923) would say. In other words, the old container of the deceased having broken down to pieces, the elders of the group pick up a young and strong body-container and work on it as they would work on freshly moulded clay to turn it into a suitable container while addressing the dead elders to ask them for many children – boys and girls – health and abundant crops, after what the newly processed notable is perceived as being filled up with life essence, and starts implementing the bodily and material culture of containers and contents in his capacity of corporate group head.

The king's three bodies as means of territorialisation/deterritorialization

The king has three bodies, or even *is* three bodies – his own, the palace, and the city. One can substantiate this statement on the basis of three main arguments. In the first place, there is a structural homology between the three bodies of the king. They are made of an envelope (the skin of the king, the enclosure of the palace and the ditch and medicines surrounding the city). The envelopes are provided with apertures. Both envelopes and apertures are the object of many technologies aiming at producing, mending and maintaining them, at ensuring that the apertures remain open so that people, goods and substances may come in or be expelled while being vetted and transformed.

Second, the king identifies not only with his bodily self, but also with the palace and the city. This identification takes place on the grounds of the identity of contents of the three bodies: the bodily/ancestral substances contained in the king's body, their extensions kept in the palace, and their produce in terms of people, livestock, crops and riches contained in the city. One may object that the saliva of the king is something different from the livestock and crops contained in the kingdom. At face value, this is true, at least for the foreign observer. However, if one considers, with the Mankon people, that the production and reproduction of people, crops, livestock and goods are the produce of the life essence originating in the dead kings and distributed by the living king through his bodily substances and their extensions, then it becomes obvious that the contents of the three bodies of the king are one and the same insofar as they originate in the unifying life substances coming from the ancestors. If one applies this scheme to the various structures of the kingdom, they appear in the full light of the logics of containers and contents.

Third and last, they have the same functions of containment, storage, intake, dispensation, excretion, transformation of the contents into one another, and of reproduction.

It remains to be discussed why and how this process of territorialisation/deterritorialization takes place. We may be satisfied that it is achieved by the governmentality of containers and contents I have described. What needs to be underscored in the first place is the fact that the kingdom of Mankon, like all neighbouring kingdoms, is a composite one. In the 19th and 20th centuries, it was made of nine exogamous clans without any common genealogical origin. Each of them had its own oral traditions of origin referring to the fact that they were, to some extent, foreign to each other. In the course of the last couple of centuries, conflicts over successions to high office, over land and raffia groves, etc., witchcraft accusations, competition over long distance and regional trade, were often resolved by the secession of given descent group segments or individuals seeking adoption in a neighbouring kingdom by being absorbed into the envelope of its city and assimilated by being rubbed with the monarchic life substances and provided with them. Likewise, Mankon was absorbing foreign groups and individuals. The practice of regional and long-distance trade, and the diplomatic relations between kingdoms translated into marriage alliance networks involving the king and the notables. Around 1900, at least 30% of the women married in Mankon were coming from the outside. More often than not, they spoke foreign languages. The large polygynous households of the notables were multilingual units. The body politics of the kingdoms did not conform by any means to the stereotype of the socially and culturally homogeneous ethnic and linguistic group. It was a composite, multi-ethnic and multilingual political entity.

Robin Horton (1971), a prominent historian of Africa, had noticed that African societies wavered between a segmentary organization conveniently exemplified by the Tiv of Nigeria, and a hierarchical organization typical of the chiefdoms and kingdoms. The segmentary organization used the idiom of kinship as a political charter, and cast itself into a single all-encompassing genealogy that helps charting the social proximity or distance of any single descent group as regards all others.

If, by any chance, a descent group moves out for some reason, it looses touch with the other groups that were close to him in space and genealogical terms. This results in what Horton called 'disjunctive migrations' – disjunctive in spatial and genealogical terms. In most parts of Africa, this disjuncture has happened in all kinds of circumstances (the impact of neighbouring, expansionist, empires, the slave trade, climatic and environmental change, etc.). If and when disjunctive migrations happen to multiply, more and more unrelated descent groups come into contact with each other and are compelled to come to terms in sharing a common territory. This creates a situation that characterizes the African frontier as analysed by Igor Kopytoff (1987), in the American sense of the term, that is, as an open space in which people and things are on the move and that calls for unending processes of political innovation. This is when the various forms of political transaction may orientate themselves towards processes of closure, thus giving rise to chiefdoms, kingdoms and empires encompassing groups of different origins.

Such a process is at the same time a territorial and a political one. Kingdoms constitute so many machines geared to producing a body politics, by manufacturing a unified space, delimited, yet open to the outside, with a given territory and a principle of unity or consent. The Mankon kingdom constitutes such a machine in which the bodily and material culture attached to the monarch and his subjects manufactures given subjectivities physically and mentally inscribed within the confines of a space defined by a body: that of the king and that of the city to which he identifies. However, it should be underscored that this machine is constantly put to the test since the extreme social inequality and sheer weight of the hierarchy foster many a conflict ending up in secession or the expulsion of unwanted persons. The king keeps expelling or losing people who go elsewhere. He welcomes and absorbs some others. A good and efficient king is one whose physical body and whose city are unaffected by leakage and cracks. It is a king who accumulates more than he loses, who has a large constituency to show for himself and put on display, and who spends his time and energy in closing down, safekeeping, and giving out unifying life substances within his kingdom.

The historiography of the western highlands of Cameroon shows that it is a zone of intensive exchange and circulation of people and things. It is quite clear as from the inception and growth of the Atlantic slave trade and its impact in the hinterland around the years 1750-1800. The practice of high polygamy and the multiplication of royal lineages around those dates are a clear indication of such a phenomenon. However, there is more and more evidence to the effect that, in the area, the African frontier opened up much earlier and that the need for closure and territorialisation may be much older than the 18th century.

In that area, the advent of food production dates back to ca. 6000 BP. The mountain environment is ecologically diversified and, as a result, quite favourable to human settlement, contrary to the romantic Latin stereotype of the mountains as inhospitable refuge areas settled by degenerate populations. The high population densities of the Cameroon Grassfields (in the 21st century, up to 350 persons per square km in rural areas) constitute the most recent stage of a much older situation. The Neolithic situation developed into a pattern of economic specialization and commodity exchange structured around areas of iron production (dating back to ca. 2500 BP) traded for palm oil produced along the escarpment of the highlands. The regional trade in subsistence goods was complemented, at least over the last four or five centuries, by long distance exchange in luxury goods between men of substance. This area pulls together all the requirements and conditions for the circulation at large of people and things: high population densities, internal socio-economic diversification, matrimonial alliance and diplomatic networks, wealth and power accumulation at the nodal points of the system of exchange, conflicts over people and access to key resources, long distance exchange networks between notables of equivalent ranks.

The territorialisation process whereby people and things that became unmoored and that roam at large, as Appadurai (1997) would say, constitutes a political constraint. Its counterpart is to be found in the deterritorialization of people who, for one reason or another, do not put up with their being assigned to the local and to be incorporated into the king's body. It is also to be found in the excremental practice of the king who expels from his city such undesirable people as witches, slaves, foreigners or asylum seekers who have failed to bring anything valuable within the confines of the city.

The territorialisation/deterritorialization process does not only concern the subjects of the king and the shaping of their subjectivity. It also concerns the things (and not only the material objects) that may be coming from the outside and may intrude into the envelope of the city by going through its apertures. Such things, in the experience and the representations of the Mankon people, may contain the best and the worst. The fear they induce may project itself in the fantasy of a certain kind of sorcery called *msa* in the north western part of the Grassfields but that has its equivalents everywhere else. The scenario of this fantasy is as follows: the adepts and initiates of msa may contact you and make interesting business proposals. If you accept them, your new business partners attract you and give you access to a marketplace or a kind of trade fair. You begin to realize that it is located in an occult world beyond the reach of ordinary people. At that point, it is already too late to back up and withdraw from it. At msa, you are compelled to purchase parcelled goods by paying with the life of your relatives euphemistically referred to as 'chicken' or 'goats'. What makes things worse is that there is no means to know anything about the contents of the parcels and to make an enlightened choice. Once you have paid and you are back home with your parcel, you unwrap it and you may find goods of enormous value such as expensive jewellery or an expensive car, or else you may find something that will spoil your household or even the whole city, such as a deadly virus. This fantasy, and the practice of protecting the city by spreading royal medicines across the paths and motorable roads giving access to its various parts, show to what extent the porosity of the kingdom to the external fluxes of people and things may generate anxiety as regards the possibility of hostile or nefarious intrusions into the various protective envelopes of the king, his subjects and the city.

Conclusion: the 'Pot-King' in the globalization era

The territorialisation/deterritorialization practiced in the Mankon kingdom goes back to a history organized around the emergence of an African frontier and of kingdom formation in the area (at a date so far unknown), the impact of the Atlantic slave trade (ca. 1750-1800), the development of forced and indentured labour (since 1910), urban migrations (since 1945), the globalization of financial, cultural and commodity fluxes and of selective international migrations (since the 1980s).

Confronted to such events in the second half of the 20th century, it became clear that the kingdom was under a serious threat of wasting away its substance. Is it loosing its contents and becoming an empty shell?

Confronted with such a challenge and such a new version of the African Frontier, king Ngwa'fo has sought to practice a selective assimilation of the incomers and to keep including the outgoing migrants at a distance. When a Member of Parliament in Yaoundé, he took the opportunity offered by the Parliamentary sessions to tour and visit his subjects who lived in the Capital town. In the early 2000s, he created an elite association named the Mankon Cultural Development Association (MACUDA), with subsidiaries in Nigeria, the United Kingdom and the United States. Such associations are found among most of the neighbouring kingdoms as demonstrated by Nyamnjoh and Rowlands (1998). For a detailed example, see Page (2007) on Bali-Nyonga. In the United-States, MACUDA has a web page ([www.macudaamerica.com]). This cyber-territorialisation constitutes a paradoxical process since it transforms the physical relation to the body of the king into a multisite, and to some extent virtual, network.

However, what would look at face value as a futile attempt at encompassing the fragments of a kingdom blown up to pieces by the globalizing forces of modernity, is actually turned into an efficient inclusion process since it joins hands with an endogenous process that Francis Nyamnjoh (2011) calls 'bushfalling'

This is a process whereby people go out of their homeland, as it were to the bush, to hunt and search for resources that can be brought back home. This process has been going on for centuries in the context of the African Frontier that offers lots of opportunities for the subjects of the kingdom to venture out of its limits in order to bring back home various kinds of external resources, and first of all hunting game. Filip De Boeck (2004) has described similar patterns around the Congo-Angolan border. The outgoing hero may assume the many different shapes of the hunter, the trader, the fetish, the white missionary, etc. He is a mutant hero. What turns bushfalling into a powerful instrument of territorialisation is the fact that people take to it in order to fetch the resources of the global frontier. Yet, this does not make sense unless one is making every conceivable effort to bring the proceeds back home, to one's relatives, and to built a house in the village and achieve a status that, at some point, will be validated by the palace and the king. Few out-migrating Mankon people contemplate severing their kinship, physical and spiritual links with their homeland and being buried in foreign soil. The practices of royal inclusion and bushfalling are further reinforced by the politics of autochtony that have developed in Cameroon and in many parts of Africa since the early 1990s as a counter to the call for more democracy (see Warnier 2011).

However, there are signs of wear and tear in the technological apparatus of royal power. Thus, after the political unrest of the 1990s, the king has felt compelled to put iron doors and gates around the palace and to keep them locked at certain times. To some extent, this runs counter the fact that the apertures of the palace (its 'mouths' – *ntsu* – in the vernacular) should allow for free passage both ways, even if people and things passing through must be vetted and must undergo some kind of transformation. It is therefore impossible to predict what will happen with the territorialisation/deterritorialization process in the years to come.

Endnotes

1. First published in French in the journal *Le Portique*, 20 (2007): 99-110, in a special issue on Gilles Deleuze and Félix Guattari entitled "Territoires et devenir", and translated by the author.

2. Richard Fardon volunteered an equivalent pun in English: being a container that takes ancestral substances into his bodily envelope to expel them again for the benefit of his subjects, the king is a pump. Being corpulent and of great bodily capacity, he is a 'pump-king', as corpulent as a pumpkin.

3. See Warnier (1999, 2004, 2006, 2007, 2009a), M.-P. Julien & J.-P. Warnier (eds. 1999), M.-P. Julien & C. Rosselin (2005, and eds. 2009).

The King of Bafut, c. 1910. Photo Diel, courtesy Photo-Archiv, Rautenstrauch-Joest-Museum, Cologne.

Containers, surfaces, apertures and contents[1]

In the first chapter, I suggested that the king may be seen as a container of ancestral substances. If this is so, it is worth investigating the theme of surfaces, containers, apertures and contents. On a world scale, the comparative archaeological and ethnographic record concerning the latter as well as ceramics, textiles, the human skin, its openings, movements from inside to outside and vice versa is considerable. Too vast to reduce to a short article on the topic which would amount to a laundry list unless one has some kind of key that will unlock various doors opening onto a common corridor.

My key will be the human body, for two reasons. First, it is itself a container, with its skin as a surface, with its openings conjoining an inside and an outside. Second, by acting in a material world, the human body supplements itself with innumerable surfaces and containers by means of which it extends beyond its own physical limits.

However, we encounter here a first difficulty. It has proved difficult to turn 'the body' into an anthropological object. The reasons for this were explored by Berthelot (1995). Basically, the social and cultural facts are not the body in itself, but the techniques of the body (see Mauss 1936), its uses, its social representations, and all the practices (sports, health care, dress, cosmetics, control, apprenticeship, etc.) attached to it. This difficulty has led most attempts towards an anthropology of 'the body' to an epistemological dead end. As a result, from an anthropologic point of view, it is more efficient to focus on bodily conducts than on the body as such. Consequently, my argument will unfold as follows.

Bodily conducts are gestures accomplished by a given subject in which his/her subjectivity is involved. They can be limited in scope, to the point of being static, like holding one's breath and staying put while playing hide-and-seek, or quite mobile, as in riding a bicycle. Second, there is no motricity without the involvement of the seven senses, that is, the conventionally distinguished five senses, to which must be added proprioception and the vestibular sense of gravitation and spatial orientation[2]. The seven senses are interconnected in such a way that, according to the neuroscientist Berthoz (1997), they are all part and parcel of a single sense: the sense of movement. There is no perception without motricity, and no motricity without the involvement of the senses. So far, my key has been transformed from 'the body' to 'motor conducts', then to 'sensory-motricity'. The next step consists in introducing a third essential dimension. As Damasio (2000) rightly pointed out, any sensori-motor conduct involves both a drive and the emotions that correspond to it: pleasure, anger, satisfaction, curiosity, etc. – most of the time, a complex and volatile mix of affects accompanied and stimulated by the production of hormones (ocitocyn, dopamine, endomorphine) affecting the central nervous system. As a result, my key becomes the 'sensori-affectivo-motor' conducts of the subject.

Much like keys that are equipped with grooves, small balls and holes, this key has several components or dimensions to it. It has a psychic dimension, made of the cognitive (not necessarily 'conscious') and emotional aspects (including 'unconscious' as repressed in the Freudian sense) of all our actions. It has an anatomo-physiological component in so far as all our actions are mediated by bodily motions, as those who are disabled know only too well.

Last but not least, it has a material component, in so far as all our 'sensori-affectivo-motor' conducts are propped against, or articulated with, a human-made material culture that has been co-produced along with the relevant gestures. The keyboard with which I type the present chapter has been manufactured very precisely to fit a human hand and to adjust to its motions. Vice versa, through a protracted apprenticeship I have devised sensori-motor algorithms that allow me to incorporate the keyboard and write as if it were a component of my bodily schema.

So now my key becomes 'sensori-affectivo-motor conducts geared to material culture'. It may sound a bit complicated, but human motricity in a human-made material world is easier to contemplate than to analyse, and for analytical reasons we need the full constellation of concepts. From an analytical point of view, the components of the key can be considered apart from one another. In agency, however, they are essentially welded and mobilized together. An acting subject is always a 'subject-acting-with-its-incorporated-objects'.

One more comment of a historical nature. At the beginning of the 20th century, Head and Holmes (1911) and others accumulated numerous observations that were put together in a path-breaking synthesis by Schilder (1923, 1935) under the expression of *Körperschema*, 'bodily schema' or 'image of the body', as a kind of bodily synthesis acquired through a long apprenticeship. Schilder (1935) insisted that the bodily schema does not end with the human skin as a limiting boundary. It extends beyond it and, from the point of view of motricity, perception and emotions, includes all the objects we use, and to which we are geared. It even includes all the material culture that lies beyond our immediate grasp. The walking stick of a blind person, following Schilder, is incorporated into the bodily schema, as is clear from the way that the perception of the environment is felt by the blind person to reside at the end of the walking stick rather than at the interface between the stick and his or her hand. Similarly, our bodily schema incorporates the domestic space, its furniture and all the appliances we can reach on a routine basis, to such an extent that, if we change the location of a given cabinet in our flat, we will have to retrain our motor algorithms to look for the cabinet in its new location instead of the previous one. Our bodily schema also incorporates the static and dynamic properties of the car we usually drive, the bicycle we ride, our favourite armchair, etc. In short, Schilder's notion of a bodily schema, enriched with all the knowledge accumulated since his time by the neuro- and cognitive sciences provides the grounds for a praxeological approach to material culture.

This approach considers material culture not only in terms of its sign value within a system of communication but in terms of its practical value in a system of agency. It departs significantly from semiotic or structuralist approaches but it does not contradict them. To be sure, material culture is good to think and to signify with, but it is also jolly good to act with, as part and parcel of any sensori-affectivo-motor conduct of the subject. This approach also departs significantly from most phenomenological approaches to 'the body' (e.g. Featherstone et al. 1991; Csordas 1994) in so far as these do not consider material culture as an essential component of 'the body' (read 'sensori-motricity') and tend to deal with 'meaning' and representations of the body rather than with the ethnography of bodily conducts. The latter would compel them to take material culture into consideration, whereas it does not have any place in their agenda. This short summary will suffice here, since I have developed the argument more fully elsewhere (Warnier 1999, 2001, 2004, 2007; Julien and Warnier eds. 1999; Bayart and Warnier eds. 2004).

The approach summarized here provides a key to opening doors on to various domains of material culture in which containers, inside, outside, apertures, surfaces and contents are all relevant. In all cases, they will be understood as essential correlates of bodily conducts and as part of the bodily schema.

The praxeology of containers, openings and surfaces

The arch-container is the human skin. The classic work here is the synthesis provided by the psychoanalyst Anzieu (1985) in his book *Le Moi-peau*, or 'The Skin-self'. A wealth of data, provided by human and animal ethology, projective tests (like the Rorschach) and dermatological observations, converge in underscoring the basic role of the skin in the ontogenesis of the human subject. The psyche is constructed as an envelope by 'anaclisis' on the anatomo-physiological functions of the skin. Anaclisis refers to the process by which many psychic experiences build upon or are propped against bodily motions and emotions. The skin provides many such basic experiences; it covers the body, it protects it, it sustains the muscles, it registers information, it is an organ of sensori-motor and of libidinal stimulation. The psychic self models itself on the experiences provided by the skin. It fulfils similar functions as regards psychic contents; it is constructed as a container which provides the basic tenets of the processes of introjection and projection studied by Ferenczi. Additionally, the skin is provided with openings through which the inside and the outside communicate and through which things, substances, information, and emotions enter or leave the body and the psyche.

The sensori-motor conducts dealing with the skin, its openings and the traffic of substances are amongst the most archaic and deeply grounded in the experience of the subject. They begin to operate before birth. Feeding, breathing, defecating, perceiving, being handled and held, washed, clothed, etc., are all activities that develop at one and the same time both the sensori-motor and the psychic components of containment and its correlates. Any subject – adult or child – will draw on such a basic repertoire in dealing with material containers that have been incorporated in bodily conducts. The main categories of material culture involved here are clothing as a second skin, all domestic containers, buildings and architecture, ships and means of transportation, or all constructions that are aimed at channelling substances: dams, canals, pumps, pipes, roads, traffic lights, and all the technology of human containment such as prisons, cells, airports, camps or various kinds.

The senrori-motor conducts associated with containment may be as diverse as opening, closing, pouring, filling, emptying, wrapping, regulating, maintaining the envelope or the limits, removing the blockages that prevent the transit of substances, mending leaks, forming a queue. Such conducts include material, psychic and sensori-motor components in various proportions, depending on the circumstances, the social context, the material culture involved, etc. Besides, they are culturally shaped. In Maussian parlance, they are 'bio-psycho-social' phenomena.

All such conducts mediate between the material culture of containers, contents, openings and surfaces, on the one hand, and the acting subject, on the other. As a result, the concerns of the subject are displaced on to, or extended into, the embodied material culture of containment: health, morality, possession and property rights, safety and security, intrusion, group belonging, privacy.

Containment as a technology of power

Michel Foucault (1975, 2001) has aptly emphasized how power is directed at 'the body' (read: to sensori-motor conducts) precisely at the point where the subject governs him/herself. Let me also emphasize here that the subject Foucault speaks of is not the conscious subject characteristic of the Cartesian tradition through phenomenology. It is rather the divided subject of his desires. Basically, power rests on agency, by acting upon the subjects and directing or helping the subjects to act upon themselves, govern themselves and act upon other subjects. All those actions – billions of them – rest on the use of given technologies of power. Such technologies include material components and know-how like those of the hospital, the school, the army barracks, the means of transport, etc. In so far as they are historically and culturally specific, Foucault calls them 'governmentalities'.

In this respect, the technology of the skin, of containment, and the associated material culture provide techniques of the self that may act as the point of departure for the construction of fully-fledged technologies of power. I will illustrate this point with an ethnographic example.

The highlands of western Cameroon have been densely settled for the last millennium to say the least. In a territory about the size of Belgium are to be found some 150 kingdoms, the largest of which have been revitalized in the last two decades of the 20th century as part of the spectacular 'come back of the kings' at the forefront of contemporary African political life.

Such kingdoms are typical examples of African sacred kingship made famous by Frazer some 100 years ago[3]. The technology of power in such kingdoms involves the mobilization of sensori-affectivo-motor conducts applied to containers and their contents. The king's body is a container of ancestral substances such as breath, saliva and semen. These substances are complemented by palm oil, raffia wine and camwood powder, a crimson pigment rubbed on people and things.

Such substances are transformed into ancestral substances through the utterance of performative words by qualified persons in the proper context of ceremonial offerings to the dead kings, or a variety of speech of a kind that has been analysed by the philosopher Austin (1962) in his stimulating book *How to Do Things with Words*. As a result, the king, in his body as a material container, possesses all the physical substances necessary for the production and reproduction of his subjects. He disseminates the aforementioned substances by projecting his breath and speech upon his subjects, by spraying them with raffia wine from his drinking horn and his mouth, and by anointing the skin of his subjects and the surface of diverse objects with palm oil and camwood powder. Since he receives reproductive substances direct from the ancestors, he is held to be the most fertile male in the kingdom. Accordingly, at the beginning of the 20th century, most kings had at least 150 wives, sometimes numbering several hundred. Nowadays the number has been reduced to a 'mere' ten to fifty wives.

The photograph of Abu'Mbi of the Bafut (see on page 102) illustrates this point well. It was taken by Diel – a German traveller – sometime around 1910. It is a still photograph taken on a glass plate with the cumbersome apparatus in use at the time. No doubt the larger *mise-en-scène* had been arranged beforehand by agreement between the photographer and the king. Despite the fact that the photographer wanted to show off an African despot, a number of features of the photograph correspond very nicely with the ethnography of the kingdom. It also fits with Foucault's argument regarding governmentality and the way this, in my view, may apply to containers.

To wit: the king cultivates corpulence. His girth is emphasized by his demeanour and the ample gown which is a second skin expanding on the first one. To his right stand a dozen of his wives, pregnant (that is, full) and naked. To his left are the offspring that issued from the king as a mon(arch)-container and from his wives. He stands in front of the door (or 'mouth' in the local language) of his personal house, where he spends his nights and receives his wives on a couch lined with the pelts or skins of the leopards with which he identifies.

The people in the still photograph do not move. In that respect, the picture is inadequate to show the motions that are essential to the governmentality that obtains in the neighbouring kingdom of Mankon where I did the bulk of my fieldwork (Warnier 1975, 1985).

The cycle of performances begins at the end of the agricultural cycle around November. People harvest the crops, put them in sacks and baskets and bring them to the house of each individual married woman. Subsequently, a number of actions are taken to rid the kingdom of its suspected sorcerers, who are believed to eat and consume the life and wealth of people. Those persons suspected of being sorcerers are subjected to an ordeal that consists of absorbing a poison taken from the bark of the tree *Erythrophlaeum guineense*. They drink the poison, validating this gesture with the following words: 'If the poison finds sorcery in my entrails, may it destroy it'. Then the convicts run out of the enclosure of the city, where they die and are abandoned in the wild, or vomit the beverage and are brought back into the city, having been declared not guilty. Let me explain: sorcery is a bad substance contained in the belly of the subject-container, and expelled both out of the city through its openings, to die in the wild or be reincorporated within the confines of the city.

The city is one of the three bodies of the king, the others being the palace and the king's own 'skin', as the human body and the self are named in the local language. The sorcerers, expelled from the city, are treated like the excrements of the body politic, and therefore of the king, who incorporates in his person the corporate kingdom. This last point is very much in line with Kantorowicz's argument in *The King's Two Bodies* (1957).

Mid-way through the dry season, or around December, the king makes offerings on the dead king's graves. He is believed to receive their life essence that, in turn, invests his own bodily substances and their extensions in the form of raffia wine, oil and camwood. Following these offerings, he gathers his people at the palace for a four-day festival during which he pours out the life substances from his own body-container in a variety of forms for the benefit of the people, and, quite literally, on to their skin, when he sprays raffia wine from his mouth on the dancers around him. As containers, the corporate king-palace-city are inalienable and therefore sacred, whereas their contents (bodily substances, goods, people) are alienable and therefore to some extent profane or mundane.

The material culture of the palace is very much focused on containers and on openings: king's graves, dwelling and storage houses, huge pots in which the raffia wine from the different lineages of the kingdom is blended, bags, boxes and bowls for camwood or the mixture of palm oil and camwood that is rubbed on people and things, bags of medicine, lodges and houses containing the paraphernalia of palace societies. The openings receive much attention: the necks of pots are shaped and decorated. The door frames of the lodges and of the councillors' hall are adorned with human and animal figures with their mouths gaping open in the act of projecting their breath and saliva on to the incomers. With respect to doors, these are noticeably small, with a high threshold and a low frame. Consequently, the act of entering a house and of extracting oneself from it amounts to an elaborate technique of the body. What is more, people bearing medicines, musical instruments or weapons must always enter the house through the narrow door walking backwards. Consequently, the material culture and the sensori-motor conducts that go along with it are shaped together in peculiar ways.

Accordingly, people, as subjects, are shaped and identified as containers. In the vernacular, there is no word for body or self other than 'skin'. Immediately after birth the newborn is rubbed daily with baby lotion for about ten to fifteen minutes thoroughly all over the body, beginning with the shaven scalp, with particular attention paid to the folds of the nostrils, ears, eyes, mouth, and moving down all the way to his legs and feet. In the past, palm oil was used instead of industrial baby lotion, and every woman and child had his or her oil container called *azo'* (calabash or clay pot). Notables owned elaborate ones for ritual purposes. In daily life, men identified with their bag and women with their basket, very much along the lines described by MacKenzie (1991) for Papua New Guinea concerning the identification of both men and women with their gendered carrying bags or containers. Going about without a bag or a basket makes one uncomfortable, lacking in interiority and substance.

I am by no means suggesting that containers openings and their associated sensori-motor conducts are part of a technology of power in all known societies. Quite the contrary. What I wish to suggest with the above example is threefold: first, that it offers an overview of the microphysics and overall paradigm of the historical governmentality specific to the sacred kingship of the highlands of western Cameroon. Second, in this particular instance, the material culture of containers should not be understood only in terms of its potential 'meaning' or for what it might 'signify' in a system of connotation or communication. Importantly, it should also be understood for what it enables in terms of perception, action, achievement, and performance on the part of the subject. The main question is to understand what this elaborate material culture of containers and containment does to the subject in terms of routinely incorporated motions, emotions and perceptions, that is, in terms of power. As a technology, it applies to the subject and shapes it. This action provides the subject with what Foucault (2001) calls 'technologies of the self' whereby one can fix one's identity and find ways of governing oneself. Besides, it submits the subject to a given 'governmentality'. A Cameroonian subject of the 'Pot-king' cannot easily operate in a contemporary Western democracy or in an acephalous society like those of the forest area of Cameroon.

However, the Mankon kingdom or the sacred kingship of Africa may not be the rare exception it seems to be at first. Hendry (1993) suggests that the Japanese have developed a 'wrapping culture' in which polite speech is a kind of wrapping of thoughts and intentions and may help in wrapping others and exercise control upon them. This dimension of social life has its material counterpart in gift-wrapping, in dressing in layers upon layers of garments, in constructions and gardens as wrapping of space, and in retinues of servants and officials as the wrapping of sorts for those wielding symbolic power. This layer of people shields them off from contact with the crowd. In fact, state formation is a process of social and spatial closure. The politics of wrapping bring us back to the material culture of containment.

Towards a praxeology of containers

In my discussion I will proceed from the larger space of the frontier and the border to the smaller artefacts of pottery and household containers. In each case, sensori-motricity provides a key for the interpretation of the material.

The open space of the frontier and the closure of the border are our point of departure. Turner's analysis of the American frontier (1893/1961), picked up by Kopytoff (1987) and applied by him to Africa, emphasizes the essential role of movement. The frontier is a vast space within which one is not only free to move about but even invited to do so ('Go west, young man') in order to fill up the emptiness and colonize it. It operates very much as an inside without any relevant outside. In other words, the notion of a clearly drawn border with its specific technologies of control is not essential to it.

In human history, the border assumes a specific dimension of control over people and things with the closure effected by the state. The state clearly imposes a limit between an inside and an outside that is provided with gates and openings through which people, animals and goods may pass in both directions. The Great Wall of China is one of the most ancient and spectacular of such material technologies; Hadrian's wall would be another example. The border is equipped with specific technologies of surveillance: patrols along its length and checkpoints at the gates where vehicles and people are searched, examined and taxed. Airport technology is the most sophisticated development of border control[4].

Cities provide an example of a smaller kind of container or border. In human history, these seem to antedate the state and are usually understood as representing the earliest forms of political organization that are not based on kinship. Much like the state, the city is composite and consists of a congeries of people of different origins collected inside what is usually a bounded space.

As compared with the state, the city provides specific sensori-motor experiences. Hall (1966) has emphasised how the city constitutes a visual, acoustic, olfactory and thermic space of a particular kind, to the extent that a traveller moving in or out of a city through its gates crosses not only a social and political threshold, but a sensori-affectivo-motor one as well. The city, indeed, can claim to possess a specific inside.

The French acoustician Louis Dandrel (personal communication) claims that each contemporary metropolis has its own acoustic signature, made up of a particular mix of sounds that depends on the type of architecture, the means of transport and the habits of the local inhabitants. There are, of course, differences among the various neighbourhoods, communities or zones of a single city, but, by and large, New York does not sound like Moscow, Shanghai or Lagos. Dandrel made recordings of the acoustic signature of various major cities. This remark could be extended to the olfactory, visual, kinesthesic and other components of urban life. Moving as part of a crowd in New York City, Rome of Shanghai does not constitute the same kind of experience, nor does moving alone.

What I wish to stress is not only that the city is characterized by its limits between an inside and an outside, which can be quite fuzzy, as, for instance, is the case with London, but also by the content of the inside, which differs from one city to the next. Moving across the limit and moving from one town to the other provide different kinds of experiences. Hall indicates some of the implications of such sensori-motor and emotional differences, especially with regard to group interactions and what Bourdieu, following Elias, would call 'different bodily and social habitus'.

The next step is to move down, as it were, the scale of containers to the house or building, with its own specific kinds of surfaces and openings. At a structural level, one of the most revealing analyses has been provided by Cuisenier in the case of French rural house (1991: 289-344). In each case, Cuisenier gives the layout of the house drawn to scale, and there is nothing new or striking about this. Juxtaposed, however, he provides a dendritic or 'tree' diagram showing the possible trajectories that allow access to a particular inner space (a vestibule, staircase, corridor, room), and from there, again, to other spaces. The diagrams show clearly the presence and potential of different patterns of movements and, therein, also, the internal organization of the content of the house.

Using the diagrams developed by Cuisenier, let me contrast the peasant house of the lower Loire valley (around the town of Saumur) with the larger farmhouse of the Jura mountains. Around Saumur, calcareous building material is readily available. In the past, builders extracted this material on the spot and trimmed it as needed. They would build several houses around a common courtyard equipped with a well and an oven for baking bread. Typically, there was a dwelling house with a door and two rooms – the kitchen and the bedroom.

Around the courtyard a building for one or two horses, another for the cows, one for the cider press and casks, a shed for tools, and a couple of barns were commonly found. In the lower courtyard, there were latrines, a pigsty and a smaller building for keeping rabbits and poultry. With the exception of the bedroom with access through the kitchen, one had to pass through the courtyard to move from one building to another; The climate is notoriously mild, so that using the courtyard as an entrance hall does not present much of a problem. In this case, the dendritic diagram assumes the shape of a common exterior trunk, with separate branches, each of which gives access to a single different specialized building as a bounded space.

In the Jura mountains, the farmhouse is a single, large, self-contained building, with everything inside: the livestock in the basement during the winter and, above, the barn, the cheese manufacturing unit, the workshop and the dwelling quarters of the household. To this day, the Jura mountains are still a livestock-rearing area known for its milk and cheese production. During the winter, the livestock, kept in the basement, served as a kind of central heating system, adding warmth to the farm-house and feeding on hay stored in the barn. The dendritic diagram of the building shows two or three entrances into it. From these the branches bifurcate several times to give access to different spaces in succession. However, in addition, there are transversal passageways to ensure that any space within the farmhouse can be reached from any other without having to get out of the building in the open, which could raise difficulties during the harsh winter.

In the Loire valley, the horses, cows, poultry and people were kept separate, each with their specific smells, sounds, food, space, and so on. In the large Jura farmhouse, they were all collected together within the same envelope/container. As a result, in terms of content and surfaces, the Loire peasant house and the Jura farmhouse differ significantly. All the dimensions of space occupation and perception underlined by Hall, such as distance, smell, sight, and so on, were organized differently in the two cases. Nor were exterior surfaces treated the same way. In the Loire valley, depending on the wealth of the peasant family, the dwelling house was far more stylish than the utilitarian buildings. This is evident from the high-quality slates, cornice, door and window frames of the dwelling house as compared with the ordinary, makeshift, somewhat poorer finish of the more utilitarian buildings. In the Jura farmhouse, there is a single surface/envelope for the whole content, and it may be rather elaborate. This is even more the case with the alpine chalet with its decorated wooden balconies and window ornaments.

Towns and houses are Neolithic innovations. This suggests that the passage from nomadic to sedentary life was accompanied by a drastic change in the closure and space articulated with equivalent changes in techniques of the body. The trend, from the political and architectural points of view, seems to have been towards more closure, departing from the openness of the nomadic camp with its marked flexibility in spatial organization and social affiliation, as suggested in Lee and DeVore's classic *Man the Hunter* (1968). It is also worth emphasizing that the advent of food production was accompanied by a major change in the domestic technology of containment, namely pottery.

Pottery provides the archetype for the actions of containing, storing, pouring, mixing, cooking, melting, heating, and so on. Its articulation with sensori-affectivo-motor conducts must also be highlighted because of pottery's close association with all daily household activities; Pottery may be provided with handles for easy grasping and a lid for better closure and treatment of the content; It is the necessary extension of the body in eating, drinking, washing and (in many societies) urinating or defecating. Surface decorations usually emphasize the opening or neck or the pot and the surface of its walls. From the vast literature devoted to pottery, let me paraphrase simply Arnold (1985) and the book by Cumberpatch & Blinkhorn (1997) and suggest that such containers may be not "so much a pot, more a way of life".

The close relationship between pottery and basketry has often been emphasized. In turn, the latter is closely related to the techniques of weaving, carpet making and, more generally, the manufacture and use of textiles. In clothing, the textiles are in close contact with the body, and provide it with a second skin. Schneider's review of the literature (1987; and chapter 13 in the *Handbook of Material Culture*, Christopher Tilley, et al. eds. 2006) on the anthropology of cloth illustrates the emotional and aesthetic dimensions of surfaces that achieve their highest realization with cloth. Cloth and textiles are gendered, and, when set in motion, they alter the proprioception and the sensori-affectivo-motor conducts in unexpected ways: either to stiffen or contain the body, or to enlarge and efface its contours or, again, by providing bounded surfaces for rest, social encounter (the 'divan'), prayer, meals or work. For example, Alec Balasescu (personal communication) noticed that, in the Middle East, the large gowns worn by some women all day long, even at home, inhibit the perception of the outlines of the female body. Nowadays, the value put on slimness conflicts with the premium formerly put on female corpulence. In such a conflicting context, the large gown makes it difficult for some women to monitor the limits of their body, even when they want to do so, and Balasescu tends to attribute this difficulty to the envelope made by the gown; Conversely, the women who remove their gown at home and dress in clothes that fit the body more closely maintain better perception and control of their body weight.

Symbolizing passages and transformations

This necessarily succinct overview still requires a few concluding remarks. First, from a praxeological and psychic point of view, the sensori-affectivo-motor conducts shored up by the human skin and containers achieve what the psychoanalytic tradition, summarized by Tisseron (1999, 2000) calls symbolization – following the term's etymological meaning: in ancient Greek, *sun bôlon*, meaning to 'put together'. Making use of containers amounts to working with and on containment, that is, putting together the things, substances and people that are introduced into a common container. It also amounts to separating things that belong together from those that do not, whatever they may be – livestock, human beings, memories, materials, liquids, and so on. The examples of the Loire peasant house and the Jura farmhouse are cases in point: through movements, living in those houses amounts to symbolizing in different ways the relationships among human beings, domestic animals, foodstuffs, etc.

Consequently, the material culture of containment helps every subject to symbolize all the relevant actions of daily life. Yet such a repertoire of actions can characterize a given society only in so far as it amounts to a technology of power, that is, to a governmentality in the Foucauldian sense of the term. Thus, the kingdoms of western Cameroon, and Japan according to Hendry (1993), provide cases where the technology of power rests on the material forms of containing or wrapping.

But then, containment, as a means of symbolizing power, the subject and daily life, is based on two processes brought out by Tisseron (1999, 2000) following Anzieu (1985), namely passing through and transformation. Containment in itself is of little value unless things, substances or people can be put together inside the container by passing through the opening cut into the surface of the container. This is why the openings of the body, or pots, houses and cities are so important and receive so much attention. This is also why the surface of the containers is usually treated with much care. The surface is the essential correlate of the opening. It must be as solid and tight as the opening is broad enough to allow the passage, and narrow enough to keep the contents inside. The surface is smoothed and decorated; It may be coated or receive a gloss or some other treatment to protect it or adorn it as well as to enhance the emotional dimension of its sensori-motor manipulation. It has to have style, both to facilitate its identification and for aesthetic satisfaction.

However, the process of passing through also entails the transformation of what passes through the opening; things will be mixed, cooked, digested, assimilated, and so on, or they will be expelled, transformed into rubbish, or combined with other materials in other containers. Thus, the process of symbolization is essentially geared to passing through and being transformed.

I have neglected many other domains that would deserve equal attention in their relationship to the sensori-affectivo-motor conducts as applied to containers. The most important one is the body itself as a container. I alluded to it only when discussing the 'skin-self' analysed by Anzieu. But this is not intended as an ethnographic survey of practices involving the skin and its openings. I have also ignored the domain of masks and masquerades, of musical instruments and the acoustic envelope provided by sounds and music, or health practices aimed at introducing substances within the body or extracting them from it, or differently, effecting a cure by treating the skin as an envelope. The same praxeological approach could also be applied to animals in so far as they are domesticated and share with humans in the household, or in so far as they provide hides, pelts and fur as surfaces suited to all kinds of purposes. I have also neglected many kinds of containers like pieces of furniture, cabinets, suitcases, boxes, etc. Nevertheless, I expect the key constituted by the sensori-affectivo-motor conducts applied here to containers can be used to open those doors that have remained closed, allowing access to their contents. Thus, investigating surfaces, containers, apertures, inside and outside as essential material correlates of sensori-affectivo-motor conducts may indicate promising future directions for research. These directions take us away from the semiotics and the 'meaning' of containers; away from the study of their utility as material contraptions; And more towards the study of different kinds of technologies of the self, different kinds of subjectivities, and different kinds of power, both at individual and at social levels. It also takes anthropology and ethnography closer to the cognitive and the neuro-sciences.

However, such a perspective does not take us away from style, aesthetics and sensori qualities of material culture. Quite the contrary. The technologies of the self and the technologies of power have style, materiality and aesthetics, especially when they concern the human body as a container in motion, emotion and the exercise of power.

Endnotes

1. First published in Christopher Tilley et al. (eds.), *Handbook of Material Culture*. London: Sage, 2006, pp. 186-195. Reproduced in a slightly different form with the kind permission of the editors whose copyright it remains.

2. Proprioception refers to the perception we have of our own body by means of the billions of captors disseminated throughout all the bodily tissues. The vestibular sense, located in the inner ear, is the sense by which we perceive the position of our body in space and its equilibrium while on the move. Both senses are crucial in relating to the material world.

3. See Feeley-Harnick (1985) for a review of the literature.

4. The interpretation of the process of closure has given rise to much debate. Lightfoot and Martinez (1995) discuss various models drawn from the archaeological record. The most basic debate revolves around the question as to whether increased mobility of persons and things gave rise to the institutions that we today associate with the state, or else, does state formation rest on other processes and, once accomplished, will it induce inter-state exchanges? A tradition that runs from Marx to Bayart (2004) through Horton (1971), Friedman & Rowlands (1977) and Appadurai (1997) argues convincingly that, as genealogically unrelated groups exchange, move about and congregate, they need to devise new political means to regulate their interactions. Closure provides a technology for creating locality, an inside, an outside, a space, and a way of mooring people and things to the body politic. In the 21st century the globalization of trade and financial fluxes goes together with a reinforcement of state control on migration and borders, and an increasingly sophisticated technology of closure directed at the sensorimotricity – and the emotions – of the migrant.

King Ngwa'fo II with young palace retainers, Mankon, no date (ca. 1910), Courtesy Museum für Völkerkunde, Leipzig.

Rebellion, defection and the position of male cadets: a neglected category (with an afterword)[1]

In 1973 I was making enquiries in the small kingdom of Songwa, where I was talking with a notable. An old woman was following the conversation. She stood up, grasped her worn down pullover with both hands and pulled it up to reveal her stomach. I saw a deep scar, that of a serious wound to judge from the length and jagged depression it had left on her lower belly. The woman explained that towards the end of the German occupation a small band of 'Kamenda' armed with breechloaders had fallen upon them, taking off women and livestock at Mauser-point, and that she had been wounded in the scuffle.

I recall the uncomfortable feeling I had at the time. The episode was not unconnected with the appropriation of women and the contributions in game, camwood and other resources embedded in the very regional hierarchy that I was discussing with the Songwa notable. Moreover, the woman recognized this. However, at that time, the scar and the scrimmage did not fit into any of my ethnographic frameworks. It could not be fitted into any analysis of pre-colonial political systems. Rather, for me, the scar bore witness to a painful event that belonged to the colonial past. It gave rise only to embarrassment and a sense of guilt on my part. Neither the incident nor the feelings it aroused were recorded in my notes. These were ethnographic notes in the strict sense of the term.

Now, twenty years later, that scar has become domesticated. It has lost its disturbing and opaque character as the evidence for an exceptional drama. It has undergone the fate of the countless events the social sciences feed on. It has become an ethnographic fact that can be included in an overview of ancient political systems. It bore witness to the disorderly rebellion of the young unmarried men (cadets) at the start of colonization and, in consequence, to their enforced subordination in the Grassfields chiefdoms in still earlier periods. It threw light on these systems with the help of new approaches that were not available to me when I began my work in 1971. In the interval I had, among other things, read and thought about Sally Chilver's paper (1967) on the relationships between Bali-Nyonga and the representatives of German colonial power.

In its essentials, Grassfields ethnography has been constructed from the point of view of the hierarchy of chiefs and notables. Women, since the classic work of Phyllis Kaberry (1952), have been the subjects of some detailed studies. In contrast, the mass of young bachelors have never, unless I am mistaken, been the subject of special studies, despite the crucial role they played in underpinning the former hierarchies, as labour during the colonial period, as recruits to the Christian missions and, from the inception of the colonial period onwards, as rebels. This lacuna is the result of four combined effects. First, an effect of social structure: speech is monopolized by the hierarchy. The cadets constituted a category of persons reduced to silence (a muted group), as were women. The ethnologist does not hear them. Secondly, an effect of theoretical approach; Anthropology, since the 1940s, in pursuing its interest in political systems, paid more attention to the hierarchy than to the *vulgum pecus*, with the exception of slaves. Thirdly, the Marxist anthropology of the years 1960-70 was more concerned to single out the relations of production than to give voice to a dominated group. Finally, the effect of a disciplinary bias: as N. Thomas has shown (1989), Radcliffe-Brown in grounding anthropology in the monopoly of the professional ethnographer over the collection of facts discarded the testimony of the missionary, the trader, the colonial officer, the schoolmaster, the convert and, by so doing, dispensed with history.

In casting a historian's eye over Grassfields societies, Elizabeth Chilver helped to neutralize this quadruple effect. One example is the history of the Bali 'irregulars' and the 'Tapenta'[2] who made their appearance along with the German penetration of the highlands. The episode of the scar belongs here. From 1891 onwards notables and cadets, nominally attached to the kingdom of Bali-Nyonga, began to hold the region to ransom on their own account. This phenomenon became more widespread after the punitive expedition of the *Schutztruppe* Commander Lt. Col. Von Pavel against Mankon and Bafut in December 1901. Armed brigandage was taken up by cadets who had broken away from authority and who were known in Pidgin as 'Kamenda', 'Tapenta' or 'Free Boys'. Here is a description given by Fr. Spellenberg of the Evangelical Mission, who was in charge at Bandjoun in 1914 (cited by van Slageren 1972:84): "[The] appearance [of the Tapenta] bodes no good. The youths in particular, who form the tail of the troop, are the bane of the country. Corrupted by the magic of the Whites, they attack men, women and children like wild beasts. They steal anything that isn't nailed down – fowls, goats and foodstuffs. Their organization has ramifications everywhere. When they are checked they cry: "Lef mi, mi big boy, mi bi Tapenta boy." (In Pidgin: Leave me alone, I'm important, I'm a Tapenta)

At this period, the phenomenon is attested from Bafut to Bandjoun. Its epicenter was the kingdom of Bali-Nyonga. However, it is likely that its equivalent was to be found throughout the so-called Bamileke chiefdoms, with resurgence during the Independence period from 1956 to 1970. At the heart of the phenomenon lies the dissemination in the Grassfields of breechloaders taken from the Germans. Elizabeth Chilver (1967) has restored some of the history of this in the course of her analysis of Bali-German relationships. We start with the attack on Mankon mounted by Zintgraff on 31 January 1891. The forces assembled by the explorer consisted essentially of Bali warriors accompanied by Zintgraff and his five German companions, their Vai bearers from Liberia, and warriors from some small kingdoms more or less closely allied to Bali. The attack proved disastrous for the Germans, four of whom lost their lives. The Vai carriers, beating a hasty retreat, abandoned their arms and provisions. On this dramatic episode of Grassfields history, see the account of Zintgraff's explorations in Bamenda by E.M. Chilver (1966).

There is little doubt that the booty found its way to the Mankon and Bafut palaces, nor that the guns were redistributed to those henchmen of fons and notables known by the Bali term of *Bigwe* (pl.), masters of the arts of brainwashing and deception. Subsequently, the dispersal of German arms increased. Following his defeat, Zintgraff called for reinforcements. These arrived in August but their bearers mutinied at the approaches to the Grassfields and made off with their arms, pillaging the villages in their path. Zintgraff's Bali allies managed to recover a good part of the material. The explorer distributed one hundred Mausers and ammunition to the Bali warriors. Meanwhile, however, the stores of the staging post of Barombi, on the Mungo, had been pillaged by bearers, who exchanged several hundred looted Mausers and carbines for women. One can see why Zintgraff said little about this reverse, more resonant of future trouble than any military defeat. There is little information about the fate of these guns. Chilver (1967:491) records that oral traditions collected in the 1920s by British colonial officers suggest that a large number were retained by the Bali and used until the ammunition ran out.

In 1910 the German Station Commander Menzel estimated that the number of breechloaders dispensed by Zintgraff in the Grassfields amounted to between 2,000 and 2,500. Both the Fons and the administration were worried and attempted to repossess them; but in 1910 the Station had only succeeded in recovering three hundred. One should distinguish between two cases. First, that of the *Basoge* or Bali irregulars who came under the authority of the Fon of Bali-Nyonga. Zintgraff, followed later by the colonial administration, had made a treaty of protection under which the Fon of Bali-Nyonga became a colonial agent. As such, he was expected to perform two essential but contradictory tasks: the maintenance of order and the recruitment of labour. Second is the case of the Tapenta who acted quite independently, accompanied by bands of young folk. In practice it is likely that the boundary between these groups was hazy. Grassfields customs consider it perfectly proper for an executive to take a percentage of every transaction. The notables controlled the networks of matrimonial exchanges, successions and marriages. They were less careful managers in other matters and could readily close their eyes to other affairs provided they got their due share. The same collusiveness was evident in the case of the traffic in children and adults.

In the course of time the notables began to realize that the Tapenta movement formed part of a larger phenomenon: the cadets, doubtless for the first time in Grassfields history, were escaping from their control. They took note of the favour which the missionaries enjoyed among young people; of the unbelievable fact that the White man baptized converts – literally initiated them – without paying any regard to their social rank; and they remarked that the cadets fled to the coast to avoid the constraints to which they had to submit in the chiefdoms. The notables were aware of this in 1911. Chilver (1967: 505) records the anxiety of the Bali who, in 1912, complained to the Governor at Buea that "many people are leaving. Nine out of ten, when they go the coast don't come back and don't send money to Bali". The missions, who on the whole welcomed young people, were not troubled by the Fons and notables. The disquiet of the latter with the missions was constrained by their fear of the administration, and also by the active friendship between the Basel Missionary Ernst and the Fon of Bali. However, in 1916 the internment of all the German missionaries by the allied forces gave the notables a chance to carry out what they had been contemplating for some fifteen years: to destroy the chapels, books, Christian emblems and schools, to disperse Christian meetings and to take the young men in hand again. The Christians were accused by the notables of being rebels. Out of spite, but not without deeper reasons, they were identified with the Tapenta. In the event, the Grassfields hierarchy had not misidentified their real adversaries: these were indeed the cadets.

Readers of Hirschman (1970) will have recognized two of the four options available to individuals in declining organizations: rebellion (that of the Tapenta) and defection (into the Christian churches or the market economy and its most important space: the coast). The scar displayed by the old woman, the Mausers, the red berets and the confused indiscipline of the cadets who exacted redress from the notables by appropriating women, livestock and anything else they could lay their hands on, indicates a rift which divided Grassfields societies on the eve of colonization. It might be objected that this crisis was caused by colonization and did not precede it. In my view, this objection does not withstand a close examination of the multiple and convergent events which accompanied the colonial episode. Certainly, by escaping to the coast, the cadets were fleeing forced labour and the death that was all too often its sole remuneration. Even so, taken all together, the instances of defection and rebellion[3], and the suddenness of that phenomenon, as well as the determined resumption of authority by the Fons and notables from 1916 onwards, indicate that the 'traditional' kingdoms were already subject to serious tensions on the eve of colonization. An effort of imagination is required to envisage the extreme demands that the Fons and their notables placed, by all sorts of practical and symbolic means, upon wives and bachelor cadets. It is, of course, inappropriate to speak of a 'crisis' since, all things being equal, political organizations such as Mankon's could have gone on reproducing themselves for a good while longer.

In my view this conflict has been insufficiently brought out in Grassfields ethnography. This remark applies in particular to my 1975 thesis and my larger work published in 1985, both influenced by functionalism. To counter a description of the kingdoms of the highlands which emphasizes the harmony of their parts, one should underline that these kingdoms rested on the shoulders of cadets, who were subjected to obligatory celibacy, to austere and meritorious work and, in some cases, to be sold into slavery. Rewards were only enjoyed by a minority of cadets, who were destined for a polygamous marriage, to succeed to a household or lineage headship or office, and to engage in the biological and social reproduction of the chiefdom. The reconstruction of these political systems by means of ethnographic enquiry, such as my own in the early 1970s, gives no access either to the situation or to the subjective experience of the cadets; An ethnographic inquiry of this kind does not expose lines of tension or potential cracks in the system.

On the other hand, when the colonizer arrived and, independently of the control of persons by notables, distributed Mauser rifles, sacraments and employment, the cadets immediately saw opening up to them opportunities for protest for which words were found ("Lef mi, mi big boy, mi bi Tapenta boy") and for action at the point of a Mauser. They could also now discern the pathways and opportunities for defection: the mission and the coast.

To summarize Hirschman (1970), individual members of organizations allegedly 'in decline' have not only the two alternatives of protest and defection, but four options in all: protest, defection, loyalty or apathy. The first two could only be offered after the arrival of the Europeans. Before 1891 they hardly existed, if at all. We have no evidence of a collective revolt of the cadets before colonization. The only recorded historical event that resembles it is the revolt of the retainers of the Bamum palace under the leadership of Nguwuo, which Nsa'ngu and his supporters managed to put down.[4]

On the other hand, cases of individual rebellion and conflicts between fathers and sons are well attested. Pradelles de Latour (1991) has exposed the intensity of parental domination among the Bamileke. In that case, a son would be devoured by the narcissism and all-mightiness of his father were it not for the role of the bride-giver, 'the father who stands at the back'. It has struck me that the hostility felt towards fathers, and the deep frustration of celibate cadets excluded from reproduction transpose themselves into rivalry between sons for access to either marriage or succession, or both. Such rivalries between sons are so strongly felt that the notables themselves found it difficult to contain them within acceptable limits. Those rivalries also involve their mothers, the wives of polygamous notables. There is plenty of evidence that they competed against one another over the advancement of their respective sons.

Defection before the colonial period was probably less difficult than might be supposed. Kingdoms were relatively open, and individuals or kin groups could migrate from one to the other. However, this option was not really viable for the great majority of cadets, who were likely to retain their status wherever they went. An unsuccessful contender for an important succession could obtain the status of notable in another kingdom only if he brought a large household or a sizeable group of lineage members with him. One could argue that such people were no longer 'cadets'.

Having reached this point in the argument, we shall advance some provisional conclusions. The revolt and defection of cadets from 1891 onwards suggests strong pre-existing tensions, and supports the hypothesis that before the colonial period the only options open to cadets were the two remaining ones described by Hirschman, loyalty and apathy. Ironically, it is the colonial situation that may supply the information required to complete the ethnography of the category of celibate cadets.

Within the limits of the present paper only a quick sketch is feasible. In the past, cadets were loyal to the hierarchy. This is seen as a praiseworthy loyalty, expressed by work, submission and attachment to the imaginary world of a notability which is conceived of and conceives itself to be a vessel brimming over with the vital substances required for social reproduction: breath, semen, camwood, oil and so on. The cadet, on the other hand, is defined and defines himself as an empty vessel lacking the means to fill itself, which means he strives to deserve. However, in the absence of reward or personal qualities, loyalty wears itself out; and then apathy sets in. Local fictions blame the losers for their misfortune (*ndon* in Ngemba-speaking kingdoms) or for the various depleting afflictions that they are seen to suffer (*atchul* in Bum for example)[5]. In the past, as in the present, one would have come upon a large number of men who were dependent on others, women in particular. Supernumerary men are to be found in all hierarchised societies, and are accommodated, as Ortner (1981) expresses it, by diversion or retrenchment. The conversations I have had with young unemployed men have made me realize that their situation is not novel, although the present economic situation has multiplied their number and increases their unhappiness as other options are now disappearing before their eyes. Loyalty no longer pays, the escape routes are blocked, and the experience of rebellion in the maquis and, more recently, in the *villes mortes* operations have shown the cadets the brutal face of power which, even before the colonial period, had identified them as dangerous categories in the population. The leader of the Social Democratic Front in the 1990s, John Fru Ndi, appeals to these categories. The preceding analysis explains why most of the Fons and neo-notables are hostile to Ndi and maintain their alliance with the President, Paul Biya. Indeed, their hostility to the cadets predates colonization and has merely been subsequently confirmed.

To conclude: this brief article is intended to illustrate Chilver's particular contribution to the anthropology as well as the history of the Grassfields. Her work provides a powerful antidote to the 'pure' ethnography put in hand by Radcliffe-Brown and continued in the tradition he founded. Chilver introduced systematically into our field of studies the sources disqualified by the famous founder of social anthropology. Among these were the accounts of the explorers and travellers (Flegel, Zintgraff, and Hutter), colonial publications (Pavel, Conrau and the articles which appeared in *Globus*, *Deutsches Kolonialblatt* and *Deutsche Kolonialzeitung*) and German and British archives, among the latter the Assessment and Intelligence Reports. She placed all these in the context of the development of anthropology in the 1920s and 1930s and the courses attended by British Colonial Officers in Oxford and elsewhere, which were followed by the studies undertaken under the auspices of the Colonial Social Science Research Council (Chilver 1971). To these she added missionary archives and, finally, the biographies of prominent Grassfielders, schoolmasters, and the *literati* straddling two worlds, such as Max Gabana Fohtung (Chilver 1962, reprinted as Fohtung 1992).

An afterword (March 2012)

The present chapter needs to be updated in view of a number of significant publications that came out since I first started to write about male cadets in the Grassfields. To begin with, it is now clear that the condition of the latter, at the turn of the 20th century, has been deciphered by many scholars including myself through the lenses of the colonial situation and of decolonization. This calls for a reassessment of the impact of colonization on the condition of male cadets.

The socio-political protest movements at Independence

From ca. 1955 to the early 1960s, Cameroon went through a process of decolonization verging on armed rebellion, mostly in Bassa and Bamileke countries. During these events, Roland Pré, the French High Commissionner in Cameroon, summarized the opinion of the colonizer that the Union des Populations du Cameroun (UPC), the nationalist pro-independence movement leading the revolt, was staffed by communist activists backed by Soviet Union and China. Roland Pré reckoned that the leaders were in a position to obtain some support from the youth and the women whose condition had worsened since the onset of colonization. This opinion set the terms of a 'Bamileke problem' that was discussed time and again in subsequent years. It identified the main protagonists of the drama: the French colonizer and its armed forces, the new Cameroonian elites expecting to harvest the benefits of independence, the traditional chiefs, the UPC nationalist leaders, and the 'masses'.

Robert Joseph (1986, 1st ed. 1977), the first noteworthy historian of the nationalist movement in Cameroon, discards the suspicion of Marxism or internationalist communism except in the case of a couple of radical leaders. By contrast, he accepts the thesis of the rebellion of Bameleke cadets against the French colonizer and the traditional authorities of chiefs and notables. Jean-François Bayart (1979: 233-281), in his seminal book on the State in Cameroon, expresses the same opinion in his last concluding chapter devoted to the tensions between the women and the male cadets on the one hand, and the stakeholders in the hegemonic alliance established by the French and the Cameroonian elites around Ahmadou Ahidjo, the first President of Cameroon.

Yet, Bayart refines considerably on previous analyses by stressing three points. The first one (p. 80) is the disappointment felt by most women and cadets with UPC leaders with the result that the ended up playing a game of their own. The second is the fact that oppressed social categories – those qualified as 'unimportant' ('*les sans importance*') by Bayart – are diversified and ranked. They themselves form a hierarchy. For example, he writes, some of the male cadets may be recruited amongst the traditional authorities by succeeding to a title, and, as a result, change camp. This simple observation accounts for the fact that, throughout the independence and post-independence periods, various political and social organizations (labour unions, youth leagues, political parties, independence movements) remained particularly unstable and fluid. The third point concerns what Bayart (1979: 256) calls the popular modes of political action, that is, actions or activities that do not seem to carry any political dimension at face value, and yet translate social and political conflicts into various domains of activity (consumption patterns, music, dress, the use of drugs or alcohol), and give them an expression. They open up a number of spaces or arenas in which the youth may play the confrontation with the colonial or post-colonial domination without taking the risk of open political dissent.

The popular modes of political action

Dominique Malaquais (2002), in her book on architecture, power and dissent in Cameroon gives a graphic account of such a popular mode of political action in Bamileke country around 1959-1960. She recounts (2002: 325-333) how thousands – even in some cases tens of thousands – of men, women, youth and children kept coming out at night to dig countless ditches across dirt and tarred roads all over the Bamileke country. These were not primarily intended to prevent the inroads of the various armed forces but to reclaim land for building and cultivation purposes, especially of food crops. In an economy that had been disrupted by the compulsory development of cash crops, the appropriation of much land by chiefs, notables and the colonial government at the expense of small holders, digging and cultivating such ditches were a means for the 'unimportant' of claiming agricultural and building land for their own use. Subsequently, the habit remained, in Bamileke country, to cultivate the roadsides.

Malaquais mentions the fact that such popular modes of political action are not recognized as such and hardly surface in official archives or in the news reports of the colonial government, nor in the major media. They may be found only in the daily newspapers that maintained journalists on the spot – mostly *Le Figaro* and *La Presse du Cameroun* – and that were read by the Cameroonian elite and the white colonists. The latter were primarily concerned with what happened in the countryside on a daily basis, for practical reasons. The historiographic problem, in this particular case as in many others, depends on a methodological one. It has to do with the kind of source and documentation put to use in writing history.

The contributions by Bayart and Malaquais open up a series of new questions regarding the historical situation of male cadets in Grassfields kingdoms from the onset of colonization to Independence. First, as Bayart said, they cannot be lumped together in a homogeneous category. They are diversified and ranked among themselves within a single kingdom. One has to distinguish between Christian converts and others, between the francophone Bamileke and their Grassfields cousins under British mandate, between the literati and the illiterate, etc.

Second, one has to question the political dimension of a broad range of activities that are not usually seen as political at face value. The digging of thousands of ditches across motorable roads, their cultivation and the building of houses on the short stretches of roads that were left intact are a case in point. This is also the case with the daily activities in Christian mission stations at the time. The Catholic clergy was still under White control and leaning heavily in favour of the policy of the French High Commissioner in Cameroon. However, since the 1920s, there was much tension, in the Catholic Church, between the White establishment and the Black clergy who felt in a position to establish a Black-controlled church. The colonial divide actually cut through the Churches and tended to reproduce, within the Church, the opposition between the elites and the 'unimportant' including the male cadets, often kept in the low status of catechist or convert.

Third, the contributions by Bayart and Malaquais underscore the fact that the split between the elite and the cadets is a historical one, that is, it depends on the dynamics of power and its change according to the political context. In order to explore it from a historical and anthropological point of view, one has to adopt a regressive analysis, starting from the later periods and working its way backwards in order to monitor the significant changes that bore upon the social condition of the 'unimportant'.

The history of violence in the Grassfields

The contribution of Dominique Malaquais underscores the significance of the historical sources and their nature. Nicolas Argenti (2007) accomplished a noticeable break-through along those lines. Whereas most anthropological and historical investigations relied so far on verbalized sources (oral traditions and history, interviews, archives, etc.), Argenti focuses his research on the memory of past events that is embodied in the performing arts, mostly masked dances and the practice of dance groups in the Grassfields, and more precisely in the kingdom of Oku. What turned out was that the memory of the domination by the notables and kings over male cadets and women, and the impact of the slave trade are embodied in these performances and could be read by implementing a careful ethnography of their practice. Argenti underlines the potential for control and violence embedded in Grassfields kingdoms. Its main target was and still is the youth, though in different ways nowadays and in the past.

Argenti's book represents a breakthrough in Grassfields studies. So far, most researchers in art history, anthropology, political history, etc., especially those with functionalist leanings, have tended to mystify and enchant the kingdoms of the Grassfields (for an example of this enchantment, see Northern 1984). These have been described as primeval idyllic communities under the guidance of paternal and benevolent kings in a gorgeous mountain environment. Their art, mostly carving, music, and dance performances, has been celebrated by countless amateurs. Argenti's iconoclastic book draws a picture that brings out the more gruesome aspects of the kingdoms, that is, the built in lines of conflict between royal and commoner lineages, elders and cadets, men and women, slave dealers and people sold in slavery. It reaches deep into the past, beyond the threshold of the first written archives, and produces a corpus of material and embodied archives that calls for more investigation in the future. It establishes the continuity of the social and political conflicts of interest between the category of the 'unimportant' and the kingdom elites under various forms: the slave trade, indentured labour under colonization, urban migrations, popular modes of political action such as music and 'jujus' (see Argenti 2004), conversion to Christianity, the domestication of globalized modernity through consumption. Argenti also underscores the lines of resistance of the cadets against the elites, in the past as well as in present-day Cameroon. This suggests that, at least in some kingdoms, there was some amount of awareness about the conflicts of interests and a potential for protest or even rebellion. We should remember this when dealing with the case of the Tapenta.

The political anatomy of domination

Yet, in my view, there is still more investigation to be done on the process of domination itself. Argenti's book (2007) rightly brings out the component of physical violence and control that inheres the slave trade (in the past), and the behaviour of the Police and Gendarmes under colonization and in contemporary Cameroon. This, however, is only one part of the picture. I have always been impressed by the compliance of the cadets I knew, ever so grateful to their father, to the king or to their *tankap* (their mother's father) for the life that had been given to them. This extends to all the ancestral principles of reproduction and wealth. So much so that, more often than not, the potential and deep conflict between elders and cadets is successfully pushed into oblivion and translated into a harsh competition amongst the cadets for whatever resource is kept out of their reach, that is, women, land, employment, money, etc. Consequently, the cadets tend to comply with the domination exercised by the hierarchy. There was, there still is, a fair degree of consent that I have underscored in my two books on the 'Pot-King' (2007 and 2009). It should be assessed and balanced against the potential for dissent underscored by Argenti.

Part of the trick comes from a discrepancy between the embodied procedural knowledge shared by all the subjects of the kingdom, and their verbalized knowledge. The procedural knowledge is propped against the bodily and material culture of containers, apertures, envelopes and contents. It is performed. It is neither explained nor exposed in so many words. It constructs the contrast between those – king and notables – who are endowed with an inside full of ancestral contents and those who, not having any direct access to the ancestors, are entirely dependent upon the elders for their access to wealth and reproduction. The imaginary of the Pot-King is a most powerful tool of domination because one cannot discuss it. It is performed, not explained or commented upon. The verbalizations, on their side, stress the generous benevolence of the elders to whom the women and cadets owe everything, including their own very life. They have no grip on the performances of the Pot-King.

This state of affairs shows that, in that particular case, domination is not achieved by the sole use of sheer force. It calls for a more sophisticated approach to domination. It would take into consideration what Béatrice Hibou (2011), following Foucault, calls a 'political anatomy of domination'. It would consider the subjectivities of the dominant and of the dominated, the compliance and consent of the latter, and the many unintended processes that contribute to producing some kind of normality.

The question of the subjectivity and the compliance and consent of the male cadets was most aptly raised by Pradelles de Latour (1991 and 2001) from a psychoanalytical point of view. Given the fact that, among the Eastern Bangwa, the male cadet is entirely submitted to the will of his father, how comes he can escape from the all-mightiness of the latter and avoid being caught in his narcissistic drive, with the effect of becoming insane? The answer given by Pradelles is that, in Bangwa, any subject is divided up between to discourses: that of his/her father, and that of the maternal grandfather, the one who has provided his daughter as a wife and a mother. The maternal grandfather is called 'the father who stands at the back'. His status is ambiguous since he is in a relationship of alliance with the father as a wife-taker and yet, he is considered as a 'father'. Thus, any subject has two fathers: the one who stands in front of him (for example when being anointed during the marriage ritual) and the other one at the back. Consequently, in Lacanian parlance, the subject is divided up between the two, as is the relationship of fatherhood. It should be stressed that, for Lacan, being a subject is not a given. It is acquired through a process of division between the act of enunciation and its contents, that is, what is enunciated, with the result that the subject is firmly established in a symbolic order. The conclusion drawn by Pradelles is that any Bangwa subject, although he/she is entirely submitted to the father (and the king), escapes the all-mightiness of the latter by being drawn away from it by the 'father at the back' who balances the discourse of the father and the paternal ancestors with another one that stands outside the sacred ideals of the father. By such means, any Bangwa subject is in a position to accept his/her fate and comply with the hierarchy without becoming insane. This contribution is most important in my view because it is grounded in a study of the subjectivity of the 'unimportant'. It avoids the shortcomings of the theory of rational choice and of functionalist political anthropology. It can be easily subsumed in a Foucauldian theory of domination that takes subjectivity into consideration.

The politics of sex in questions

Then there is the question of the politics of sex. As far as I can see, in Mankon as in most parts of the Grassfields, the control on genital sex was quite tight in the past and well into the 20th century. Genital sex was limited to married men and women. Male bachelors were effectively barred from it. I have quoted my sources and my interpretations in this respect in my book on the 'Pot-King' (2007: 233-266). On the basis of his fieldwork in Babungo, Ian Fowler (personal communication and 2012) expresses some scepticism in this regard. Eugen Zintgraff (1995: 324), the first White visitor of Babungo, he says, claims that unmarried males did engage in illicit heterosexual relations. Fowler himself was told of sexual practices that testify of more tolerance as regards the sexuality of women and youth of both sexes than in Mankon. For example, he says (personal communication) that sexual intercourse inter crura between unmarried youth was mentioned to him as both acceptable and pleasurable. This is in agreement with what Robert Brain (1977) had been told among the Eastern Bangwa (Fontem) where unmarried girls took lovers with whom they slept and obtained much erotic satisfaction short of penetration. When the girl married, the husband gave a gift to the lover for having refrained from full intercourse during his love affair. If I trust my many elderly informants (see for example the testimony of Julia in Warnier 2007: 242 – she was just one among many others and there is more evidence to the same effect), such practices would have been abhorrent in Mankon. I do not find any reason to mistrust what has been said to me, though I agree with Fowler (2012) when he claims that sexuality is a most difficult topic to investigate, and one in which we have to rely on oral testimonies that require much critical interpretation.

In order to reconcile what seem to be rather conflicting views of the politics of sex in the Grassfields, I would be tempted to conclude that there was a fair amount of variations and diversity in such matters from one kingdom or community to the next. We cannot assume that all the kingdoms of the Grassfields operated the same way. They shared a common civilisation indeed, but with much variation according to their own history and to the place they occupied in the regional ecumene. In my book on regional hierarchies (Warnier 1985), I tried to point out significant differences between the kingdoms of Bafut, Mankon, Nkwen, Bambili and Bambwi, and to identify the various parameters, mostly their location in the regional system viewed from a Leachean point of view, that could contribute to explaining such variations.

Moreover, Nicolas Argenti (personal communication) and I came to the conclusion that social practices that were named and talked about in one community went unnamed and repressed in another one. Or else, they obtained, but in a significantly different ways. For example, this is the case with the excrements of the king or the community, that is never explicitly mentioned as such in Mankon, as far as I am able to ascertain, whereas around Ide, in the Metchun valley, according to Masquelier (1978: 55), the last of the six Ide villages was considered as his 'anus' and explicitly designated as such. Whenever the six villages held a forum, the Ifakpa village, being the last one along the line, had to shout towards the outside the bad words voiced during the meeting as so many excreta. In that particular case, there was an elaborate discourse, putting crude words on the practice, whereas, in Mankon, regarding analogous kinds of practice, there was a taboo on such an explicit discourse. True enough, there were significant differences in the political organization of the two communities, since the Mankon had a powerful king, whereas the Ide had none and were running their affairs through public forums of discussion.

Similar comments could be made concerning many other practices. For example, it was generally believed, all over the Grassfields, that the truth regarding any dead person could be found in its bodily contents. In some kingdoms such as Bafou (see Miaffo 1977 and Salpeteur 2009), this belief provided the rationale for fairly systematic vernacular public autopsies (that are being revitalized in the early 21st century). However, many other kingdoms relied more on an external post mortem examination and on divination, as seems to have been the case in Mankon.

We may conclude tentatively that there were significant variations in practice and discourse from one kingdom to the next. I do not think we may extrapolate from one kingdom to the next or from one community to the Grassfields as a whole. Yet, there are undoubtedly underlying assumptions obtaining all over the highlands, such as the governmentality of containers, apertures, envelopes, and contents, that translate into many different empirical practices and discourses. Such underlying assumptions constitute the basic tenets of Grassfields civilization.

It is now time to return to the question of the possible rebellion of male cadets during the last two centuries and to conclude by summarizing two points:

1. One has to distinguish between various social categories within the general category of the 'unimportant' and rank them in a hierarchy of domination. Women constitute a category of their own. In the past, they enjoyed a fair degree of economic autonomy due to their involvement in agriculture and to their capacity to cooperate in work organizations, in dance groups, and, in some cases, in protest mobs such as the well documented *Anlu* (see Ritzenthaler 1960).

Male cadets, by contrast, formed a category that exhibited a fair degree of internal diversification. Some of them were selected, often early in life, to serve at the palace (see Photograph on page 108), or to succeed to high office. This was the highest-ranking sub-category – that of the potential successors. Down below, one would find a series of other categories, from those who would perhaps be given a wife in their lifetime, thanks to the work of their mother, those who would stay in the household as labourer, and at the bottom of the hierarchy, those who would be sold into slavery, and, under colonization, recruited as forced or indentured labour. This category is still more or less in existence, with the youth who have no prospect for access to work, land or money, neither in the Grassfields, nor in town for those who were born there.

2. One can match specific individual options as identified by Hirschman (1970) to each of these categories. The category of the would-be successors has always favoured loyalty to the elite, and compliance with the tenets of political domination. The exit option could not be contemplated before the onset of colonization. It became possible when Christian missions, urban migrations and the development of market economy opened up specific spaces in which escapees could set their foot. It can be empirically documented. Apathy was the preserve of those who stayed in the household as low-ranking unmarried labour. The voice option, in the form of protest or rebellion, is the most difficult to document from an empirical point of view. There is at least one reason for this: in order to identify it, one would have to have access to the subjectivity of those engaged in protest or rebellion. We know about the Tapenta and about UPC activists, but we know precious little about the subjective experience of the enrolment of the rank and file into a Tapenta gang or into the UPC. We have access to the various and conflicting statements of the leaders (such as Um Nyobé or Moumié), though these statements were obscured by the many polemics and ideological interpretations that have piled up upon them.

By contrast, we do not have any access to the lived experience of the rank and file who did not leave any oral or written articulate discourse or statement. Besides, when a case for protest can be made, it remains to be determined against whom it is or was directed: the kingdom hierarchies, the colonizer, the White religious establishment, the armed forces of the colonial or post-colonial State, the Government. It has to be established in each particular case. The research conducted by D. Malaquais (2002) shows that the women and youth who dug thousands of ditches across the roads in Bamileke country around 1959-1960 were not members of the UPC. They developed a 'popular mode of political action' aimed at appropriating the local space, arable and building land, and exercise a modicum of autonomy in the general pandemonium. Did it amount to protesting? And against whom? This is far from clear insofar as the picture was not accompanied by any kind of verbalized caption stating what the action was all about. I would now extend this conclusion to the Tapenta. However, this would not rule out the possibility of the Tapenta being henchmen of some kings such as the king of Bali-Nyonga. Clearly, there is still much research to be done, especially in Mission archives, to document this episode, and shed some light on the history of domination and dissent in Grassfields history.

One last thing about the Hirschmanian options: any given subject may successively try different options in his lifetime. Loyalty may fail to pay off in the end, in which case the subject may test the exit option and migrate to the town or to the Mission station. In case of success (see Warnier 1993 concerning the itineraries of accumulation and the material culture of success), the migrant may revert to the loyalty option, acquire a palace or lineage title, and built a house in his village of origin. But in case of failure, he may come back to the village for want of a better prospect and stay there as an apathetic bachelor.

Endnotes

1. This chapter was first published in a edited volume in honour of Mrs. E.M. Chilver under the title "Rebellion, Defection and the position of Male Cadets: A Neglected Category", in I. Fowler & D. Zeitlyn (eds.): *African Crossroads. Intersection Between History and Anthropology in Cameroon*, Providence, Oxford: Berghahn Books, 1996: 115-124.

2. According to E.M. Chilver, this is a pidginisation of 'interpreter' (pers. communication).

3. By religious conversion, providing service for Europeans, the market economy, the 'Kamenda' adventure, the disregard for the hierarchy, the reference to the White man rather than to the Fon.

4. The analysis of this complex incident, which took place in a kingdom which was in many ways atypical of the rest, would involve too long an excursus. An account of it is to be found in Tardit's monograph of the Bamoum kingdom (1980: 170-99).

5. I have described these in Warnier (1993).

The Mankon palace[1]

The Surroundings

Details of the location of the palace can be seen on Map 1, which shows that the Fon's marketplace, the dancing field, the palace itself, and the patch of secondary forest, all follow a general north-south line. The whole complex, not including the forest, is about 400m long and extends over a low hill, rising to an altitude of 1260m between the dancing field and the palace. The dancing field and the marketplace slope down towards the north (with an average slope of 3.3 per cent), and the palace extends over the southern slope of the hill, which is somewhat steeper, as can be seen from the number of stairways connecting the various yards and buildings (Map 3). The palace is surrounded by a number of higher hills, which have fairly steep slopes, and an *Hyparrenia* grass cover which was formerly used as thatch for roofs. Compounds and farms occupy the lower parts of the hills and all the valleys as well as the other hills, to the north and northeast.

A secondary forest to the south of the palace (*kekfure* = 'forest')[2] extends right to the walls of the Fon's quarter, into which two doors allow easy passage. Tsendi of Ala'a Akuma, to whom I owe most of my information, justifies the presence of this grove on purely practical grounds: it allows the Fon to hide in case of need! However, there is more to it than that: the Fon entertains a spiritual relationship with the forest, his ancestors, the animals and other beings living there. He may retire into the sacred forest at times of illness and uncertainty to be reassured and strengthened.[3]

Besides the forest, all the land surrounding the palace complex is compound and farm land. Nowadays, it is of an orchard type, with open farms of maize, groundnuts, *Colocasia*, plantains, yams and various green vegetables cultivated under shade trees (*Dracaena arborea, Markhamia tomentosa, Ficus natalensis*, and other *Ficus*) or trees of economic importance (*Kola nitida, Elaeis*, avocado, mango, eucalyptus). In the 19th century, European-introduced species were of course absent and the farms were hedged with lines of *Ficus, Dracaena*, kola trees, etc., supporting a lattice of raffia stems to keep the goats in the fields, or out of them, as the case may be. Between the palace and the Mezam river extend the flat hydromorphic banks of the river, on which the women can cultivate dry season crops, and where the Fon has fairly large tracts of land.

The Marketplace *miti fo* in 1973 (Map 1)

The market is held every eighth day, on one of the two weekly holidays on which the deaths of the last two Fons are commemorated. The market takes place on *Samne*, on which Angwa'fo II died, in 1920. The day on which the market is held is not the only connection between the market and the palace. Public announcements are broadcast there, and the proximity of the palace allows an easy maintenance of order by the masker Mabu' should a dispute occur.

In the 19th century, the marketplace was small, serving only local functions, the regional trade being handled by trading households. Only local exchanges took place there and few foreign traders attended.

Characteristically, the market day was not synchronized with those of the large markets with regional functions such as *Tad* in Medig, *Kwor* in Nyang Funam, and *Keu* in Ngwokong, known from the day of the *Meta'* week on which they took place. Those were synchronized, and fixed ne varietur, whereas the Mankon market day changed with each new Fon. The marketplace is a rectangular space, approximately 60 by 80m. A single row of mud blocks houses with zinc roofs surrounds the area on all four sides.

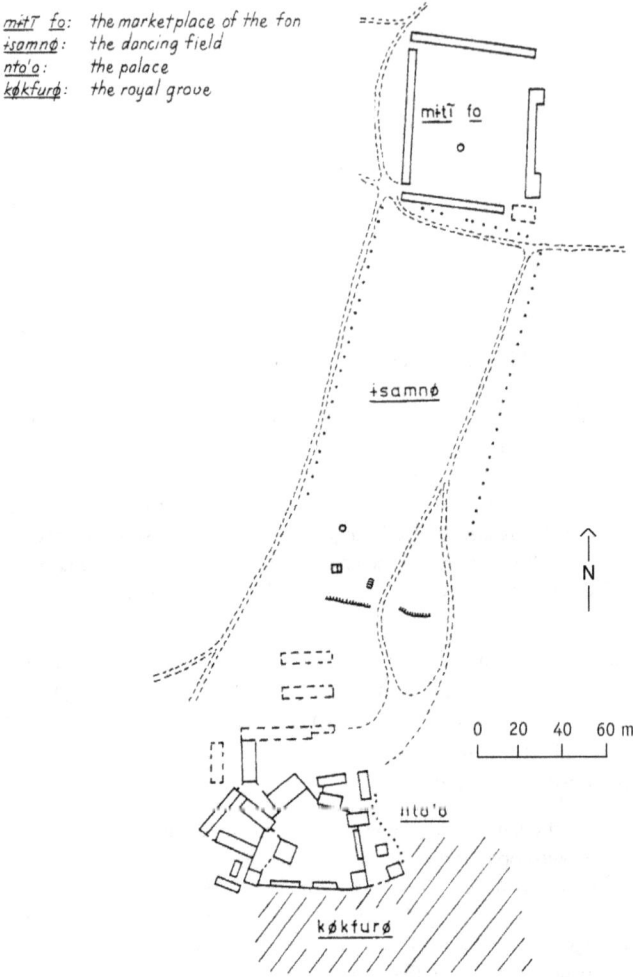

mɨtī fo: the marketplace of the fon
tsamnø: the dancing field
nto'o: the palace
køkfurø: the royal grove

Map 1. The Mankon Palace Precinct

Besides the houses, the structures that can be seen on the marketplace are a water tap, a raised stone about 50 cm high, and a kola-nut tree. The raised stone falls under the category of *netchwere*, that I would call, for want of a better term, a 'ritual' stone. It stands for a given space and represents it. It focuses the ceremonial and ritual actions concerning the said space. Once a year, at the time of *ngang fo* ('the medicine of the Fon'), palace retainers put apotropaic medicines around it. That seems to be its only function. The kola-nut tree is about 15 m high. It is surrounded by a mat enclosure, about 2.5m in diameter, supported by Ficus poles. Within the enclosure, there is a *Markhamia tomentosa* (*ewa* in Mankon) much smaller than the kola tree, and a *Dracaena sp.* of a larger species than the very common *Dracaena deisteliana* (*nkeng* in Mankon), yet not of the *arborea* species (*ndobe* in Mankon), and known in Mankon as *nkengnkeng*. Immediately outside the enclosure, pressing right against it, are tufts of the hard *Sporobolus africanus* called *maala'a* or *mabyen* in Mankon. All those plants are protected, that is, people do not cut or uproot them. The only information I could discover on that association was that, besides providing shade, it protects lost and found items that can be thrown into the mat enclosure, where palace retainers collect them and safe keep them until they are claimed.

The Dancing Field [*samne*] in 1973 (Maps 1 and 2)

The dancing field is also a rectangular space, 170m long and 75m wide, extending immediately south of the marketplace, between the latter and the palace buildings. Its function is to accommodate large gatherings held in connection with palace activities: the annual dry season festival, death celebrations of Fons and palace officials, the ritual *nisa'*, etc. It is covered in grass, except on its higher part (the last 40m), where the area around the Fon's seat and various structures is kept free of vegetation. Rows of cypresses line it on all except the southern side. Photographs taken in 1959 by Ritzenthaler (published in 1962:69 and 71), at the time of the death ceremony of Fon Ndi' Furu show a number of large trees that have been felled since that date.

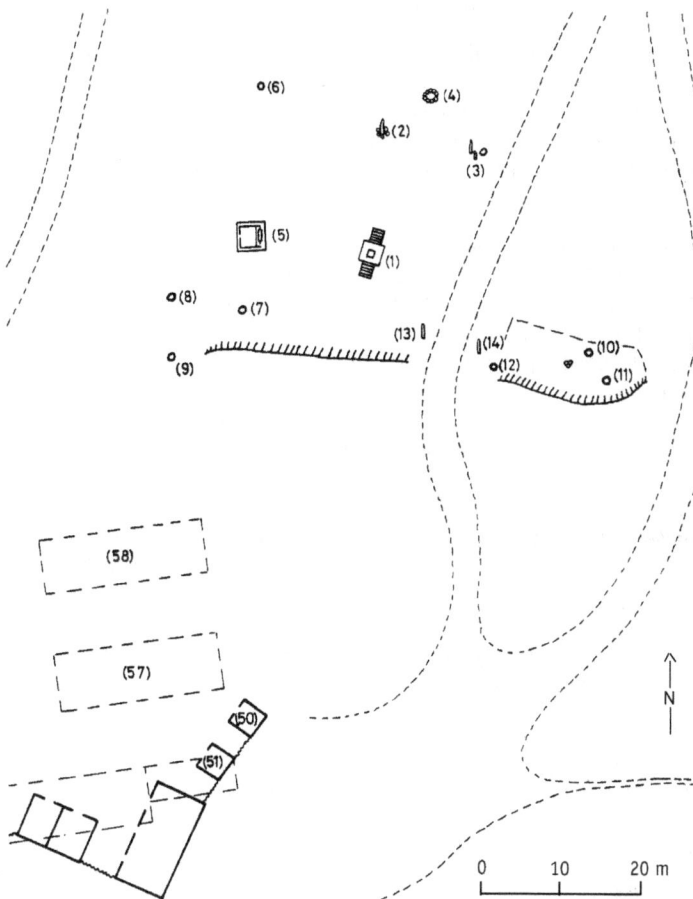

Map 2. The Higher Section of the Dancing Field

121

Most of the structures that can be seen in the higher part of the dancing field, nearest to the palace, are connected with its ceremonial functions. The throne of the Fon (*adi'i angangne fo*: 'the place where the Fon sits' - **1** on Map 2), is a stone and cement platform onto which one can climb by two stairways, one facing the field, and the other on the opposite side. On the platform, there is a square seat of cemented stones on which the Fon may sit, usually on a leopard's pelt or a valuable rug, with another one under his feet, surrounded by a couple of palace retainers either on the platform itself, or about it. On ceremonial occasions such as the annual dance, a couple of palace retainers, standing on the platform, blow ivory oliphants, while another one beside the platform occasionally plays a double iron gong.

In front of the throne are three structures: a raised basalt monolith (**2** on Map 2), 180cm high, surrounded by a few small specimens of *ewa* (*Markhamia tomentosa*). This raised stone falls into the category of netchwere or 'ritual stone', as the presence of *Sporobolus* and *Markhamia* indicates. People refer to it simply as *ngo' mbye bwerefo*, that is, 'the stone beside the throne of the Fon'. Two other basalt raised stones (**3** on Map 2) can be seen some 12 m to the east of the first one. The taller one is 185cm, the smaller one is ca. 70cm high. A tree *ewa* (*Markhamia tomentosa*) grows next to them. Those two stones are again called netchwere. The only function of structures **2** and **3** is to receive the apotropaic medicines put in various places by palace retainers at the beginning of the agricultural cycle. No other ritual is performed on them or in connection to them.

North of the netchwere is a low earth platform about 40cm above ground level, circular in shape, and supported by a small dry stone wall (**4** on Map 2). The two forked posts (*letya* in Munggaka, *ati mbom abinge*, that is: 'customary sticks of the dance' in Mankon) of the Lela borrowed from the Bali, and performed during the annual festival, are stuck into the platform. For a photograph of two similar posts taken in Bafut, see Ritzenthaler (1962: 128)[(4)]. The platform is called *bombabinge*, that is: 'building the dance' (the annual festival is called *abingefo*, that is: 'the dance of the Fon').

Fifteen meters west of the Fon's throne is a small hut (**5**) built on an earth platform this time supported by a cemented stones wall. It is called *Ndere Takumbeng* – *Takumbeng* being used to designate either a society or the whole of Mankon. *Ndere* seems to be used only in connection with the hut of Takumbeng and could probably be translated as 'the shrine of Takumbeng', It is divided up into two chambers of unequal size. The one facing east, which is entirely open and rather shallow, shelters the slit-gong used in sending coded messages from the palace. It is similar to the one seen on Plate 33 of Ritzenthaler's monograph of Bafut (1962:70). The other chamber shelters an altar (*nebete*) made of a few stones. This chamber is walled on all four sides, and access to it is through a small doorway cut into its western wall. The shrine of Takumbeng, as can be seen on Ritzenthaler's photograph, is a raffia stem structure that is not plastered with mud like any ordinary house. Instead, it is entirely covered with dried young leaves of the raffia palm. Every year, at the approach of the dry season, *Takumbeng Ala'a tsum*, that is, 'Takumbeng country all' or 'all the members of Takumbeng' are summoned to the dancing field. Only members of the lineage societies called Takumbeng – men and women – are allowed to join in. Each lineage lodge brings a young raffia palm stem (*ntsara*). The leaves are split into two, and stuck into the raffia lattice of the shrine, in an act of fictitious building. Following this gathering, the Fon and Nkwa, a notable of the clan Bon Anyerengum, perform a libation on the altar of Takumbeng, in the shrine, a rite on which I do not possess any information.

It must be noted that the young stems of the raffia palm (*Raphia humilis*) appear connected with the palace in various ways. They can be seen hanging above the door on *Nechwim* (the grave-shrine of the Fon), some could be seen on the steps of the Fon's throne on the day known as *nzwi Mesongong*, before the beginning of the annual festival. The calabashes of raffia wine sent to the palace have a stopper made of two raffia leaves pointing straight out of the neck of the calabash.

The landscape of that part of the dancing field is completed by two *Ficus* trees (**6** and **7** – *ewome* in Mankon), a kola-nut tree (**8**), an avocado tree (**9**), two *Markhamia tomentosa* (**10**) and (**11**), and one cypress (**12**). The southern limit of the field is marked by an earth bank. The motorable road leading to the palace used to pass between two raised stones (**13** and **14**), near the Fon's throne, but has now been diverted 25 m further east. These two stones are not 'ritual' ones (netchwere) since their sole function is to materialize the gateway of the dancing field. They are simply called *ngo'* (stones).

The Palace (*nto'o*) in 1973 (Map 3)

a. The Structures

The Mankon palace can easily be divided up into four quarters: those of Kwi'fo, the Fon, the 'women of the palace', and lastly, the public quarter. In each quarter, the basic unit is the yard (*esang*) with its surrounding buildings. As it is in other palaces (see Shanklin on Fuli and Laikom & Pradelles on Bangoua, Tardits on Bamoum, in the edited volume of *Paideuma* 31, 1985), the yards may be closed by walls, buildings, and fences, or open, depending on whether access to them is restricted or free for all.

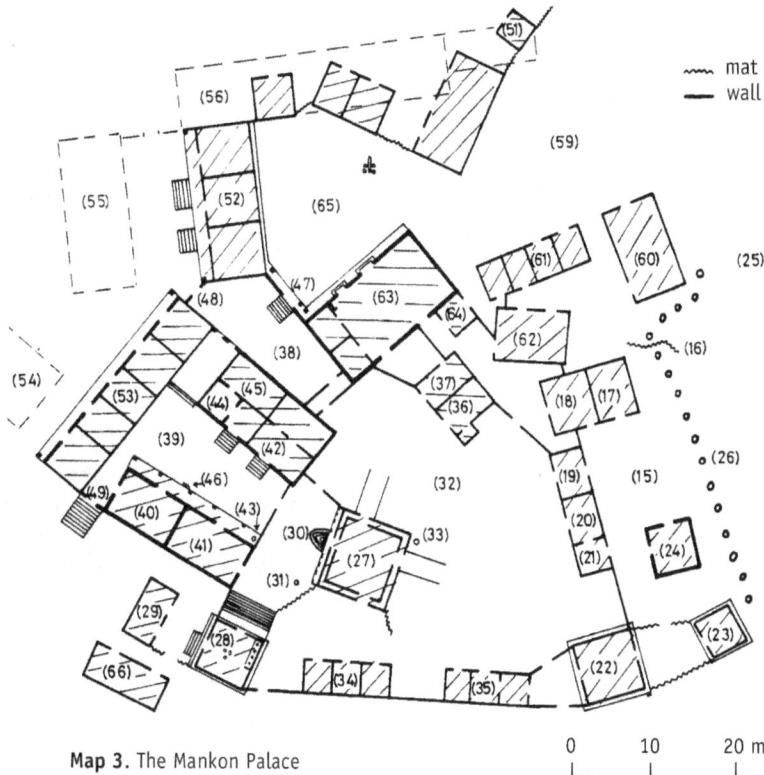

Map 3. The Mankon Palace

b. The quarter of Kwi'fo

The quarter of *Kwi'fo* is known as *Abye Kwi'fo* or simply *Abye Kwi'* (15 on Map 3). In 1973 its northern limit was marked by a mat fence (16). The first building that one meets on entering the quarter is *Nda Ngang* ('the house of medicine'), partitioned into two: a store room for the medicines (17) and the meeting room of the medicine men (18), with a double entry: one on the side of Kwi'fo; the other on the side of the Fon. It is in Nda Ngang that the apotropaic medicines to be put on the 'ritual' stones and other places are prepared. Next to it is found *Nda Menang* (19), 'the house of the secret', which is the name of the palace masker in charge of arresting people accused of witchcraft, or crime, and which seems to have been connected with the slave-trade. This house has a double entry allowing contact between the Fon and Kwi'fo officials. Next to it is a store room (20) and next again *Nda Mesongong* (21): the palace war lodge that plays a leading role in the war rituals performed at the beginning of the annual dance. Again, royal notables and Kwi'fo officials can have access to it, each of them from its own side. This also obtains in the last building on the line: *Nda Ala'a* ('the house of the country' – 22) whose members, some of them of royal status, some of them commoners, used to have a monopoly on the organization of communal hunting. Nda Ala'a shelters a *nebwe'tene awem* ('altar of hunting') on which rituals used to be performed to insure success in hunting. Societies other than Nda Ala'a could also meet in the building, e.g. *Alub Ala'a*, and *Mbebvure*. The latter has an altar in the building. In the same building an esoteric rite takes place occasionally, which gathers four people around the Fon, and has to do with the welfare of the country. Also, in the past, some of the notables met in the house before an armed conflict to perform a ritual aimed at insuring success. In this ritual, the grass *mabyen* (*Sporobolus africanus*) that is allowed to grow near 'ritual' stones and other similar structures was tied in a knot. We shall see that the same knot was used in the arrest of people accused of witchcraft by the masker Minang (Further details on Nda Ala'a are given in Warnier 1975: 213-14, 238-40, 249-53, and passim).

Opposite Nda Ala'a to the east, is found *Nimoni Kwi'fo* (**23**), or 'parlor of Kwi'fo', where until the 1920's, when there were nearly one hundred young retainers at the palace, they assembled to play music and listen to the instructions of either one of the three Kwi'fo officials (*Foti, Bechi* and *Awambeng*). The retainers also chatted, rested and drank as well as played music in *Azoga Kwi'fo* (**24**) further to the north. It is made of a roof resting on four strong pillars. Along its southern wall is a raised platform the functions of which are not known to the author.

In the past, the Kwi'fo complex of buildings had nine other components that have not been maintained as 1,3their functions have disappeared. To the east of the entrance to Abye Kwi' were eight houses in which the young men of the category 'retainers of the palace' (sg: *ntsenda nto*') used to have their living quarters (**25**). Others – the 'retainers of Abye Kwi' ' – used to stay at night in the buildings opening on Abye Kwi' itself.

Lastly, another house, *Nda Ngu* ('the house of the poison ordeal' – **26**) used to stand approximately where it is indicated on the map. This is where Kwi'fo officials prepared poison to be administered to persons accused of witchcraft.

c. The Fon's Quarter

The heart of the Fon's quarter is made of two buildings: the *Atsum* or 'lake' (**27**), which is the Fon's dwelling. It is built on a raised platform sustained by stone walls, and it is surrounded on all sides by a corridor closed to the outside by a wall of date palm trunks (*Phoenix reclinata*), raffia stems, and raffia mats. On its western side (that of the main entrance), it has an open shallow verandah. On that side, the roof is supported by a row of double date palm trunk pillars. The roof is thatched, and it is crowned by a small thatched steeple (*ko'ti*) which contains apotropaic medicines.

The other important building is *Nechwim* (**28**), the shrine in which the late Fons are buried. Three Fons are buried in the Nechwim of Ndzu' Mankunge: Ndi' Furu II alias Fomukong who died c. 1870-75, Angwa'fo II who died in 1920, and Ndi' Furu III who died in 1959. I was told that at the old palace of Ala'a Nkye, each fon was buried in a separate Nechwim. Every week (of 8 days), the last two Fons are remembered on the day of their death: Angwa'Fo II on the day Samne, Ndi' Furu III on *Zinka'ni*. Those two days are traditional holidays for the whole Mankon population.

The Nechwim has two doors: one that opens up on the Atsum yard, the other one that opens up on a small courtyard located outside the Fon's enclosure, and that faces *Nda Anyechye* (**29**) also called *Nda Ntsenda Nechwim*: 'the house of the servant of Nechwim', in which some palace retainers of royal status used to have their living quarters. The others stayed in the Nechwim, with the high-ranking palace officials. The shrine was also the meeting place of palace officials, notables of the royal clan and the retainers of royal status who were sometimes referred to as Takumbeng. The sitting order, in the house, is as follows: the Fon in the North-east corner, between him and the northern door, a retainer. To the western side of the door: Ndifomukong, Mumafomukong, and Tabyen, successor in the line of the first-born of Angwa'fo II. Along the western and southern walls, all the other Muma and Ndifo. The shrines were located along the eastern wall. Above the western door of the Nechwim, on the outside, a couple of raffia palm stems are fixed, and plastered with the rumen of the rams sacrificed every year on the late Fon's graves. Between the Atsum and the Nechwim is *esang Atsum* ('the yard of Atsum' – **30**), closed on its western and northern sides by stone walls with doors, and on its southeastern side by a mat fence. In the yard is *abwerefo* (**31**): 'the seat of the Fon', on which the Fon can rest while meeting with the people (retainers, royal officials and women of the palace) who have access to the yard. The yard to the other side of the Atsum is *esang nto*' ('the yard of the palace' – **32**), access to which is far more restricted than to esang Atsume: the royal notables going to Nda Ala'a, Nda Mesongong, or Nda Minang may pass through. In addition to them, only the retainers and the women of the palace who have paid a due (which was 20 brass rods at the end of the 19th century) and a few notables could go there. The yard is vast, ornamented with shrubs, flowers, a bitter cola tree and a plum tree. The Fon has a stone seat (33): *abwere ankware nkye*, 'seat take water' where he can 'take water', that is, wash himself – the word *suge* (to wash) being inappropriate in the case of the Fon. Along the southern wall of the yard are two buildings: *nto' aba'* ('the palace of aba' – 34) nowadays partitioned into a kitchen, a dining room and a pantry; and *nto'o melu'* ('the palace of the raffia wine' – 35). The latter is partitioned into three store-rooms, two of which have recently been handed over to Kwi'fo whose retainers can reach it through Nda Ala'a, and a small yard located between them and the Kwi'fo store rooms. To the north of the yard is a toilet and a bath-room and *Tsa bangye binto'* ('the hall of the women of the palace' – 37) which has two doors: one opening onto the palace yard, the other one opening on a small yard which allows people who do not have access to the palace yard to reach it. There, the women of the palace can assemble with the Fon and Maafo.

Until perhaps the 1920s, the Fon's quarter extended westwards to include two yards: *ntsu ebu'* ('the mouth of the entrance' – 38), *esang nto'* ('the yard of the palace' – 39) and the buildings to which they gave access. Nowadays, these two yards and their buildings have been turned to public use. On the spot marked (40) there used to be *Tsa bonto'* ('the hall of the children of the palace'), where resident sons and daughters of the

The Atsum of Bafut ca. 1910. Although this photograph was not taken in Mankon, it is included here to illustrate a palace setting in the past. The Mankon Atsum was (and still was a century later) similar. At the top of the steps, the fon, with women of the palace on his right and children on his left. Courtesy of Photo-Archiv, Rautenstrauch-Joest-Museum, Köln.

Fon met. This building was pulled down by Fon Ndi' Furu together with the next one, *Atsume Afotchu'* ('the dwelling of Fo Tchu' – 41 – that refers to the Fon of Mbu' who used to stay when visiting his very close friend Angwa'fo II). The two buildings were replaced by long stone and mud-block buildings partitioned into two rooms which kept the names of the buildings they replaced. Nowadays, the Fon gives public audiences in

Tsa bon nto' to which any visitor is automatically directed. Private audiences are given in Atsume Afotchu', and in a small lounge (42) furnished with bookshelves and comfortable armchairs. The Fon has a seat (43) at the end of the verandah in front of Tsa bon nto' and Atsume Afotchu', where he sits on every *Zinka'ne* for a couple of hours in the afternoon, and where he hears and discusses matters concerning the palace. The spot offers a number of advantages: from where he is seated, the Fon can see incoming visitors who are more numerous on the Mankon holiday. Some of them are directed to the public audience hall or to a private one, where the Fon will join them later on, while others take their turn in the queue which naturally lines up under the narrow verandah in front of the Fon, at sufficient distance to allow the Fon to have private conversations in a low voice when needed.

There is another building (44) in which the Fon's clerk has his office along with a small anteroom. The palace Museum (45) is also located there. This building does not seem to have any traditional name, but I may be misinformed on that point.

King Nka'fo III in the couryard of the palace (esang nto', n° 39 on the map 3) shortly after his succession in 1959. In the background, the atsum (n° 27 on map 3). Courtesy of the Mankon Palace.

A last feature is worth mentioning in connection with this yard: that is the netchwere *nala'a*: the 'ritual stone of the country' (46). It is a cluster of three or four small stone boulders of different sizes that seem to have been dumped in no particular order. It is a shrine where the Fon must sacrifice a goat to reconcile any member of the royal clan who has left Mankon on exile, and has come back. The goat, plus various gifts are brought by the returned exile. The commoners have the equivalent shrine in the 'hall of the notables' (62).

One can leave the palace yards (or enter them) through three gates or *ntsu nto'* (sg: 'mouth of the palace' – 47, 48 and 49). In the past, access to the palace yards, reached by passing through those gates, was restricted to the women and the children of the palace, palace retainers, notables of the royal clan, and men who had made the necessary payments. They could not enter, however, without having removed shoes and caps, and left all weapons outside. Nowadays, anyone can enter and only a few people leave their sandals along the walls outside the gates with such things as walking sticks, umbrellas and hats.

The palace layout is such that the most important buildings (the Atsume, the Nechwim, Nda Ala'a, and Nimoni Kwi'fo) are lower than the less important ones on the hill side, and that the normal access is from above, through the less important yards and buildings, to the ones with higher status, and more restricted access. This disposition obtains in most traditional compounds, where the house of the household head is located lower than all others, and can be reached only from above.

d. The quarter of the 'women of the Palace'

It extends to the west-northwest of the Fon's quarter. In the past, the quarter of the 'women of the palace' (*bangye beunto'*, sg: *mangye nto*) was made of individual huts. Some of them (e.g. **50** and **51**) were still visible in 1973, but Ndi' Furu had pulled down a number of them, to replace them by stone and mud-brick buildings covered with zinc roofs (**52** and **53**). In 1973, I did not survey the women's quarter. In 1980, the Fon pulled down all the buildings that did not meet sufficient standards of comfort, hygiene and safety, and built five new buildings (**54, 55, 56, 57** and **58** - see Map 2), partitioned into individual rooms. The whole quarter has been landscaped with a bulldozer, and it gives an orderly impression that contrasts with the intricacies of the old quarter. I did not survey the quarter in 1982, and the location and dimensions of the buildings marked in dotted lines are only approximate. Among those living in the women's quarter is *Maafo*, the real or titular mother of the Fon.

She has her own residence: *atua Ma* ('the head of Ma'), and her own yard: *asang Ma* ('the yard of Ma'). Women of the palace have never been secluded, and access to their quarter is free for all. Kin and friends can visit them and pay homage to Maafo. As part of the rebuilding program of the palace, one of the 'houses of the women of the palace' (sg.: *nda bangye beunto'* – **53** on the map) was turned to other uses: the inner partitions were pulled down, large windows were carved into the walls, and new partitions erected to make a large conference or reception hall, corridors, and various other rooms.

e. The 'public' quarter

Approaching the palace from the dancing field (which is the normal approach), the first yard encountered upon reaching the palace is *isamne Mbebvure* ('the dancing field of Mbebvure' – **59**). The members of the society Mbebvure whose head is Tamandam, the clan head of Bon BeNdi' Siri, has exclusive rights over rituals directed towards cleansing a burnt down house from pollution, and sending fire on the houses of criminals or on an enemy village. The society met at Nda Ala'a where it had a shrine (*nebe'te Mbebvure*).

To the south of this yard stood three buildings: a school for the children of the palace (**60**), a building divided into four rooms used, from east to west, as (a) an office for the 'Mankon State Union' – a kind of credit union created by the Fon around 1960; (b) a store room for foodstuffs used by the women of the palace; (c) a store room where the debris of corn thrashing were piled up; and (d) a store room for a kitchen (**64**) located nearby. The third building was *Tsa Bikum* (the hall of the notables' – **62**) where the council of the Mankon notables holds its meetings. The Tsa Bikum shelters a *netchwere nebikum* ('ritual stone of the notables'), on which the Fon sacrifices a goat for the reconciliation of returning exiles of commoner status. The school and the building (**61**) have been pulled down recently, and replaced by a new large building the functions of which I have not ascertained.

Around 1981, a cement-block wall was erected between the 'dancing field of Mbebvure' and the next yard: *sang Nda Mukong* ('the yard of the House of Spears' – **65**). There is an iron gate in the wall, which now marks the entrance to the palace in a more formal manner than the small door (**47**) named 'the mouth of the palace'. There used to be four raised stones in the middle of the yard of the 'House of Spears'.

These have recently been replaced by one basalt monolith about 120 cm high, surrounded by a few boulders. It is a 'ritual' stone or netchwere also called *ngo' ngang fo* ('the stone of the medicine of the Fon') because palace retainers put the apotropaic medicines around it, as on all other netchwere. On the southern side of the yard is Nda Mukong ('the House of Spears') – a large stone and brick building which replaces an old hall whose functions were connected to warfare. It seems that the hall used to be the meeting place for all the leaders of the Mankon war clubs or *ta manjong* (sg: 'father of warrior lodge'), and that male visitors to any quarter of the palace left their spears and cutlasses there before going any further.

127

The present Nda Mukong is used for public gatherings, such as students' meetings during the 'Mankon student's week', or when a Mankon lineage pays a group visit to the palace. This is why a kitchen (**64**) was added to it, because no such gathering can take place without some food being shared. In the same building are found a small office and a library. The yard of the house may be put to use on the same occasions as the house itself, in which case it serves as a small dancing field.

I should finally mention a few public buildings, to the south of the palace, namely *Nda abyang Takumbeng* ('the house of arbitration of Takumbeng' – **66**), built around 1977, to serve as a customary court which could arbitrate conflicts that the civil or criminal courts of the Cameroon State would not handle, such as failing to attend communal work, breaking Mankon laws, adultery with a woman of the palace and land disputes. The judges are appointed by the Mankon council. Besides this building, are couples of store-houses, and below them, outside the area covered by the map, a pigsty.

f. The furniture of the Palace

The Mankon palace was burnt to the ground in 1901 so that nothing of the 19th century furniture is left. The offices and reception halls are now equipped with European style furniture: cushion armchairs, wooden chairs, tables, benches, bookshelves, etc. The more 'traditional' buildings (the Atsum, the Nechwim, and the whole of Abye Kwi') are furnished in a traditional way, although I cannot give any description because I did not visit them, with the exception of Azoga Kwi', Nda Mesongong, and Nda Ngang. There, the furniture is made of logs, raffia stem benches and stools, wooden carved stools, raffia stems shelves and baskets for storage. The houses of the women of the palace used to be furnished in a rather 'traditional' manner: a cooking hearth with three stones at the centre, beds, stools, and shelves made of raffia stems, a tray hanging above the fire, and maize hanging from the ceiling. Wooden mortars and pestles, aluminum cooking pans, plastic buckets, and enamelware complete the kitchen equipment, while clothing and valuables are kept in a wooden trunk or a couple of suitcases.

Kwi'fo retainers keep the paraphernalia of Kwi'fo at the palace, that is, double iron gongs, the 'bag of Kwi'fo', the tall drum, harps, sisal hoods donned by maskers, and whistles, etc. Four large slit gongs (sg. *Kwinga*) can be seen at the palace. Two are used for calling notables in asang Nda Mukong, the third is in Ndere Takumbeng and the fourth one on the marketplace. In addition, the palace keeps a number of important objects, such as an *azo'*: a wooden carved bowl used in mixing camwood powder and palm oil for the ritual anointing of people (e.g. daughters upon marriage, successors); a 'cutlass of the country' (*mungwi mala'a*; a butchering board for noble game (*awate or aka'te*) and a 'pot of the ground' (*antong shye*) used for cooking animals found dead; the musical instruments of royal societies and dances; the Wukari or Bamum-Bamileke tie-dye indigo cloths displayed on ceremonial occasions; and the flag displayed on the dancing field during the Fon's annual dance.

For want of space, this paper cannot deal with the inhabitants of the palace (the Fon, the retainers, the women of the palace, the palace notables), nor with the yearly cycle of palace activities (the annual festival, the various rituals, the poison ordeal), for which I can only refer the reader to what I wrote in 1975, 1985 and in the present volume.

Problems of Classification

There is a direct correspondence, in the palace, between segregated spaces (marketplace, dancing field, the various quarters, yards and buildings) on the one hand, and various social, political and economic groups and functions on the other hand. This is commonplace and does not require any special comment. By contrast, the disposition of space, the choice of building materials, of vegetation, and so on, is not haphazard and rests upon a series of classifications specific to Mankon culture (that shares to some extent many of the Grassfields conventions) and that provide the palace complex with symbolic meanings immediately perceptible by the Mankon people (see Rowlands' contribution in the 1985 edited *Paideuma* volume). An adequate understanding of the Mankon palace would require spelling out this series of classifications – an exercise that, in turn, would have to be based on the description of various types of compounds, buildings, functional spaces other than the palace. This has not been done. Yet, I wish to mention two out of many possible leads in that direction, as a pointer to the fact that the preceding ethnography amounts to describing Chinese ideograms without knowing anything of their meaning, and second, as a kind of programmatic statement for a future deciphering exercise. They concern stones and vegetation.

a. Stones

From a functional point of view, stones may serve as seats, grave markers, space markers, and shrines. The last two categories of stones deserve some comments regarding their names, the material used, and associated materials. The space markers are called *netchwere* (as against *ngo'*: stone). They stand in the middle of the space that they mark, and not at its limits, and are most of the time oblong raised monoliths of black basalt and less often rounded boulders of granite or similar material. The three hearth stones of any dwelling house fall into this category. In the house of any compound head, a fourth, bigger one, called *ndom netchwere* ('husband of netchwere') is erected by one of the three hearth stones. Such stones stand for a certain space: the compound, the yard of the palace, the marketplace, the entire country, and constitute a means to connect or disconnect a person to a given space (e.g. a daughter going away upon marriage) or to protect the space from evil influences. In the open, they are associated with *Ficus spp.* trees, and, at the palace, with *Sporobolus africanus* and *Markhamia tomentosa*, and receive apotropaic medicines. Indoors, they receive frictions of palm oil. They may receive blood offerings, as in the case of the two stones *netchwere nala'a* and *netchwere nebikume*, through which returning exiles are reconciled. A detailed analysis of all the rituals performed in connection with those stones is required. The colour of the stones also needs investigation, as the Mankon contrast black and white stones that are often put at the centre of a compound's yard. Ideally, it should be possible to make a social geography of Mankon from such space markers.

The other category of stones is that of the *nebe'te*, which can be translated by 'shrine' or 'altar'. It is made of boulders assembled in a rough circle with an empty space at the centre, or is built with dried mud. It is connected with hunting, warfare, the dead elders, and presumably other beings, each altar being specialized along a certain line of communication. The functions of space-markers and shrines seem to be fulfilled by trees in Bangoua according to Pradelles de Latour (1985).

b. Vegetation

The classificatory code underlining the use of vegetation is quite obscure, but it is obvious that there is one. Everywhere, chieftaincy is associated with a grove. The *Markhamia tomentosa* is a royal tree. In Mankon, the *Sporobolus africanus*, grown at various places around the palace, appears as a ritual ingredient in conflictual contexts. It is tied in a knot during war rituals, and sent, also tied in a knot, as a summons to people accused of witchcraft. The various *Ficus spp.* are planted in the yards of newly founded compounds, or between chiefdoms during peace-making rituals. The treatment of vegetal matters is significant: chopped into bits, split into two, or intact, fresh, dried or fermented (hence, warm). Unless a systematic study of these various aspects is made, it will be impossible to verbalize the significance of the Mankon palace, which is immediately perceived in a non-verbal manner by the Mankon people.

Endnotes

1. First published in an edited volume of the journal *Paideuma* (31, 1985, pp. 15-29, on Grassfields royal palaces). Most of the information on which this paper is based comes from the Fon of Mankon, Felix Akuma Ntumna of Matru Fon, Nkwenti Ngang of Nto', H.N. Labah of Ala'a Bekam, Jonathan Ndifomukong of Banong, Ntsu Nto' (Mr. Charles, the Fon's clerk), and above all Tsendi of Ala'a Akuma. The latter was born before 1900, recruited as a *Ntsenda Nto'* around 1911, and he served at the palace until about 1926. Botanical identifications were made at the National Herbarium of Cameroon, Yaoundé, except for the *Sporobolus africanus* identified by Didier Rousvoal, Institut de Recherche Agricole, Bambwi. I am grateful to Liza Sandell for editing the present article.

2. The phonetic transcription of Mankon words has been highly simplified, in particular with regard to its vowel system. In this paper its nine vowels have been reduced to seven: both anterior and central 'e' have

been represented by e, anterior and central 'o' by o, and the tense i, a central vowel to be distinguished from the front vowel, has been rendered by the latter. See J. Leroy (1977), especially pp. 43-74, for a study of the Mankon language and its phonology.

3. In the years 2000s, Ngwa'fo has reclaimed a few hectares of land around the sacred forest and allowed them to revert to a tree cover. In 2009, on the occasion of his jubilee, one could see that a secondary forest had grown on its own. This is one more indication that the grass cover of the Grassfields is man-made and is maintained only insofar as bush fires and land cultivation destroy the shrubs and trees on a routine basis.

4. Richard Fardon (2006) has documented the transfer of the Lela cult from the Chamba to the Bali and the neighbouring chiefdoms of the Bamenda plateau.

General conclusion

13. New directions for research

The first twelve chapters of this book have been written and published over a period of thirty years. They exhibit significant shifts in theoretical and methodological paradigms. Those shifts impact upon the internal consistency of the whole volume. The present, concluding, chapter is meant to provide a synthesis and some amount of consistency in the overall historical picture, however provisional it may be. It is also intended to open up new lines of investigation for future research.

In this chapter, I propose to turn upside down the chronological hypothesis regarding kingdom formation that I had developed in my 1985 book (Warnier 1985). That is, instead of considering the Grassfields as a peripheral area to the modern world system that took shape in the 16th century, I would hypothesize that the highlands were a secondary, yet somewhat autonomous, centre of wealth and power accumulation. Accordingly, instead of dating kingdom formation in the Grassfields to the impact of the Atlantic slave trade in the hinterland of the Bight of Biafra around the 18th century, I would hypothesize a much earlier process of increasing complexity and concentration of power.

This shift calls for a new paradigm as regards the interpretation of Grassfields history and a new chronological framework. It also calls for a shift in the theoretical approach, from social anthropology *à la* Radcliffe-Brown to a historical and comparative socio-anthropology of politics based on the work of Weber and Foucault. Accordingly, it also calls for new methodological tools to take into account material culture and sensori-motor repertoires in addition to verbalizations in their capacity to provide an access to the subjectivity of the Grassfielders.

In a nutshell: I will look at the Grassfields not as a peripheral area in the modern world system, but as a *centre* of development and accumulation calling for a revised historical *chronology*, a shift in *theoretical paradigm* and a change in *methodology*. This overall shift rests on a different interpretation of the historical data that I shall now unravel, at some cost, since I will have to repeat a few things I have already written in various chapters of the present volume.

In the late 1970s, when I expanded on my research interests from the Mankon kingdom to encompass the Bamenda Plateau at large, I soon noticed that a regional approach was required to analyze what Edmund Leach (1954) called a 'political system', by overriding cultural, linguistic and kingdom boundaries. This is what my 1985 book was all about. Its first part was devoted to analyzing the regional trading networks in subsistence goods. These were structured around a basic pattern of exchange between two items in universal demand all over the Grassfields, that is: palm oil produced along the western escarpment of the highlands, and iron implements produced on a large scale around the geographical centre of the Grassfields, some 80 km away from the palm oil belt (see chapters 3 and 5 in the present volume). Around those two basic items, given local communities specialized in the production of raffia textiles, ceramics, small livestock, grains, root crops and miscellanea. Such productions were specifically designed to meet the regional demand on the marketplace. They were surplus products on top and above the household production for domestic consumption.

The goods were carried by human porterage from the producing areas all the way to half a dozen regional marketplaces, the meeting days of which were fixed and synchronized with all others within the eight days week. Large trading households in the Mankon kingdom participated in this pattern on a daily basis. Their male staff met trade partners on the various regional marketplaces with whom they established formal friendships and marriage alliances.

Long before the colonial conquest, there were local currencies in iron, salt, brass, beads and, when the Hausa trade reached the area in the mid-19th century, cowries. The traders increased their capital and the size of their business thanks to rotating credit associations between peers, from which kinship ties were excluded. This helped the traders to withstand the pressure put on them by their kin groups, which is a major obstacle to capital accumulation in Africa.

On top and above this regional trade in subsistence goods, the notables and kings engaged in long distance trading in luxury goods with one another in three major directions: towards the middle Benue valley to the northwest; towards Adamawa to the northeast; and towards the harbours along the Atlantic coast to the south and southwest (see Map in chapter 2). In the 19th century, the items of trade were slaves (in all three directions), kola nuts and salt in bulk, ivory, cotton textiles, and European imports such as guns, gunpowder, Manchester cloth, Toby jugs, brass rods and manillas (see chapters 6, 7 and 8 in the present volume). This long distance trade came along with political alliances between kings and high-ranking notables of equivalent ranks in different polities.

It can be easily understood that the political economy of the whole system rested on local and regional social and political hierarchies. Within a kingdom like Mankon, the king stood at the top. He was at the same time the monarch of the whole kingdom and the head of the royal descent group. He still is, at the beginning of the 21st century, at the time of the 'come back of the kings' in Africa (see Perrot et Fauvelle-Aymar, eds. 2003). In addition to the royal clan, Mankon is made of eight other, commoner, clans that do not share any common origin. Genealogies and oral traditions converge to stress the fact that the kingdom was, right from the start, a composite one. The myth of origin underscores the federal and mixed nature of the body politics.

The Mankon hierarchy is therefore structured around the king, the nine clan-heads (including the king), the lineage heads within the clans (32 of them altogether), the heads of the lesser descent groups and households. The practice of high polygamy being the rule (the king had more than eighty wives until the 1960s, and the high-ranking palace and descent group notables had up to 30 wives until the 1920s – and sometimes, though rarely, up to ten nowadays), it will be clear that half of the male population was kept out of marriage and genital sexuality until fairly recently (see chapter 11 in the present volume). In Mankon, in the 1970s, there was still a tight control on the sexuality of girls, women and bachelors. Until the 1920s, all over the Grassfields, low-ranking bachelors were sold out as slaves, (and some women as well), bringing revenue and means of bride-wealth payment to the highest rungs of the kingdom hierarchy, and thus financing social and political inequality and the intensification of labour in the sphere of subsistence goods for local consumption and for the market.

It should be made clear that this description, focused on trade and exchange networks, does not provide any explanation as regards the causes of this state of affairs. My argument is not a Marxist one. It does not consider that the economic organisation shapes the social and political organisation in the last instance. I take trading as an indicator, a manifestation, so to speak, of the high level of mobility of persons and things in the area. My argument is focused on mobility, not on trading as such. Mobility, as it will be made clear, is the key issue – trading and its organization being only one aspect (albeit quite important) of the mobility of persons and things.

The historical conundrum: centre or periphery

In my 1985 book, I addressed the question of the history of the Mankon kingdom and of its chronology. This was not simply a quest for origins. It was a question in political analysis. I wanted to find some kind of explanation for the existence of a regional hierarchy, with inegalitarian, composite, multilingual and powerful kingdoms in some places, and much more homogeneous, egalitarian polities in other places, mostly along the southern, western and northern fringes of the highlands.

In Mankon, genealogies and associated royal graves, gave evidence for the demographic expansion of the royal clan around 1800, with the creation of three new lineages within the clan. Very high royal polygamy (with up to 150 wives in the larger kingdoms) also seems to date back from the same period. The institutions of the slave trade, with a licence owned by seven of the nine clans, gave evidence of the centrality of the Atlantic and inland trade in the later political economy of the kingdom (see chapter 7 in this volume). The historians of the coastal polities (Austen 1977, Austen and Derrick 1999, Latham 1973, Northrup 1978, Wirz 1972) gave evidence of the rapid development of the slave trade from 1750 onwards. It was clear for all the historians that the densely populated Grassfields provided the bulk of the trade and had a reputation for that. Brain (1972: 14-15, 120), who conducted research among the western Bangwa, on the edge of the highlands, claimed that "the slave trade was the backbone of Bangwa economy". It left a deep imprint on marriage alliance systems.

Since 1976, I had been conducting research with Michael Rowlands on the same kingdoms, and with the very same informants (see Rowlands 1979). We traded all our notes. I was deeply influenced by his volume on *The Evolution of Social Systems*, co-edited with Jonathan Friedman (1977) and in particular by their 'epigenetic model' of social transformation published in the same volume. It rested on a basically Marxist model combined with an approach to social reproduction in terms of regional networks and a centre/periphery system.

From our common investigations and analyses, I concluded tentatively by underscoring the existence of two centre/periphery systems (Warnier 1985: 224, 297-301). A regional one, with a few major kingdoms including Mankon in a central position; and a sub-continental one, with the coastal area in a semi-peripheral position, and the Grassfields at the periphery of the modern world system through the coastal polities. Although I did not explicitly quote Wallerstein, I had in mind his *Modern World System* (1974-1989). I saw kingdom formation as the local response to the impact of the Atlantic trade on inland societies that fed it with tens of thousands of slaves year after year, thus financing the construction of a political hierarchy while intensifying agricultural and manufacturing labour, and promoting the diversification of the regional economy. Besides, a fairly strong political control on the population must have been required to extract slaves contingents without making use of armed violence. Indeed, slaves were not obtained through raiding, but by taking them within the kin groups and the kingdom (Warnier 1989, 1995 and chapter 7 in this volume). Such a system of control was not achieved by direct and authoritarian surveillance and punishment, but by what Foucault would see as technologies of the subject shaping given kinds of persons while subjecting them to a sovereignty (see Warnier 2007).

The emergence of those kingdoms ca 1750-1800 made sense in that respect. It coincided with the indirect connection of the Grassfields to the world market and their inclusion at the periphery of the world system through the Atlantic coast. Yet, as from the year 2000, it seemed to me that the whole scheme was rather shaky. The Grassfields exhibited many features of a centre of development. Their internal dynamics was much too strong, and the impact of the coastal trade too weak and too late in their history to be the sole cause of kingdom formation. The process of increasing complexity could have been much older than I thought at first. The highlands could not be seen as a periphery to the world system. My scheme may have been walking on its head.

It can be seen that there are actually two different, yet related, debates: the first one concerns the chronology of kingdom formation: did Grassfields kingdoms emerge during the 18th century or much earlier? The second one concerns the much debated causes of kingdom formation (alias concentration of power, centralization, complexity, etc.), whether they should be seen in the development of trading, or in conquest, competition over scarce resources, mobility of persons and things, disjunctive migrations, etc. I find it difficult to disentangle the two debates. However, the second one being far too complex to be discussed in a short concluding chapter, I wish to concentrate on the first one – concerning the chronology – although I must take a number of clues from the second one and suggest some lines of investigation.

Revisiting the chronology: a summary of the evidence, with the latest developments

Accordingly, I now wish to summarize two kinds of data that would support the view that the Grassfields have been the arena of highly complex sociopolitical phenomena (that is, a 'centre' of sorts) in a larger world system for a very long time. The first kind of evidence belongs with a batch of hard data on the history of the area examined in chapters 2, 3 and 4 of the present volume. The second belongs with more circumstantial evidence. It should be made clear that, at this juncture, I lack some of the archaeological and historical data that would allow me to claim with certainty that the Grassfields have been a centre of development for centuries if not millennia. My general conclusion is of a rather negative nature: I think that there is enough evidence to rule out my first chronological hypothesis that kingdom organization developed at the periphery of the world system out of egalitarian, lineage, societies such as are found at the periphery of the Grassfields, or, more obviously, in the forest area of Cameroon, in the Fang-Beti-Bulu area as analysed by Abega (1987), Laburthe-Tolra (1981, 1986), and Mallart-Guimera (1981).

However, our present knowledge is sufficient to rule out the accepted wisdom of massive migrations as late as the 17th century by people coming from the surrounding lowlands. Those migrants were said to have displaced or absorbed sparse local populations. The scheme obeyed the trope of the mountains as refuge areas relatively ill suited for human settlement as it obtained in Latin countries such as France and Spain in the 19th c, as against the British trope of the mountains as places of origin for the human colonization of unhealthy marshy plains. This accepted wisdom is most aptly summarised in the synthesis provided by Tardits (1981).

As regards population history, the general pattern was that of an early and dense settlement, as early as the inception of food production (6000 BP), developing at a very early stage a basic division of labour, a system of regional specialization and trade between iron and palm oil productions as soon as iron metallurgy became efficient enough to provide the whole area in basic agricultural implements (perhaps around 2000 to 1500 BP).

The more circumstantial evidence

Thurstan Shaw (1976) remarks the presence of a densely and anciently settled population around the Niger Delta, Igbo land and the Tiv countries south of the Benue river, based on the domestication of yams and a nearly complete diet provided by yams and palm oil right from the inception of the Neolithic. This area includes the Grassfields. Besides, the cereals of African origin such as sorghum grow in the northern half of the Grassfields. As a result, the populations of the highlands have been in a position to benefit from a prosperous agriculture right from the beginning of food production.

There has been much speculation about the possible correlation between the introduction of Asian food crops in the area under consideration, and the diffusion of Bantu languages following the so-called 'Bantu migrations'. Whether this has been the case or not, the importance of Asian food crops (especially plantain and banana) in rituals, as well as research done by Mbida et al. (2000) indicate an early introduction of those crops around the southern Cameroon forest margins. Lastly, the introduction of American crops, especially groundnuts, dates back to the earliest European contacts with the coastal areas. It must be kept in mind that the Grassfields lay within 200 km from the coast as the crow flies. However, manioc and maize only met with any success around the beginning of the 20th century. Maize replaced sorghum, and manioc provided a poorer substitute for yams as from 1918.

The general conclusion is that the Grassfields agrosystems developed an excellent carrying capacity right from the start of the Neolithic, with the two main African crop complexes (root crops and cereals), complemented at a later date by the Asian and the American ones. They were also fed by an abundant palm oil supply, by hunting and by small livestock production. This, in itself, does not constitute any proof of high population densities, but it makes them possible and most likely when compared with the very high language density and diversity that must have been the result of fairly generous population dynamics, and with the early deforestation process shown by paleopalynological investigations (Maley 2001).

It must be added that the highland environment is quite favourable to human settlement. Rainfall averages 2000 mm per year. Water is plentiful, even during the dry season. The relief is such that the water does not stagnate. Consequently, water born diseases and parasites are almost non-existent in the area. Thanks to the altitude, the impact of malaria is considerably attenuated. However, because of the very same altitude (ca. 1200 to 1400m for the settled areas, the mountains culminating in the range 2600-3000m – hardly any village being built above the 1400m contour line), the temperature may fall fairly low at night, especially during the dry season (down to 4 to 10°C.), and respiratory conditions may create health hazards. All in all, the environmental setting reinforces the hypothesis, carried by linguistic and agricultural evidence, of high population densities for very long periods of time, with a pattern of regional economic specialisation and trade between local communities. However, we are far from any hard evidence on the demographic history of the area.

Another batch of evidence comes from somewhat patchy, yet crucial, information regarding long-distance trade. Trade in salt for iron with the coastal areas pre-dates European contacts (Warnier 1985: 173-178) and, according to early witnesses, was voluminous. This is an indication for the existence of an efficient iron industry for export in the Grassfields before 1500. The trade in salt and cotton cloth with the middle Benue may be equally ancient, perhaps with slaves as a token of exchange. It may be assumed that the twin pattern of regional and long distance trading is very old, dating back perhaps to the first centuries of the iron age ca 2000 BP. There is a fair degree of certainty regarding the regional trade, but less so regarding long distance trading.

However, the proof for wealth accumulation ca 1000 BP cannot be disclaimed in Igbo Ukwu, excavated by Thurstan Shaw (1977) some 350 km away from the Grassfields as the crow flies. So far, nothing equivalent has been found in the Cameroon highlands, but it should be stressed that no archaeological research of any significance has been conducted in the area, except in the rock shelters bearing witness to the earlier periods. I do not take trading as an indication of increasing complexity or concentration of power. As Northrup (1978) indicated for southeastern Nigeria, 'trade without rulers' is well documented. I take trading as an indicator of the increasing mobility of persons and things over large areas. And mobility seems to be a key issue in the institution of sacred kingship in Africa.

Indeed, last but not least, the research I conducted since the early 1990s on kingship and containers in the Grassfields has convinced me that the 150 odd kingdoms of the highlands belong with the sacred kinship variety distributed all over Sub-Saharan Africa (Warnier 2007).

Sacred kingship, in its turn, must be correlated with a number of significant hard facts. The Mankon kingdom, like all Grassfields kingdoms, is a composite one. It is made of genealogically unrelated descent groups coming from all over the place. Each household is a multilingual and, so to speak, multiethnic group. Consequently, the basic and most fundamental problem faced by any of those kingdoms is to device technologies that could and should be implemented to produce some kind of bounded locality and to assign people and things to it in order to counteract the powerful fissiparous forces that tend to shatter the kingdom into pieces (see chapter 9 in this volume). Such technologies develop around the Pot-King as a sacred king. The governmentality of containers is a means of shaping and building a material envelope, of attracting into it people and things that are unmoored and roam around at large outside its envelope, as part of the African frontier (see Kopytoff ed. 1987). It is a means of unifying those people and things kept within the envelope by giving out to them the unifying bodily contents of the king together with their reproductive powers, for them to ingest or smear on their skin. It is a means of expelling from the kingdom the bad things and substances as so many excreta: witches, unwanted people, slaves, bad medicines, foreign trade goods inherent with destructive powers. The technologies of power are matched by the technologies of the self that are implemented by the subjects of the king: working on their skin, their bodily envelope, their openings, their house as a container, its only door as its mouth, etc. It is a matter of opening up, closing down, screening, vetting, absorbing or expelling people, things and substances.

The technology of sacred kingship grounded in the logics of containers and containment explains many features such as the murder of the king when the bodily envelope of the king is found to be decrepit and leaking out, with the result that it is feared that the ancestral life substances are not properly stored and distributed, and the prosperity of the kingdom is wanting. In such a case, it is required to get rid of the old pot-king just as if it were a cracked calabash, to be replaced by a brand new one. It is a practical and mundane process. This pattern is found, with considerable variations, all over the Grassfields. It is too widespread in Sub-Saharan Africa to be a recent innovation. It cannot be seen as a response to the Atlantic slave trade, but to the local development of regional and long distance mobility and displacement of people and things combined with wide-ranging cultural models of political organisation of great antiquity. In other words, I find myself in agreement with the theory expressed by Robin Horton (1971) who claimed that chiefdoms and kingdoms are a means of coping with what he calls 'disjunctive migrations', that is, the fact that groups of people – and individuals as well – may shift places within what Kopytoff (1987) later called the African frontier, to find themselves in contact with unrelated groups. As a result, such neighbouring groups have to find a means to built up some kind of encompassing political organization. In other words, the mobility of persons and things over large areas is the key issue, whatever the causes of mobility may have been. We know what they were in the last two centuries (conflicts over succession to high office, witchcraft accusations, competition for land and resources, Chamba and Fulani raids, trading patterns, inter-chiefdom marriage alliances, etc.). There is no doubt that several of them obtained in earlier periods, but, to some extent, they escape historical or archaeological documentation. By contrast, trading patterns can be documented. This is why they are important elements in my argument. I take them as a strong indication of the mobility of people and things.

If high population densities, linguistic diversification, high levels of mobility and sacred kingship as a means of producing locality are ancient features in the Grassfields, then, it is most likely that kingdoms must have originated one to two thousand years ago, with particular kingdoms emerging and disappearing in succession in various places.

Then, if we go one step further along those lines, we may hypothesize that the sacred 'Pot-King' believed to contain vital substances and the source of all wealth in people, crops and livestock, together with the kingdom hierarchies, are conducive to wealth accumulation by kings and notables, to the intensification of labour, to its regional specialisation, and to a spectacular cultural production and diversification that has been documented by scholars over the last 100 years. This is precisely what a centre of development is all about. I have sketched the description of it and of its peripheries in my 1985 book.

The larger world system

Since the publication of Wallerstein's *Modern World System* (1974-1989), global history has revisited its main thesis by taking the notion of a world system away from Northern Europe and the Atlantic, and by applying it with equivalent scientific requirements on a global scale. The most recent synthesis of those debates has been published by Beaujard, Berger and Norel (eds. 2009). They underscore the fact that there cannot be any smaller centre of development such as the Grassfields that is not connected to other neighbouring centres within larger spheres of interactions or 'world systems'. They provide a complex model of what a system may be, and of the causes of differential wealth, power and knowledge accumulation in the various parts of the system. These causes are quite numerous and diverse. In that respect, the views of Beaujard and his colleagues diverge from the cruder Marxian models so widespread in the 1970s and 1980s, often based on an obsolete labour theory of value. This would require a discussion that is unfortunately beyond the scope of the present conclusion.

If I follow their more sophisticated model, the concluding remarks to the present contribution should be as follows: what could be the likely candidates as centres connected to the Grassfields within the African spheres of interaction, and, beyond Africa, to the world systems? I accept the thesis of the existence of a 'Euroasiatic and African world system', with four phases of expansion and decline, as delineated by Beaujard, Berger and Norel (eds. 2009). This world system took shape around 2500 BP. It had its centre of gravity around the Indian Ocean. As a global system, this would be a convincing candidate, linked to the Grassfields through the Nile valley, Southern Sudan, and the Chad region, in consonance with the hypothesis of a Nilotic connexion from Igbo-Ukwu expressed by John Sutton (2001). True enough, Beaujard, Berger and Norel do not deal explicitly with sub-Saharan Africa. Their model, however, is quite open to a sub-Saharan extension.

In view of available data, the connexion of the Grassfields to the later North Atlantic world system through the coastal polities must have had a local impact in the 18th century at the earliest. Yet, given the strength of the regional and local exchange networks, it is hard to believe that the latter did not previously belong with larger spheres of interaction. Neither could it be said that the impact of the North Atlantic world system would have been dominant in the area earlier than the late 19th century. That is, to make it clear, I am now of the opinion that the regional and sub-continental centres of development date back to pre-contact times and kept much of their autonomy and local dynamics until they were superseded by the direct impact of the world market with the inception of colonization. Until then, they were shielded by the coastal middlemen from any direct impact of the world market. The coastal polities kept a monopoly on the interactions with the hinterland (see Austen, Derrick and Derrick, 1999).

The chronology of the emergence of centralized polities in the area, along the lines of the sacred kingship, would thus be as follows: as from the inception of the Neolithic around 6000 BP and that of the iron age in 2500 BP, population densities increased on the long run, presumably with ups and downs, together with the mobility of people within the regional ecumene. Centres of economic development, concentration of wealth and power, mobility, specialization and trade emerged, together with a concern with locality, closure, conflict management and the unification of the diverse components of the local polities. The circumstances and the causes of such an increased mobility producing a frontier situation as an open space conducive to new patterns of political organization remain quite obscure and, so far, beyond our reach. Only the end result is known, that is, the frontier situation that has prevailed in the last millennium at least. Sacred kingship provided the answer to the specific concerns of a frontier situation. As from 1750 and the increasing impact of the slave trade, kingdoms benefited from the coastal trade and intensified the concentration of wealth and power, together with high polygamy. In Sub-Saharan West central Africa, other neighbouring sub-centres may be found in the Yoruba and middle Benue regions, in Bornu and around lake Chad, that are definitely of pre-contact origin.

May I insist on the fact that this sketch is partly a matter of educated speculation. It is intended to put aside the Eurocentric view of the Grassfields as a periphery of the 'Modern world system', and to open up a new space for historical, archaeological, linguistic, and anthropological research by pushing back into the past the terminus a quo of kingdom formation. Regarding the two debates at hand concerning the chronology and the causes of increasing complexity, I consider the first one as conclusive. By contrast, the second one leaves open a number of important questions regarding mobility, trading, specialisation, the definition of wealth and value, the tenets of sacred kingship, etc. The two debates may have disturbing implications, particularly as regards the endogenous background to social inequality, slavery and the inland slave trade. At the same time, they make it possible to conduct research in Grassfields history on the grounds of the more local political, cultural and economic dynamics rather than on Eurocentric ones.

A theoretical statement

As from 1971, when I first arrived in Mankon, onto the mid-1980s, I made use of two basic theoretical paradigms. The first one was derived from British social anthropology, itself moulded by Durkheimian sociology as interpreted by Radcliffe-Brown. The second one was derived from a broad interpretation of Marxism, with an interest in political economy and history, through such contributions as that of J. Friedman and M. Rowlands (1977) regarding an epigenetic model of the evolution of social systems. Under the first paradigm, one had to identify the social structures (descent groups, the king, the regulatory societies, etc.) and their functions (religious, political, economic, etc.). In the 1950s, with the contribution of the Manchester School, one more dimension was added to it, that is, conflicts, conflict resolution, change and socio-political dynamics.

Those paradigms proved to be quite useful and productive in bringing out many important features of the Grassfields situation. Yet, a lot of data could not be fitted in either one of them. I am alluding here to everything pertaining to the king as a container, to material culture, to sensori-motor repertoires, to the processes of subjectivation. As an example, let me quote the gesture made by the king when he sprays raffia wine from his mouth onto the surrounding crowd. Where can I fit such a gesture in a paradigm derived from Marxism or British social anthropology? Nowhere, it seems to me.

In the mid-1980s, I therefore found myself in a situation well documented by Kuhn (1970) as regards the structure of any scientific revolutions: when one or several existing paradigms cannot accommodate a growing number of empirical observations, one has to device a new paradigm in order to accommodate them. This is what I started doing in the late 1980s.

This is not the appropriate place to propose extensive and detailed developments regarding this shift in paradigm. I will only mention its two basic components. The first one has to do with the body, its techniques, the bodily motions and emotions as propped against the material culture of containers, apertures and contents. Here, the basic theoretical references are provided by Marcel Mauss, the tradition established by Paul Schilder on the *Körperschema*, and the neuro-cognitive sciences.

The second one concerns the technologies of power and the technologies of the subject insofar as they are based on the implementation of bodily and material cultures. Right from the start, in 1971, I intended to analyse the political systems exemplified by Grassfields kingdoms and the regional hierarchies they formed. But at the end of the 1980s, it became clear that those *political* systems should be analyzed not only in terms of structures and socio-political relations of production but also in terms of the technologies of power that address the body and the subjectivity of the king and his subjects. The basic references here, were provided by Max Weber and Michel Foucault. Weber was concerned with the comprehensive interpretation of socio-political phenomena in their historical setting, such as the spirit of incipient capitalism. In order to do so, he thought, the sociologist has to document the way such phenomena manifest themselves in the daily life and practice of given people. The words Weber used to point out such daily routines are all derived from the German word *Tag* (day): *täglich, Alltäglichkeit*, etc. Reading Weber involves paying attention to detailed and fine grain empirical descriptions of such daily routines as keeping logbooks of accounting, attending church service and the like. On his side, Michel Foucault has insisted on the way power is addressed to the body of the subject and how given governmentalities subject them to a sovereignty. Such governmentalities address the body insofar as any subjectivity is embodied. Just as Weber was interested in minute daily routines, Foucault advocated the construction of a political anatomy of details. In the case of Foucault, and Weber as well, and as against the Durkheimian approach, the sociology of daily life, lifestyles, the techniques of the self, and the technologies of power addressing the body, provided an object of scientific enquiry that was clearly a historical one. Change, conflict, social and political dynamics were part and parcel of it. In a nutshell: one had to contribute to a historical, comparative, and comprehensive sociology of politics intent on describing bodily practices, daily life and the production of given lifestyles and subjectivities.

On my own, I would not have contrived to produce such a theoretical framework lest it had been in the making with a number of scholars working in the field of political analysis, especially in France. This was the case in the 1960s with Guy Hermet and Jean Leca and, in the wake of their path-breaking research, with Jean-François Bayart (1979, 2004), Béatrice Hibou (2006, 2011), Romain Bertrand (2005), etc. They built up a powerful, lively and extensive research network reaching out far and wide, to establish connexions with such scholars as John Londsdale and Peter Geschiere. My own contribution focused on the mediation achieved by bodily and material cultures in the process of subjectivation. It required a methodological shift that needs a modicum of explanation.

A methodological statement

Ever since the psychologist Jean Piaget (1962) and his researches on children's development in the 1920s, most psychologists make a distinction between two kinds of human knowledge. One is an embodied procedural knowledge (that is, knowing how to do things like writing with a pen, riding a bicycle, playing the piano, etc.); the other one is a verbalized knowledge (that is, knowing *that* London is the capital town of Great Britain and Yaoundé that of Cameroon). The first one is directly related to the body, to bodily practices and material culture. It is no less human than the verbalized knowledge. Most of the time, the two go hand in hand, as when writing a text expressing some verbalized knowledge, with a pen and paper, or with the keyboard of a computer.

Going back to the theoretical statement made just above, my approach to the 'Pot-King' and to the governmentality of containers, envelopes, apertures and contents called for a sophisticated enquiry on procedural, embodied knowledge. The corpus of verbal statements, texts, oral traditions, etc. usually collected by anthropologists while doing fieldwork, proved to be inadequate if one wanted to document bodily and material culture. The corpus that was needed had to rest on descriptions of objects and associated gestures. For example, one could take raffia bags and their various contents and uses, and complement the corpus with other types of containers, including the human body, pots, calabashes, houses, the palace, etc.

What matters with such a corpus is not the sign value of objects and gestures in a coded system of communication or connotation, but their praxic value in a system of agency; not what they mean, but what they achieve in terms of producing given types of subjectivities. Semiotics and structuralism are quite efficient tools of investigation as far as signs and symbols are concerned. They are next to useless when one wishes to address the question of the bodily and material technologies of the subject and their efficacy in shaping given subjectivities.

Yet, one cannot oppose the two kinds of knowledge. Both need to be documented, each one on its own right. The analysis of political systems makes a big leap forward when it does not rest only on verbalized knowledge, on interviews, on the accounts of the 'rational choices' of the individual but on the potential harmony, tensions or even contradictions between the two kinds of knowledge with a given subject or a group of subjects. This is when both discourses and practice win the consent of the subjects and achieve an hegemony or a subjection of sorts. This is what I have tried to explain in my book devoted to *The Pot-King* (2007). One may discuss a verbal statement. One cannot discuss camwood or the palm oil used to anoint a bride or a successor. Yet, both contribute to shaping the subject.

Most people will probably agree that it was indeed the case in the past, but that the impact of modernity and of post-independence politics will have disturbed this kind of governmentality beyond recognition. This is indeed open to discussion, but there are many indications that the Mankon kingdom has not yet jettisoned its ancient constitution. Not only many techniques of the body and techniques of the self hold on fast, but the shock of modernity may very well have been absorbed by the old technologies of power as we shall now see.

The domestication of modernity

In Braudelian parlance, a civilization is a *longue durée* phenomenon. It does not easily yields to sudden changes. It endures to some extent through the demographic, economic and political changes taking place in *moyenne durée*, and to sudden historical events. Braudel had underlined the fact that no historical analysis could entirely dispense with these three dimensions of human history. This, in my view, helps understanding the invention and consumption of a genuinely African modernity in the Grassfields (see Rowlands 1996). The frontier situation carries on through the colonial and independence periods. The colony constitutes an open space, with new subjects stepping in (the colonizer, the trader, the military, the missionary) with all their material culture and economic organization (the material culture of the Mission station, the school, the hospital, the factory, the means of transport) and the global financial, cultural and commodity fluxes.

In the 20th century, the existence of such an African frontier raises a number of problems that are nothing new in the history of the Grassfields, that is, how to produce locality and a bounded space, how to assign people and things to the local, how to vet things and people that are good to take on board from those that should be kept out or expelled once they have been taken in and found to be useless or nefarious?

Right from the first direct contacts between Grassfields kingdom and the intrusive colonizer, the repertoires of action provided by the governmentality of containers were activated. Galega, the king of Bali-Nyonga, decided to take Eugen Zintgraff within the envelope of his kingdom and to 'eat' him so to speak. He sent his envoys to meet the German explorer before he even set foot on the highlands, to attract him to Bali (see Zintgraff 1895). Subsequently, the same repertoires were used to absorb or expel the missionaries, the biomedical system, the commodities of the globalized market, the nation-state, the labour market. All these items were emblematic of the globalized modernity. Each one of them raised specific problems as regards their potential for wealth procurement and accumulation or for the disruption of existing hierarchies. Vetting out these items, taking them inside or keeping them outside the kingdom have been and still are, matters for conflict. Suffice it to mention the imaginary of witchcraft, *famla*', or the occult marketplaces as a kind of lottery producing either the doom of the village or its wealth and wellbeing. Either the village is spoiled or is enriched and fed by these incorporated foreign substances.

Whatever the case, kings and kingdoms hierarchies have been in the forefront of the invention of an African modernity in which they made an efficient use of the governmetality of containers, down to this day. This is one amongst the many reasons of the enduring, yet ambiguous vitality of African kingdoms in general, and Grassfields ones in particular, as analysed by Perrot and Fauvelle-Aymar (2003).

Yet, the governmentality of containers seems to reach its limits with urban and international migrations. Right from the beginning of the 20th century, the kingdoms lost part of their population to the coastal plantations, the growing towns, and the market economy in its different forms. After World War II, and even more so from the 1970s onwards, this population drain reached alarming proportions, at a time when the envelope of the kingdom, materialized by the ditch in Mankon, became useless and irrelevant as people moved out of it to cultivate land and build their compounds outside its confines. The bounded space of the city seemed to have lost its limits. The king found it more and more difficult to produce and monitor the envelope of his own body politics. The answers, to this day, seem to have been manifold. For one thing, like many of his peers, the king has created an association – the Mankon Cultural Development Association (MACUDA) – that provides an institutional envelope by means of which the local and diasporic elites can be encompassed. For example, it has a subsidiary in the United States, with a web page of its own ([www.macudaamerica.com]). The king has also created a museum at the palace, with a sophisticated catalogue (Notue and Triaca 2005) and a web page. The palace has an electronic address. Thus the king has made an efficient use of the new technologies of information and communication that translate the physical envelope of the kingdom into a virtual one.

However, this attempt would probably be to little avail if it were not geared to an active politics of autochtony supported by the Cameroon State as a divide and rule reply to the democratization movements of the 1990s. Every Mankon subject is encouraged to maintain a physical relationship to his land of origin, to patronize the yearly festival, to built a house in Mankon and to be buried in Mankon soil (see Warnier 2011 and Page 2007). Of course, this concerns above all the administrative, professional and business elites rather than the vulgum pecus. However, has not the latter belonged in the past with some kind of waste that the kingdom could dispense with? That is, provided the elite stays inside the kingdom by implementing the politics of belonging and by the various means that are offered to it, is the kingdom really threatened by the domestication of modernity and the subsequent broadening of its limits? I suppose not, but only the future will tell.

In that respect, one thing is noteworthy: in December 2009, Ngwa'fo celebrated his Golden Jubilee – fifty years on the Mankon throne – the first fifty years of independence. The Jubilee combined specific celebrations with the annual dry season festival – the Abweng-afo. It was very well attended. It received delegations from a number of other kingdoms, together with the official visit of the Governor of the North-West Region and of members of the diplomatic corps. The Mankon elite from Cameroon and abroad crowded the palace. A 53mn documentary film provides a graphic account of the event (Zips & Zips-Mairitsch 2010). On such an occasion, it was possible to measure the vitality of the kingdom and of the king as a container of its vital substances. All the rituals were dutifully performed with compliance and faith in their efficacy as so many technologies of the subject.

To conclude: the thirteen chapters of this book put together, although they do not appear in the chronological order of their dates of publication, reflect the shift in paradigm and in methodology I have explained in the present conclusion, to the effect that the Grassfields civilization is well and alive and its history needs to be thoroughly revisited.

Bibliography

ABEGA, S.C., 1987, *L'Esana chez les Beti*, Yaoundé, Clé.

ALLEN, W. & THOMSON, T.R.H., 1848, *A Narrative of the Expedition to the River Niger*. London : Richard Bentley, 2 vol.

ANZIEU, D., 1985, *Le Moi-peau*, Paris, Dunod.

APPADURAI, A., 1997, *Modernity at Large: Cultural Dimensions of Globalization*. Minneapolis, MN: University of Minnesota Press.

ARDENER, E.(1968) "Documentary and Linguistic Evidence for the Rise of the Trading Polities between Rio del Rey and Cameroons, 1500-1650", in I.M. Lewis, ed., *History and Social Anthropology*, London: Tavistock: 81-125.

ARGENTI, N. (2004) "La danse aux frontières. Les mascarades interdites des femmes et des jeunes à Oku", In : J.-F. BAYART & J.-P. WARNIER (eds.), *Matière à politique. Le pouvoir, les corps et les choses*, Paris, Yaoundé, CERI-Karthala-UCAC, pp. 151-180.

— (2007) *The Intestines of the State. Youth, Volence, and Belated Histories in the Cameroon Grassfields*. Chicago : The University of Chicago Press.

ARNOLD, D.E. (1985) *Ceramic Theory and Cultural Process*. Cambridge : Cambridge University Press.

ASOMBANG, R.N. 1988 "Bamenda in Prehistory : The Evidence from Fiye Nkwi, Mbi Crater and Shum Laka rockshelters", Ph.D. Thesis, Institute of Archaeology, London University. Unpublished.

AUSTEN, R.A. (1977) "Slavery among Coastal Middlemen : The Duala of Cameroon », in S. Miers & I. Kopytoff, eds., *Slavery in Africa*. Madison : University of Wisconsin Press : 305-333.

AUSTEN, R. & DERRICK, J. (1999) *Middlemen of the Cameroon Rivers. The Duala and their Hinterland c. 1600-c. 1960*. Cambridge : Cambridge University Press.

AUSTIN, J.L. (1962) *How to Do Things with Words*. Oxford : Oxford University Press.

BAIKIE, W.B. (1856/1966) *Narration of an exploring voyage up the rivers Kwora and Binue, commonly known as the Niger and Tsadda in 1854*. London : Frank Cass.

BARBIER, J.-C. (1981) "Le peuplement de la partie méridionale du plateau bamiléké", in : C. TARDITS (éd.), *Contribution*, Vol 2, pp. 331-354.

BARTHES, R. (1957) *Mythologies*, Paris, Éd. du Seuil.

BAYART, J.-F. (1979) *L'État au Cameroun*, Paris, Presses de la Fondation nationale des sciences politiques.

—(1989) *L'État en Afrique. La politique du ventre*. Paris, Fayard.

—(2004) *Le gouvernement du monde. Une critique politique de la globalisation*, Paris, Fayard.

BAYART, J.-F. & WARNIER, J.-P. (eds.) (2004) *Matière à politique. Le pouvoir, les corps et les choses*, Paris, Yaoundé, CERI-Karthala-UCAC.

BEAUJARD, Ph., BERGER L. & NOREL, Ph., (2009) *Histoire globale, mondialisations et capitalisme*, Paris, La Découverte, coll. Recherches.

BERTHELOT, J.-M. (1995) "The Body as a discursive operator, or the aporias of a sociology of the body", *Body and Society*, I (1): 13-23.

BERTHOZ, A. (1997) *Le sens du mouvement*, Paris, Odile Jacob.

BERTRAND, R. (2005) *État colonial, noblesse et nationalisme à Java. La Tradition parfaite*, Paris, CERI-Karthala, coll. Recherches internationales.

BLACKMORE, H.L. (1961) *British Military Firearms, 1650-1850*. London : Herbert Jenkins.

BOHANNAN, P. & L. (1968) *Tiv Economy*, London: Longman.

BOSERUP, E. (1965) *The conditions of agricultural growth: the economics of agrarian change under population pressure*. London: Allen & Unwin.

BOUCHAUD, P.-J. (1952) *La côte du Cameroun dans l'histoire et la cartographie, des origines à l'annexion allemande*, Douala, Institut français d'Afrique noire ("Mémoires" n° 5).

BRAIN, R. (1972) *Bangwa Kinship and Marriage*. Cambridge : C.U.P.

— (1977) *Friends and Lovers*. Frogmore, St. Albans: Paladin.

BRÁSIO, A. (1955) *Monumenta missionaria Africana. África occidental*. VI. 1611-1621, Lisbon: Agência general do ultramar.

BRUN, S. (1913) "Samuel Brun, des Wundartzet und Burgers zu Basel. Schiffarten...", in D. RUYTERS, *Toortse der zeevaert, door Dierick Ruiters (1623). Samuel Brun Schiffarten (1624). Uitgegeven door* S.P. *L'Honoré Naber*, Gravenhage, M. Nijhoff ("Werken uitgegeven door Linschoten-vereeniging" 6).

CALDWELL, J.C. (1982) "Comments on Manning : 'The enslavement of Africans : a demographic model'", *Revue Canadienne des Études Africaines* (RCEA-CJAS), XVI (1).

CARNOCHAN, J. (1973) "Lexicostatistics and African languages", in: C. RENFREW (ed.) *The Explanation of Culture Change*, London: 643-46.

CAROTHERS, J.C., (1954) *The Psychology of the Mau Mau*. Nairobi: Government Printer.

CHAMPAUD, J. (1973) *Atlas régional Ouest II*, Yaoundé, ORSTOM.

CHILVER, E.M. (1961) "Nineteenth-century trade in the Bamenda Grassfields, Southern Cameroon", *Afrika und Übersee*, XLV, 233-58.

— (1962, ed.)*Portrait of a Cameroonian. An Autobiography of Maxwell Gabana Fohtung*. Cyclostyled edition.

— (1966) *Zintgraff's Explorations in Bamenda, Adamawa and the Benue Lands, 1889-1892*. Buea: Ministry of Primary Education and Social Welfare and West Cameroon Antiquities Commission.

— (1967) "Paramountcy and Protection in the Cameroons: the Bali and the German, 1889-1913", In: P. GIFFORD & W.M. ROGER LOUIS (eds.): *Britain and Germany in Africa*. New Haven: Yale Univ. Press. Pp. 479-511.

— (1971) "The Secretaryship of the Colonial Social Sciences Research Council: a Reminiscence". *Anthropological Forum* 4(2), 103-12.

— (1981) "Chronological synthesis: the western region, comprising the Western Grassfields, Bamum, the Bamileke chiefdoms and the Central Mbam", in: Cl. TARDITS (ed.) *Contribution*, II: 453-73.

CHILVER, E.M. & KABERRY, P. (1968) *Traditional Bamenda. The Pre-Colonial History and Ethnography of the Bamenda Grassfields*. Buea: Ministry of Primary Education and Social Welfare, and West Cameroon Antiquities Commission.

— (1971) "The Tikar problem: A non-problem". *Journal of African Languages*, 10 (2): 13-14.

CLINE, W. (1937) *Mining and Metallurgy in Negro Africa*. Menasha, Wisconsin: G. Banta Publishing C°.

CSORDAS, Th. (ed.) (1994) *Embodiment and Experience. The existential ground of culture and self*. Cambridge: Cambridge Univ. Press.

CUISENIER, J. (1991) *La maison rustique : logique sociale et composition architecturale*, Paris : Presses Universitaires de France.

CUMBERPATCH, C.C. & BLINKHORN, P.W. (eds.) (1997) *Not so much of a Pot, More a Way of Life*. Oxford: Oxbow Books.

CURTIN, P. (1969) *The Atlantic Slave Trade: A Census*. Madison: University of Wisconsin Press.

CURTIN, P. & VANSINA, J. (1964) "Sources of the Nineteenth Century Atlantic Slave Trade", *Journal of African History*, V (2): 185-208.

DAMASIO, A. (2000) *L'Erreur de Descartes*, Paris, Odile Jacob.

DAPPER, O. (1668) *Neukeurige beschrijvinge der Afrikaensche gewesten van Egypten, Barbaryen, Lybien...*, Amsterdam, J. van Meurs.

DAVID, N. (1980) "Early Bantu expansion in the context of Central African prehistory: 4000-1 B.C.", in L. Bouquiaux et Al. (ed.), Paris, SELAF, Vol III., pp. 609-647.

— (1981) "The archaeological background of Cameroonian history", in : C. TARDITS (ed.), *Contribution de la recherche ethnologique à l'histoire des civilisations du Cameroun*, Paris, CNRS, Vol. I : 79-100.

DE BOECK, F. (2004) "La frontière diamantifère angolaise et son héros mutant", in J.-F. BAYART & J.-P. WARNIER (éds.), *Matière à politique. Le pouvoir, les corps et les choses*, Paris, CERI-Karthala (Coll. Recherches internationales), pp. 93-128.

DE MARET, P. (1980) "Preliminary report on 1980 fieldwork in the Grassfields and Yaoundé, Cameroon", Nyame Akuma, XVII: 10-12.

— (1982) "New Survey of archaeological research and dates for West-Central and North-Central Africa", *Journal of African History*, XXIII, (1): 1-15.

DEVEREUX, G. (1967) *From Anxiety to Method in the Behavioral Sciences*. The Hague, Paris : Mouton.

DILLON, R. (1973) *Ideology, Process, and Change in Pre-Colonial Meta' Political Organization (United Republic of Cameroon)*. Ph.D. dissertation: University of Pennsylvania.

DONGMO, J.-L. (1981) *Le dynamisme bamiléké*, Yaoundé, CEPER, 2 vol.

DRUMMOND-HAY, J.C. (1925) *Intelligence Report on the Ndop Plain Area*. Unpublished, Buea Archives.

DURELL, G. (1958) *The Bafut Beagles*. Harmondsworth: Penguin.

FAGE, J.D. (1978) *A History of Africa*, London: Hutchinson.

FARDON, R. (1988) *Raiders and Refugees. Trends in Chamba Political Development 1750 to 1950*. Washington DC: Smithonial Institution Press.

— (1990) *Between God, the Dead and the Wild. Chamba interpretations of Ritual and Religion*. Edingburgh: Edinburgh University Press for the IAI, London.

— (2006) *Lela in Bali. History through Ceremony in Cameroon*. New York, Oxford: Berghahn Books. Cameroon Studies – Volume 7.

FASSIN, D. (2000) "Les politiques de l'ethnopsychiatrie. La psyché africaine, des colonies britanniques aux banlieues françaises", *L'Homme*, 153 : 231-250.

FEATHERSTONE, M., HEPWORTH, M. & TURNER, B. (eds.) (1991) *The Body: Social Process and Cultural Theory*. London: Sage.

FEELEY-HARNICK, G. (1985) "Issues in Divine Kingship", *Annual Rev. of Anthropology*, (14): 273-313.

FISHER, H.J. (1972-73) "He Swalloweth the Ground with Fierceness and Rage: the Horse in the Central Sudan", *Journal of African History*, 13 (3): 369-88, 14 (3): 355-79.

FISHER, H.J. and ROWLAND, V. (1971) "Firearms in the Central Sudan", *Journal of African History*, 12 (2): 215-39.

FOHTUNG, M.G. (1992) "Self-portrait of a Cameroonian, Taken down by Peter Kalle Njie and Edited by E.M. CHILVER", (Published version of *Portrait of a Cameroonian: an Autobiography of Maxwell Gabana Fohtung*, cyclostyled for private circulation in 1962), Paideuma 38, 219-48.

FOUCAULT, M. (1975) *Surveiller et punir*, Paris, Gallimard.

— (2001) *L'Herméneutique du sujet*. Cours au Collège de France, 1981-1982, Paris, Gallimard.

FOWLER, I. (1989) "Babungo: A Study of Iron Production, Trade and Power in a Nineteenth Century Ndop Plain Chiefdom (Cameroon)". PhD: London University.

— (1993) "African Sacred Kings; Expectations and Performance in the Cameroon Grassfields", *Ethnology*, 32 (3): 253-268.

— (2011) "The Oku Iron Industry in its Regional Setting", in: B. CHEM-LANGHËË & V.G. FANSO, *Nso' and its Neighbours*. Bamenda, Langaa RPCIG, pp. 51-88.

— (2012) "Kingdoms of the Cameroon Grassfields". *Reviews in Anthropology*, online publication, London: Routledge.

FOWLER, I. & ZEITLYN, D. (eds.) (1996) *African Crossroads. Intersections between History and Anthropology in Cameroon*. Providence, Oxford: Berghahn Books.

FRIEDMAN, J. & ROWLANDS, M.J. (1977) "Notes towards an epigenetic model of the evolution of civilisation". In: J. FRIEDMAN and M.J. ROWLANDS (eds.), *The Evolution of Social Systems*. London: Duckworth, pp. 201-278.

Geggus, D. (1989) "Sex Ratio, Age and Ethnicity in the Atlantic Slave Trade: Data from French Shipping and Plantation Records", *Journal of African History*, XXX (1): 23-44.

GESCHIERE, P. & KONINGS, P. (éds.) (1993) *Itinéraires d'accumulation au Cameroun*, Paris, Karthala.

GHÓMSI, E. 1972 "Les Bamiléké du Cameroun: Essai d'étude historique des origines à 1920", Thèse de doctorat de troisième cycle, Paris.

GODELIER, M. (1989) "Sexualité, parenté et pouvoir", *La Recherche*, XX, 213: 1141-1155.

GOLDIE, H. (1862) *Dictionary of Efik Language*. Glasgow: Dunn and Wright. (Reprinted at Ridgewood, NJ: Gregg Press, 1964).

GOUCHER, C.L. (1981) "Iron is iron. 'til it is rust: trade and ecology in the decline of West-African iron-smelting", *Journal of African History*, XXII (2): 179-189.

GREENBERG, J.H. (1966) *The Languages of Africa*, The Hague: Mouton.

GRZYMSKI, K. (1981) "The greatest-diversity concept and African history", *Current Anthropology*, XXI, iv: 506-507.

GUTHRIE, M. (1967-1971) *Comparative Bantu. An Introduction to the Comparative Linguistics and Prehistory of the Bantu Languages*. Farnborough: Gregg Press, 4 vols.

HALL, E.T. (1966) *The Hidden Dimension*. New York: Doubleday.

HANSON, C.E. (1955) *The Northwest Gun*. Lincoln, Nebraska: Nebraska State Historical Society.

— (1964) "Trade guns". In: H.L. PETERSON (ed.), *Encyclopedia of Firearms*, London: George Rainbird.

HARTLE, D.D. (1969) "An Archaeological Survey in the West Cameroon", *West African Archaeological Newsletter*, XI, 35-39.

HAWKESWORTH, A.G. (1926) "An assessment report on the Bafut area of the Bamenda Division, Cameroons Province, Nigeria". Unpublished, Buea Archives.

— (1931) "Assessment Report on Bafut and Babanki, Bamenda Division, Cameroon Province, Nigeria." Unpublished. Buea Archives.

HAWKINS, P. & Brunt, M. (1965) *Soils and Ecology of West Cameroon*. Rome: F.A.O., 2 Vol.

HEAD, H. and HOLMES, G. (1911) "Sensory Disturbances from Cerebral Lesions". *Brain*, 1911-1912: pp. 34-102.

HENDRY, J. (1993) *Wrapping Culture: Politeness, Presentation, and Power in Japan and other Societies*. Oxford: Clarendon Press.

HIBOU, B. (2006) *La Force de l'obéissance. Économie politique de la répression en Tunisie*, Paris, La Découverte.

— (2011) *Anatomie politique de la domination*, Paris, La Découverte.

HIRSCHMANN, A. (1970) *Exit, Voice and Loyalty: Responses to Decline in Firms, Organisations and States*. Cambridge, Mass.: Harvard Univ. Press.

HOMBERT, J.-M. (1979) "Grassfields lexicostatistics", unpublished report to the GBWG.

HOOK, R.J. (1934) "An intelligence report on the associated village groupe occupying the Bafut N.A.A. of the Bamenda Division of the Cameroon Province". Unpublished, Buea Archives.

HORTON, R. (1971) "Stateless Societies in the History of West Africa", In: J.R. ADE AJAYI and M. CROWDER (eds.), *History of West Africa*. NY: Columbia Univ. Press. Vol. I: 78-119.

HUTCHINSON, T.J. (1967) *Ten Years' Wandering among the Ethiopians*. London: F. Cass (reprinted in "Cass Library of African Studies. Travels and Narratives" 28. 1ˢᵗ ed. 1858).

— (1970) *Impressions of Western Africa*. London: F. Cass (reprinted in "Cass Library of African Studies" 63. 1ˢᵗ ed. 1858).

HUTTER, F. (1902) *Wanderungen und Froschungen im Nord-Hinterland von Kamerun*. Braunschweig: F. Viewveg.

HYMAN, L. (1979) *An Annotated Index of Proto-Grassifleds Bantu Roots*, working document for the Grassfields Bantu Working Group, mimeo.

HYMAN, L., VOORHOEVE, J. & BOUQUIAUX, L. (eds.) (1980) *L'Expansion bantoue*, Paris, SELAF, 3 vol.

INIKORI, J. E., ed. (1982) *Forced Migration. The Impact of the Export Slave Trade on African Societies*. London: Hutchinson.

Jeffreys, M.D.W. (1942a) *Report on the Local Iron Industry, Bamenda Division*. Unpublished, Bamenda Provincial Archives.

— (1942b) *Addenda to B. 2142/64 of 12th Feb. 1942*. Unpublished, Bamenda Provincial Archives.

— (1942c) "Sexual inhibition in the Negro", *Man*, 54: 95-96.

— (1951) "Neolithic Stone Implements (Bamenda, British Cameroons)", *Bulletin de l'IFAN*, XIII, I, (1970), 3-11.

— (1970) "A Neolothic site in Southern Cameroon", *The Nigerian Field*, XXXV, I, 3-11.

— (1972) "Stone implements from Sabga mineral spring, West Cameroon", *West African Journal of Archaeology*, II (1972), 114-18.

Joseph, R. (1986) *Le mouvement nationaliste au Cameroun*, Paris, Karthala (éd. originale en anglais, Oxford, Clarendon, 1977).

JULIEN, M.-P. & ROSSELIN, C. (2005) *La culture matérielle*, Paris, La Découverte, Coll. « Repères ».

JULIEN, M.-P. & ROSSELIN, C. (éds.) (2009) *Le sujet contre les objets... tout contre. Ethnographies de cultures matérielles*, Paris, CTHS.

JULIEN, M.-P. et WARNIER, J.-P., (eds.) (1999) *Approches de la culture matérielle. Corps à corps avec l'objet*, Paris, L'Harmattan.

KABERRY, P. (1952) *Women of the Grassfields*. London: H.M.S.O.

KANTOROWICZ, E.H. (1957) *The King's Two Bodies. A Study in Medieval Political Theology*. Trad. Fr. : *Les Deux corps du roi. Essai sur la théologie politique au Moyen Âge*. Paris, Gallimard, 1989, nouvelle édition 2000.

KEA, R.A. (1971) "Firearms and Warfare on the Gold and Slave Coasts from the Sixteenth to the Nineteenth Centuries", *Journal of African History*, 12 (2): 185-213.

Koelle, S.W. (1854) *Polyglotta Africana*, reprint 1963: P.E.H. HAIR & D. DALBY (eds.) Graz, Austria: Akademische Druck – U. Verlag-anstalt.

KOPITOFF, I. (ed.) (1987) *The African Frontier: the Reproduction of Traditional African Societies*. Bloomington and Indianapolis, Indiana: Indiana University Press.

KUHN, T. S. (1970) *The Structure of Scientific Revolutions*. Chicago: The University of Chicago Press.

LABURTHE-TOLRA, Ph. (1981) *Les Seigneurs de la forêt*, Paris, Publications de la Sorbonne.

—(1986) *Le Tombeau du soleil*, Paris, Le Seuil/Odile Jacob.

LATHAM, A.J.H. (1973) *Old Calabar 1600-1891 The Impact of the International Economy upon a Traditional Society*. Oxford: Oxford University Press.

LAW, R. (1975) "A West Africa Cavalry State: the Kingdom of Oyo", *Journal of African History*, XVI (1): 1-15.

—(1986) "Dahomey and the Slave Trade: Reflections on the Historiography of the Rise of Dahomey", *Journal of African History*, XXVII (2): 237-267.

LEACH, E. (1954) *Political Systems of Highland Burma*. London: Bell.

LEE, R.B. & DE VORE, L. (eds.) (1968) *Man the Hunter*. Chicago: Aldine.

LEO AFRICANUS, J. (1665) *Pertinente Beschryvinge van Africa met alle Landen... Getrokken en vergadert uyt de Reys-boeken van Johannes Leo Africanus...*, Tot Rotterdam, by A. Leers.

LEROY, J. (1977) *Morphologies et classes nominales en Mankon* (Cameroun), Paris, SELAF.

—(1980) "The Ngemba group: Mankon, Babangu, Mundum I, Bafut, Nkwen, Bambwi, Pinyin, Awing", in: L. HYMAN & J. VOORHOEVE (eds.), *L'Expansion bantoue*. Actes du colloque International du CNRS, Viviers (France) – 4-16 avril 1977, Vol. I : Les classes nominales dans le bantou des Grassfields, Paris, SELAF (NS 9), p. 111-141.

—(2003) *Grammaire du mankon, langue du Bantou des Grassfields*, Thèse de Doctorat ès lettres, Université de Paris III – Sorbonne Nouvelle.

—(2007) *Le Mankon. Langue bantoue des Grassfields (Province Nord-Ouest du Cameroun)*, Paris, Péeters.

LEROY, J. & VOORHOEVE, J. (1975) "Vowel contraction and vowel réduction in Mankon". *Studies in African Linguistics*, 6 (2), 125-149.

LETOUZEY, R. (1968) *Étude phytogéographique du Cameroun*, Paris, Éditions Paul Lechevalier.

LIGHTFOOT, K.G. & MARTINEZ, A. (1995) "Frontiers and boundaries in archaeological perspective", *Annual Review of Anthropology*, 24 : 471-92.

LOVEJOY, P.E. (1983) *Transformations in Slavery: A History of Slavery in Africa*. Cambridge: Cambridge University Press.

MACKENZIE, M. (1991) *Androgynous Objects: String Bags and Gender in Central New Guinea*. Chur: Harwood Academic.

MALAQUAIS, D. (2002) *Architecture, pouvoir et dissidence au Cameroun*, Paris, CERI-Karthala, coll. Recherches internationales.

MALEY, J. (2001) "Elaeis guineensis Jacq. (oil palm) fluctuations in central Africa during the late Holocene: climate or human driving forces for this pioneering species?" *Vegetation History and Archaeobotany*, 10: 117-120.

MALLART-GUIMERA, L. (1981) *Ni dos ni ventre*, Paris, Société d'ethnographie.

MANNONI, O. (1984) *Psychologie de la colonisation*, Paris, Éditions Universitaires (1ʳᵉ éd. 1950).

MARLIAC, A. (1981) "L'état des connaissances sur le paléolithique et le néolithique du Cameroun (prospections de 1968, 1969, 1970, 1971)", in Cl. TARDITS (ed.) *Contribution de la recherche ethnologique à l'histoire des civilisations du Cameroun*, Paris, CNRS, Vol. I, 27-77.

MAUSS, M. (1950/1936) "Les techniques du corps", *Sociologie et anthropologie*, Paris, PUF, 331-362, (1ʳᵉ éd. 1936, *Journal de psychologie*, XXXII, 3-4).

MASQUELIER, B. (1978) *Structure and Process of Political Identity. Ide, A Polity of the Metchum Valley (Cameroon)*. Ph.D. Dissert., Univ. of Pennsylvania. Univ. Microfilms Int. N° 78-24745.

MBIDA, C.M., VAN NEER, W., DOUTRELEPONT, H. & VRYDAGHS, L. (2000) "Evidence for Banana Cultivation and Animal Husbandry During the First Millenium BC in the Forest of Southern Cameroon", *Journal of Archaeological Science*, 27: 151-162.

MEILLASSOUX, C. (1986) *Anthropologie de l'esclavage: le ventre de fer et d'argent*, Paris, PUF, coll. Pratiques théoriques.

METCALF, G. (1987) "A Microcosm of why Africans Sold Slaves: Akan Consumption Patterns in the 1770s", *Journal of African History*, XXVIII (3): 377-394.

MIAFFO, D. (1977) *Rôle social de l'autopsie publique traditionnelle chez les Bamiléké*, Mémoire de DES de sociologie, Université de Yaoundé, multigraphié.

MIAFFO, D. et WARNIER, J.-P. (1993) "Accumulation et ethos de la notabilité chez les Bamiléké", In : P. GESCHIERE et P. KONINGS (eds.), *Itinéraires d'accumulation au Cameroun*, Paris, ASC-Karthala, pp. 33-70.

MIERS, S. & KOPYTOFF, I. (eds.) (1977) *Slavery in Africa*. Madison : University of Wisconsin Press.

MOISEL, M. (1913) *Karte von Kamerun*, Berlin.

MORIN, S. (1982) "Rapport de mission dans les Grassfields et en pays bamiléké", Yaoundé, ISH, unpublished report.

NAIR, K.K. (1972) *Politics and Society in South Eastern Nigeria, 1841-1906. A Study of Power, Diplomacy and Commerce in Old Calabar*, London : F. Cass.

NEWTON, R. (1934) "An intelligence and re-assessment report on the village groups occupying the Ngemba N. A. A. of the Bamenda Division". Unpublished, Buea Archives.

NORTHERN, T. (1984) *The Art of Cameroon*, Washington DC : Smithonian Institution.

NORTHRUP, D. (1978) *Trade without Rulers: Pre-colonial Economic Development in South-Eastern Nigeria*, Oxford: Clarendon Press.

— (1981) "The Ideological Context of Slavery in Southeastern Nigeria in the 19ᵗʰ Century", in: P.E. LOVEJOY (ed.): *The Ideology of Slavery in Africa*. Beverly Hills CA: Sage: 101-122.

NOTUE, J.-P. & TRIACA, B. (2005) *Mankon. Arts, Heritage and Culture from the Mankon Kingdom*. Milan, 5 Continents Editions.

NYAMNJOH, F.B. (2011) "Cameroonian bushfalling: Negotiation of identity and belonging in fiction and ethnography", *American Ethnologist*, Vol. 38, n° 4, pp. 701-713.

NYAMNJOH, F.B. & ROWLANDS, M.J. (1998) "Elite Associations and the Politics of Belonging in Cameroon", *Africa*, 68 (3) : 320-337.

ORTNER, S. (1981) "Gender and sexuality in hierarchical societies : the case of Polynesia and some comparative implications"». In : S.B. ORTNER and H. WHITEHEAD (eds.) : *Sexual Meanings : the Cultural Construction of Gender and Sexuality*, Cambridge : CUP, pp. 359-409.

PEREIRA, D.P. (1956) *Esmeraldo de Situ Orbis. Côte occidentale d'Afrique, du Sud marocain au Gabon*, éd. et trad. par R. Mauny, Bissau, Centro de estudos da Guiné portuguesa (*Memorias* 19), (1ʳᵉ édition, 1892).

PAGE, B. (2007) "Slow Going: the mortuary, modernity and the hometown association in Bali-Nyonga, Cameroon". *Africa*, 77 (3): 419-441.

PAIDEUMA. *Mitteilungen zur Kulturkunde* (1985) Special issue (31) on: Palaces and chiefly households in the Cameroon Grassfields.

PARLEBAS, P. (1999) J*eux, sports et sociétés. Lexique de praxéologie motrice*, Paris, INSEP.

PAVEL, Oberstleutnant, (1902) "Report on the punitive expédition against the Bangwa, Bafut and Bandeng". *Deutsch. Kolonialblatt*, 13 : 90-92, 162-3, 238-9.

PERROT, C.-H. et FAUVELLE-AYMAR, F.-X. (2003) *Le retour des rois. Les autorités traditionnelles et l'État en Afrique contemporaine*, Paris, Karthala.

PIAGET, J. (1962) *Le Langage et la pensée chez l'enfant*, 5ᵉ ed., Neuchâtel, Paris : Delachaux et Niestlé.

POLE, L.M. (1974) "Iron smelting procedures in the Upper Region of Ghana", *Historical Metallurgy*, 8 (1) : 21-31.

PRADELLES DE LATOUR, Ch.-H. (1985) "Le palais du chef dans une chefferie bamiléké : Bangoua", *Paideuma* (31) : 31-48.

— (1991) *Ethnopsychanalyse en pays bamiléké*, Paris, EPEL, (2ᵉ édition : *Le crâne qui parle*, 1999).

— (2001) *Incroyance et paternités*, Paris, EPEL.

RICHARDSON, D. (1989) "Slave Exports from West and West-Central Africa, 1700-1810: New Estimates of Volume and Distribution", *Journal of African History*, XXX (1): 1-22.

RITZENTHALER, R. & P. (1960) "Anlu: A Women's Uprising in the British Cameroons", *African Studies*, XIX, 151-156.

— (1962) *Cameroons Village. An Ethnography of the Bafut*. Milwaukee: Milwaukee Public Museum.

ROWLANDS, M.J. (1979) "Local and long-distance trade and incipient state formation in the Bamenda Plateau in the late 19ᵗʰ century". *Paideuma*, 25 : 1-19.

— (1985) "Notes on the Material Symbolism of Grassfields Palaces". *Paideuma*, (31) : 203-213.

— (1996) "The Consumption of an African Modernity", in: M. J. Arnoldi et Al. (eds.) *African Material Culture*. Bloomington and Indianapolis: Indiana Univ. Press, pp. 188-212.

RUDIN, H.R. (1938) *Germans in the Cameroons, 1884-1914*. New Haven: Yale University Press.

SALPETEUR, M. (2009) "Du Palais à l'autopsie. Les doublures animales dans une chefferie bamiléké (Cameroun)", Thèse de doctorat en anthropologie, Paris, Museum National d'Histoire naturelle.

SCHILDER, P. (1923) *Das Körperschema. Ein Beitrag zur Lehre vom Bewusstsein des eigenen Körpers*. Berlin, J. Springer.

— (1935) *The Image and Appearance of the Human Body ; Studies in the Constructive Energy of the Psyche*, London : Kegan Paul (trad. fr. *L'Image du corps*, Paris, Gallimard, 1968).

SCHNEIDER, J. (1987) "The anthropology of cloth", *Annual Review of Anthropology*, 16: 409-48.

SHARWOOD-SMITH, B.A. (1926) "A report on the Mogamaw and Ngemba speaking families of the Widekum tribe of the Bamenda Division". Unpublished, Buea Archives.

SHAW, T. (1976) "Early Crops in Africa: A Review of the Evidence", in: J.R. HARLAN, J.M.J. DE WET & A.B.L. STEMLER (eds): *Origins of African Plant Domestication*, The Hague: Mouton ("World Anthropology"): 107-154.

— (1977) *Unearthing Igbo-Ukwu*. Ibadan: Oxford University Press.

STALLCUP, K., (1980) "La géographie linguistique des Grassifelds", in: L. HYMAN et Al. (eds.), *L'Expansion bantoue*, V, i: 43-58.

STALLCUP, K., & HYMAN, L. (1975) "The Grassfields Bantu Working Group". Unpublished communication to the 6th Annual Conference on African Linguistics, Columbia, Ohio, 11-13 April 1975.

SUTTON, J. (2001) "Igbo-Ukwu and the Nile". *African Archaeological Review*, 18(1): 49-62.

TAMWA HAMKONG, J. (1983) *Relations économiques traditionnelles entre le Haut-Noun et Yabassi*, Yaoundé, Université de Yaoundé, Département d'histoire, mémoire de DIPLEG, MIMEO.

TARDITS, Cl. (1980) *Le Royaume bamoum*, Paris, Armand Colin.

—(1981) "L'implantation des populations dans l'Ouest Cameroun", in Cl. TARDITS (éd.) *Contribution*, op.cit, II, 475-84.

TARDITS, Cl. (éd.) (1981) *Contribution de l'ethnologie à l'histoire des civilisations du Cameroun*, Paris, CNRS, 2 vol.

TCHOUANGO-TIEGOUM, P. et NGANGOUM, B.F. (1975) *La Vérité du culte des Ancêtres en Afrique chez les Bamiléké*. Nkongsamba, éd. Essor des Jeunes, multigraphié.

THOMAS, N. (1989) *Out of Time : History and Evolution in Anthropological Discourse*. Cambridge : Cambridge University Press (Cambridge Studies in Social Anthropology 67).

THOMASON, S.G. & KAUFMAN, T. (n.d.) "Toward an adequate définition of creolization", 57 pp.

TILLEY, C. et Al. (eds) (2006) *Handbook of Material Culture*. London, Thousand Oaks, New Delhi : Sage Publications.

TISSERON, S. (1999) *Comment l'esprit vient aux objets*, Paris, Aubier.

—(2000) *Petites mythologies d'aujourd'hui*, Paris, Aubier.

TURNER, F.J. (1893/1961) "The significance of the frontier in American history", in R.A. BILLINGTON (ed.), *Frontier and Section: Selected Essays*. Englewood Cliffs, NJ : Prentice Hall, pp. 28-36.

TYLECOTE, R.F. (1965) "Iron smelting in pre-industrial communities", *Jnl. Of the Iron and Steel Institute*, (April) : 340-8.

VAN SLAGEREN, J. (1972) *Les origines de l'Église évangélique au Cameroun*, Yaoundé, Clé.

VOORHOEVE, J. (1971) "The linguistic unit Mbam-Nkam", *Journal of African Languages*, 10 (2) : 1-12.

—(1976) « Bantu/Bane. Communication to the 12th Congress of the West-African Linguistic Society, Ile-Ife, 14-20 March 1976. Unpublished.

WAINWRIGHT, G.A. (1945) "Iron in the Napatan and Meroitic ages", *Sudan Notes and Records*, 26 : 5-36.

WALLERSTEIN, I. (1974-1989) *The Modern World-System*. 3 vol., San Francisco, New York : Academic Press.

WARNIER, J.-P. (1975) *Pre-Colonial Mankon : the Development of a Cameroon Chiefdom in its Regional Setting*. Ph.D. Dissert, Univ. Of Pennsylvania, Univ. Microfilms Int. N° 76-3227.

—(1979) "Noun-classes, lexical stocks, multilingualism, and the history of the Cameroon Grassfields', *Language in Society*, VIII: 409-23.

—(1980) "Les précurseurs de l'École Berlitz: le multilinguisme dans les Grassfields du Cameroun au XIXᵉ siècle", in: L. HYMAN et Al. (eds.), *L'Expansion bantoue*, Paris, SELAF, II. 827-844.

—(1983) *Sociologie du Bamenda pré-colonial*, Thèse de Doctorat ès lettres, Université de Paris 10 - Nanterre.

—(1984) "Histoire du peuplement et genèse des paysages dans l'ouest camerounais", *Journal of African History*, XXV (4) : 395-410.

—(1985a) *Échanges, développement et hiérarchies dans le Bamenda pré-colonial – Cameroun*. Stuttgart, Franz Steiner Verlag Wiesbaden. Studien zur Kulturkunde 76.

—(1985b) "The Mankon Palace", *Paideuma*, 31 : pp. 15-29.

—(1989) "Traite sans raids au Cameroun". *Cahiers d'Études africaines*, 113, XXIX, pp. 5-32.

—(1992) "Rapport préliminaire sur la métallurgie du groupe Chap", In : J.-M. Essomba (éd.), *L'archéologie au Cameroun*, Paris, Karthala, 197-212.

—(1993) *L'Esprit d'entreprise au Cameroun*, Paris, Karthala.

—(1995) "Slave trading without slave raiding in Cameroon", *Paideuma* (41): 251-72; (reproduced in this volume, chapter 6).

—(1996) "Rebellion, Defection and the Position of Male Cadets : a Neglected Category ", In : I. Fowler and D. Zeitlyn (eds.), *African Crossroads. Intersection between History and Anthropology in Cameroon*. Providence, Oxford : Berghahn Books : pp. 192-213.

—(1999) *Construire la culture matérielle. L'Homme qui pensait avec ses doigts*, Paris, PUF.

—(2001) "A Praxeological approach to subjectivation in a material world", *Journal of Material Culture*, 6 (1) : 5-24.

—(2004) "Métallurgie ancienne, identifications et domestication de la violence au Cameroun", In : J.-F.Bayart & J.-P. Warnier (éds.), *Matière à politique. Le pouvoir, les corps et les choses*. Paris, Yaoundé, CERI-Karthala-UCAC, pp. 181-194.

—(2006) "Inside and Outside, surfaces and containers". In : C. Tilley et Al. (eds.) *Handbok of Material Culture*. London : Sage, pp. 186-195.

—(2007) *The Pot-King. The Body and Technologies of Power*. Leiden, Boston : Brill (African Social Studies Series).

—(2009a) *Régner au Cameroun. Le Roi-pot*, Paris, CERI-Karthala, Coll. Recherches internationales.

—(2009b) "Les politiques de la valeur », web page of the Fonds d'analyse des sociétés politiques (Fasopo) [www.fasopo.org], online journal *Sociétés politiques comparées*, janvier 2009.

—(2011) "Territorialization and the Politics of Autochtony", in : H. Anheier & Y.R. Isar, *The Culture and Globalization Series. Heritage, Memory & Identity*. Los Angeles, London : Sage, pp. 95-104.

Warnier, J.-P. and Fowler, I. (1979) "A Nineteenth-century Ruhr in Central Africa", *Africa*, XLIX (4) : 329-51.

White, G. (1971) "Firearms in Africa : an Introduction". *Journal of African History*, 12 (2) : 173-84.

Wilhelm, H. (1981) "Le commerce précolonial de l'ouest (plateau bémiléké-grassfields, régions bamlum et bafia)", in : C. Tardits (éd.), *Contribution*, op. cit, II, pp. 485-502.

Wilkinson-Latham, R. (1977) *Antique Guns in Colour to 1865*. Poole; Dorset: Blandford Press.

Williamson, K. (1970) "Some food plant names in the Niger Delta", *International Journal of African Linguistics*, XXXVI : 156-167.

—(1971)'The Benue-Congo Languages and Ijo", *Current trends in Linguistics*, 7 : 245-306.

Wirz, A. (1972) *Vom Sklavenhandel zum Kolonialen Handel : Wirtschaftsraume formen in Kamerun vor 1914*. Freiburg : Atlantis Verlag.

Zintgraff, E. (1995) *Nord-Kamerun. Schilderung der im Auftrage des auswärtigen Amtes zur Erschliessung des nördlishen Hinterlandes von Kamerun während der Jahre 1886-1892 unternommenen Reisen*, Berlin : Verlag von Gebrüder Paetel.

Zips, W. & Zips-Mairitsche, M. (2010) *The Golden Days of the Kingdom*. 53mn Documentary film.

Table of illustrations

www.ingramcontent.com/pod-product-compliance
Lightning Source LLC
Chambersburg PA
CBHW081740270326
41932CB00020B/3345